D1277688

INTRA-INDUSTRY TRADE AND ADJUSTMENT

Intra-Industry Trade and Adjustment

The European Experience

Edited by

Marius Brülhart
University of Manchester

and

Robert C. Hine
University of Nottingham

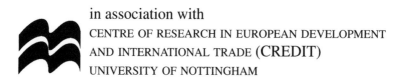

in association with
CENTRE OF RESEARCH IN EUROPEAN DEVELOPMENT
AND INTERNATIONAL TRADE (CREDIT)
UNIVERSITY OF NOTTINGHAM

First published in Great Britain 1999 by
MACMILLAN PRESS LTD
Houndmills, Basingstoke, Hampshire RG21 6XS and London
Companies and representatives throughout the world

A catalogue record for this book is available from the British Library.

ISBN 0–333–62304–5

First published in the United States of America 1999 by
ST. MARTIN'S PRESS, INC.,
Scholarly and Reference Division,
175 Fifth Avenue, New York, N.Y. 10010

ISBN 0–312–21568–1

Library of Congress Cataloging-in-Publication Data
Intra-industry trade and adjustment : the European experience / edited
by Marius Brülhart and Robert C. Hine.
p. cm.
Includes bibliographical references and index.
ISBN 0–312–21568–1 (cloth)
1. European Union countries—Commerce. 2. Industries—European
Union countries. I. Brülhart, Marius. II. Hine, R. C.
HF3496.5.I58   1998
382'.094—dc21   98–16157
                                                                         CIP

This book is printed on paper suitable for recycling and made from fully managed and
sustained forest sources.

10   9   8   7   6   5   4   3   2   1
08   07   06   05   04   03   02   01   00   99

Printed and bound in Great Britain by
Antony Rowe Ltd, Chippenham, Wiltshire

This book is dedicated to the memory of

Johan Torstensson

1964–1998

in appreciation both of his friendship and of his distinguished contribution to scholarship in the economics of international trade.

Contents

List of Contributors   ix

Preface   x
David Greenaway

1 Overview   1
   Marius Brülhart and Robert C. Hine

PART I: THEORY AND MEASUREMENT

2 Intra-Industry Trade: What Does the Theory
   Predict and How Robust Are the Empirical Estimates?   13
   Johan Torstensson

3 Marginal Intra-Industry Trade and Trade-Induced
   Adjustment: A Survey   36
   Marius Brülhart

4 Vertical and Horizontal Intra-Industry Trade:
   An Analysis of Country- and Industry-Specific
   Determinants   70
   Robert C. Hine, David Greenaway and Chris Milner

5 A Survey of Intra-Industry Trade in
   the European Union   98
   Marius Brülhart and Robert J.R. Elliott

PART II: COUNTRY STUDIES

6 Belgium   121
   P.K.M. Tharakan and German Calfat

7 France   135
   Mohamed Harfi and Christian Montet

8 Germany   151
   Heinz-Dieter Smeets

Contents

9 Greece   168
   Alexander H. Sarris, Pyrros Papadimitriou and
   Athanassios Mavrogiannis

10 Ireland   188
    Marius Brülhart, Dermot McAleese and
    Mary O'Donnell

11 Italy   213
    Gianpaolo Rossini and Michele Burattoni

12 The Netherlands   225
    Jacob Kol and Bart Kuijpers

13 Portugal   239
    Manuel Porto and Fernanda Costa

Index   252

List of Contributors

Marius Brülhart	University of Manchester
Michele Burattoni	Università di Bologna
German Calfat	University of Antwerp, UFSIA
Fernanda Costa	Universidade de Coimbra
Robert J.R. Elliott	Manchester Metropolitan University
David Greenaway	University of Nottingham
Mohamed Harfi	Université de Montpellier I
Robert C. Hine	University of Nottingham
Jacob Kol	Erasmus University Rotterdam
Bart Kuijpers	Erasmus University Rotterdam
Athanassios Mavrogiannis	University of Athens
Christian Montet	Université de Montpellier I
Dermot McAleese	Trinity College Dublin
Chris Milner	University of Nottingham
Manuel Porto	Universidade de Coimbra
Mary O'Donnell	University of Limerick
Pyrros Papadimitriou	University of Athens
Gianpaolo Rossini	Università di Bologna
Alexander H. Sarris	University of Athens
Heinz-Dieter Smeets	Heinrich-Heine Universität Düsseldorf
P.K.M. Tharakan	University of Antwerp, UFSIA
Johan Torstensson	Lund University

Preface

The chapters in this volume are the fruits of a major multinational programme coordinated from the University of Nottingham. The programme was funded under the European Union's Stimulation Plan for Economic Science (SPES). SPES was created to encourage collaboration between researchers across the EU. SPES support on this particular initiative brought together researchers from eight of the Member States in a comparative analysis of intra-industry trade in Europe. As this volume and a related series of journal articles testify, that collaboration proved to be very successful. Moreover, it has also proved to be durable in that a number of sub-sets of these researchers have moved on to collaborate on other projects.

I am very grateful for the support provided by the EU and for the efforts which colleagues put into what turned out to be a stimulating and informative programme. Finally I would like to record my thanks to Marius Brülhart and Bob Hine for their expert editorial work on this important volume.

David Greenaway

1. Overview

Marius Brülhart and Robert C. Hine

1.1 INTRODUCTION: A TRADING WORLD

Increasing openness to international trade has been one of the most conspicuous features of the global economy in the second half of the twentieth century. Trade growth has consistently outpaced income growth, and there are no reasons to doubt that this trend will continue in the next millennium. International trade has boomed because it was freed of numerous barriers that had previously obstructed exchanges across country borders. Barriers to trade fell both through advances in technology, most importantly in the transport and telecommunication sectors, and through policy-led liberalization. Policy liberalization occurred at the global level, mainly through successive rounds of GATT negotiations, as well as among numerous regional country groups. As the significance of national boundaries diminishes, economies become more exposed to international competitive pressures to which they must adapt or face economic decline.

The normative conclusions from economic theory are uncharacteristically consistent when it comes to free trade. With the exception of a few highly specific scenarios, theory tells us that complete trade liberalization produces net gains in economic welfare. International specialization and competition enhance the quantity and variety of attainable output. However, trade theory also suggests that the removal of trade barriers can impact considerably on countries' production structures and income distributions, and that the net welfare effects of incomplete liberalization can be ambiguous. Even where economic integration is a positive-sum game, it produces losers as well as gainers. A focal issue in this debate are the transitional costs which occur as economies adapt to international competition. Some adjustments may be easily accomplished – such as minor product re-design. Others may be more far-reaching and difficult to achieve quickly, in particular when they necessitate occupational or geographical mobility of the work force. The severity of trade-related economic restructuring is, therefore, a hotly debated topic in international economics as well as in public policy discourse. Given the likely continuation of trade

1

liberalization at both the global and the regional levels, the adjustment issue is set to rise further in prominence on the economic research and policy agendas. This book is dedicated to some specific theoretical aspects of trade-related structural adjustment and to the relevant developments in 12 EU[1] countries. The theoretical emphasis is on the concept of intra-industry trade (IIT), the international exchange of very similar products. An extensive literature has developed on this topic over the last three decades. IIT has received much attention both from economic theorists, who found it in contradiction to their established models of international trade and therefore had to adapt their modelling framework, and from policy-minded economists, who came to believe that IIT generally entails less severe structural adjustment pressures than an expansion of inter-industry trade flows. In spite of the large quantity of academic investigations conducted on this topic, the latter source of interest in IIT, that is its perceived link with smooth structural adjustment, has been subjected to surprisingly little explicit scrutiny. The present volume is designed as a step towards closing this gap in the literature.

1.2 EUROPEAN INTEGRATION AND STRUCTURAL ADJUSTMENT

The empirical contributions to this collection all refer to the link between changes in EU trade and changes in production patterns. There are many reasons why the European experience provides a valuable case study. Most importantly, the EU is the world's most advanced regional integration project, and it consists of industrialized market economies. The post-war economic evolution of the EU might, therefore, bear strong similarities to impending changes in regions which are currently at an earlier stage of economic development.

The general features of EU integration are well documented. Early formation of a customs union among the original six member countries in the 1960s appeared relatively frictionless, as fast growth helped to offset adjustment pressures in sectors affected by trade liberalization, and substantial non-tariff barriers continued to shelter large parts of the national economies from international competition. Slower growth and rising unemployment in the 1970s and 1980s brought the distributional implications of European integration into sharper focus. In response to the change in economic climate, as well as to enlargement, redistributive EU regional and industrial policies were expanded continuously. The increase in the budget share of the Structural Funds amounts to an implicit acknowledgement that gains and losses from integration were distributed unequally among regions and industries. The debate on structural adjustment issues reached its peak intensity in the late 1980s, during the negotiation of the Single Market programme. Again, considerable net gains were anticipated from the removal of non-tariff barriers, but many economists also predicted substantial costs arising from the inevitable economic restructuring as firms adapted to intensifying EU-wide competition. Similar considerations motivated the establishment of the Cohesion Fund as a redistributive mechanism to prepare countries for monetary union.

1.3 THE RELEVANCE OF INTRA-INDUSTRY TRADE

The expectations of severe adjustment pressures after completion of the Single Market were based on two main developments, both of which are connected to the phenomenon of IIT. First, the discovery of high and growing IIT levels in the 1970s had produced a wave of new thinking by trade theorists that shifted the emphasis of the models away from country-specific trade determinants, generically termed 'comparative advantage', towards industry-specific factors such as increasing returns and external economies. Models of the 'new trade theory', and the derived 'new economic geography', generally predicted that a fall in trade barriers would promote concentration and relocation of industries near their largest markets.[2] Second, most economists agreed on the hypothesis that high levels of IIT were indicative of relatively low trade-induced adjustment costs. Some studies in the late 1980s found evidence of stagnating IIT growth, and therefore concluded that adjustment pressures were becoming more severe. The rapid growth of trade flows among EU countries was hence expected to result in growing factor-market friction which in turn could fuel protectionist sentiment and undermine the integration project.

Part I of this book provides a summary of the current state of play in IIT research. In Chapter 2, Johan Torstensson discusses the most widely quoted theoretical explanation of IIT, the monopolistic-competition model of the 'new trade theory'. He specifies the predictions of this model for IIT patterns and tests whether econometric estimates thereof are statistically robust. This analysis shows that earlier empirical tests may have been somewhat deceptive, as most of the detected relationships between IIT and its determinants proved to be statistically fragile. This finding justifies recent efforts to decompose IIT according to its horizontal and vertical components (see Chapter 4). Extending the monopolistic-competition model to a three-country setting, Torstensson finds that intra-union IIT can develop non-monotonically as regional integration proceeds; rising at early stages of regional integration, but falling again as intra-union trade barriers fall below a critical threshold. Recent signs of a partial IIT trend reversal in the EU (see Chapter 5) might be explained by the factors identified in this model.

Two developments have dominated the empirical literature on IIT in the early 1990s: the introduction of the concept of *marginal* IIT (MIIT), and the measurement of *vertical* IIT (VIIT). Chapter 3, by Marius Brülhart, provides an overview of recent work on MIIT. This concept was developed because the traditional Grubel-Lloyd (GL) index of IIT is a static measure, in the sense that it describes trade patterns for one time period. It was shown that the observation of a high proportion of IIT does not justify *a priori* any prediction of the likely pattern of change in trade flows. Industrial adjustment, however, is a dynamic concept, relating to the reallocation of resources over time. Even an observed increase in static IIT levels between two periods could 'hide' a very uneven change in trade flows, attendant with *inter-* rather than *intra*-industry adjustment. Hence, it has been argued that an analysis of traditional IIT measures should at least be complemented by a survey of MIIT patterns.

In Chapter 4, Robert C. Hine, David Greenaway and Chris Milner survey recent empirical work, disentangling vertical and horizontal IIT. They present their (by now widely applied) method to separate the two types of IIT in empirical work. Putting their methodology into practice on a trade data set for the UK, they show that vertical IIT is more prevalent than horizontal IIT. This poses a number of challenges to the common explanatory models of IIT, which are based on large numbers of firms and horizontal differentiation of traded goods. The UK analysis suggests that small-number oligopoly models are more successful in explaining horizontal IIT, whereas models based on large numbers of firms are a better approximation of industries dominated by vertical IIT.

Chapter 5, by Marius Brülhart and Robert J.R. Elliott, provides the most comprehensive and sectorally disaggregated overview of IIT patterns yet compiled for the EU, using five-digit bilateral trade data and spanning the 1961–92 period. This survey draws together the main results computed by the authors of the country studies in Part II of this volume. The results allow a first verification of the speculative diagnosis made by several economists in the late 1980s that the secular IIT growth of the post-war decades might have been reversed. Evidence of IIT stagnation is found for the 1980s, but a pervasive increase in IIT in the run-up to the 1992 Single-Market deadline suggests that it would be premature to diagnose a reversal of the upward trend in IIT. Chapter 5 also provides a first set of comparable MIIT results for the EU countries. These figures indicate that inter-industry adjustment pressures were not exceptionally strong during the implementation of the Single Market.

1.4   THE EXPERIENCE OF EU MEMBER COUNTRIES

Part II of this volume is a collection of eight country studies. These exercises have several features in common. First, they all draw on an identical set of SITC five-digit trade data, from which various IIT measures are calculated. Furthermore, they all complement traditional IIT indices by the computation of new measures capturing marginal and vertical IIT. Each of the country studies supplements trade data by national industry statistics, thus producing sectorally disaggregated data sets matching trade with structural variables such as output and employment. However, Part II is more than a collection of country studies replicating a methodology on similar data. The analyses differ considerably in their emphasis, their time coverage and in the nature of national data used.

It would be inappropriate to review the specific points made in each country study here. We choose instead to compile a comparative table of the results obtained through correlation exercises linking various measures of trade change with measures of structural change. This provides a first, albeit crude, test of the generally assumed relationship between IIT and structural adjustment. Table 1.1 lists the data sets that were used in the country studies to calculate Pearson coefficients of correlation between variables representing different types of trade structure and variables of sectoral employment change.

Table 1.2 summarizes the results of these studies. It is apparent that most of the correlation coefficients are relatively low and statistically insignificant. This should not surprise, since employment changes in industry are determined by many other factors and only indirectly by

Table 1.1   Correlation studies of trade and adjustment: coverage

Study	Country	Initial year $(t-n)$	End year (t)	No. of industries
Tharakan and Calfat[1]	Belgium	1980	1990	78
Harfi and Montet[1]	France	1979	1990	201
Smeets	Germany	1980	1987	95
Sarris, Papadimitriou and Mavrogiannis[1]	Greece	1978	1985	64
Brülhart, McAleese and O'Donnell	Ireland	1980	1990	70
Rossini and Burratoni	Italy	1979	1987	36
Kol and Kuijpers	Netherlands	1972	1990	36
Porto and Costa	Portugal	1986	1989	81
Hine, Greenaway, Milner and Elliott[1]	U.K.	1979	1987	182

[1] results reported in Table 1.2 not reported in country reports of Part II, but available from the authors on request.

Table 1.2   Correlation studies of trade and adjustment: results

Studies	Correlation coefficients between percentage employment changes in each industry and various trade variables						
	ΔX^1	ΔM^1	GL_{t-n}	GL_t	ΔGL	A^2	B^2
Tharakan and Calfat	0.08	0.09	−0.02	−0.02	0.00	−0.05	0.15
Harfi and Montet	0.18*	0.13	0.04	0.06	0.02	0.14	0.30*
Smeets	0.07	−0.22	0.09	−0.02	−0.16	0.01	−0.13
Sarris, Papadimitriou and Mavrogiannis			−0.03		0.03	0.28*	
Brülhart, McAleese and O'Donnell	0.32*	0.17	0.13	0.12	−0.03	0.19	0.31*
Rossini and Burratoni	−0.02	0.16	−0.13³	−0.08	0.13	0.05	−0.16
Kol and Kuijpers³	0.50*	0.69*	−0.42*	−0.11	0.43*	0.37*	0.24
Porto and Costa	0.56*³	0.03³	0.20	0.25*	0.06	0.27*	
Hine, Greenaway, Milner and Elliott	0.29*	0.19*	0.04	0.03	0.02	0.24*	0.15

* statistically significant at 95 per cent confidence level (two-tailed t tests).
[1] percentage changes; [2] measures of MIIT (see Chapter 3); [3] absolute employment changes

trade patterns. More surprisingly, the evidence suggests that growth in imports relates positively to employment gains. Increased imports do not seem mainly to have crowded out domestic jobs, but they seem to accompany booming sectors, where either intermediate goods are imported to sustain growing domestic production, or the growth in domestic demand is such that it can absorb both higher imports and greater domestic production. Obviously, this conforms with the typical IIT scenario, where both domestic and foreign producers carve out their separate market niches through differentiated products.

What about the relevance of various trade measures for the analysis of structural change? The results on traditional IIT measures support the doubts formulated on theoretical grounds (see Chapter 3). None of the correlations between employment change and *changes in the GL index* is statistically significant. Statistical significance is found in only one study for correlations with *base-year* or *end-year GL indices*. Some more encouraging results emerge if we look at measures of MIIT. The *A index* produces positive coefficients in eight out of the nine studies, and statistical significance is found in four. The *B index* has produced statistically significant positive correlations in two studies, but in two other studies it has given rise to negative (that is counterintuitive, though not statistically significant) correlations.

These findings provide some empirical confirmation that MIIT measures relate more closely to structural change than static or 'comparative-static' IIT indices. However, the results should be interpreted cautiously for two reasons. First, the variable representing adjustment costs needs to be specified more adequately. Most correlation and regression analyses use percentage employment changes as an inverse proxy for adjustment costs. This is not consistent with the theoretical definition of adjustment, which encompasses frictional unemployment arising from both inter- and intra-sectoral labour movements as well as wage differentials, not net increases or decreases in total sectoral employment. Percentage employment changes are a measure of net employment performance rather than of adjustment costs.

The second shortcoming of the correlation methodology arises from its one-dimensional nature. Bivariate analysis cannot take into account multiple determinants of adjustment. Regression analysis using (M)IIT as one of several regressors and a measure of adjustment as the dependent variable can overcome this problem. Some country studies in Part II include exploratory regression studies of this kind (Tharakan and Calfat, Sarris *et al.* and Hine *et al.*). These exercises produce interesting results, but they are not comparable, since they use very different, largely *ad hoc*, specifications, which highlights the need for more theoretical work on an integrated and testable theory of trade and structural change.

1.5 CONCLUSIONS

Some important positive results can be distilled from the empirical analyses of this book. First, it is found that the European IIT turn-around, diagnosed by several economists in the late 1980s and early 1990s, and interpreted with some anxiety about increasing inter-industry adjustment pressures, was at most a temporary and partial phenomenon. On average, intra-EU IIT levels continued their upward trend until 1992. Fears of stronger inter-industry adjustment during the implementation of the Single Market were also allayed by the finding that MIIT was no lower in that period than in previous time intervals.

Second, this research produced important conceptual advances. New measures of MIIT were developed and tested with some success. A general consensus emerged that MIIT is the more relevant concept for the analysis of structural adjustment than traditional 'static' measures of IIT. Furthermore, this book reports on the development of new measures to disentangle vertical from horizontal IIT. It is found that the bulk of IIT is vertical. This too leads us to believe that the adjustment consequences of conventionally measured IIT may have been understated.

The contributions of this book also motivate a number of clear directions for further research. Our data sample ending in 1992, it would evidently be interesting to have more up-to-date IIT results for the EU in the 1990s. However, it remains to be seen whether the quality of intra-EU trade statistics collected under the border-control free post-1992 regime will be of sufficient accuracy to permit an extension of the existing series. More importantly, it is apparent that further theoretical work is needed to elucidate the adjustment issue. The discussion of IIT and adjustment has so far been conducted in a rather informal fashion. Stronger theoretical foundations should be particularly helpful to future empirical work, as past efforts have been constrained by the lack of consensus on the adequate specification for an econometric model of trade-related adjustment. There is also scope for more effort to find better proxies for structural adjustment. It might be illuminating, for instance, to look at gross labour flows as well as wage data instead of changes in stocks, since those are the variables which define structural adjustment in its proper sense.

Notes

1. Even though the analysis in this book refers to developments prior to the ratification of the Maastricht Treaty, we use the term European Union (EU, rather than EC or EEC) throughout for simplicity.
2. For a comprehensive survey, see Helpman and Krugman (1985). The integration-induced adjustment problem is treated explicitly by Krugman and Venables (1996).

References

Helpman, Elhanan and Krugman, Paul (1985) 'Market Structure and Foreign Trade', Cambridge (Mass.), MIT Press.

Krugman, Paul and Venables, Anthony J. (1996) 'Integration, Specialization and Adjustment', European Economic Review, vol. 40, pp. 959–967.

Part I
Theory and Measurement

2. Intra-Industry Trade: What Does the Theory Predict and How Robust Are the Empirical Estimates?*

Johan Torstensson

2.1 INTRODUCTION

The focus of this book is on intra-industry trade (IIT) in Europe and new methods introduced to analyse this trade. The aim of this chapter is to serve as a background to subsequent chapters. It is not primarily meant as a comprehensive survey. Rather, the aim is to complement the now classic study by Greenaway and Milner (1986) and the new survey by Greenaway and Torstensson (1997).

The focus of this chapter is, therefore, fairly narrow: many overviews of IIT, including Greenaway and Milner (1986, 1987) and Greenaway and Torstensson (1997), deal with a number of aspects such as normative conclusions from models that are capable of generating IIT. Here, I deal exclusively with the specific issue of determinants of the country and industry pattern of IIT. I examine the most widely used model of IIT, its predictions about the pattern of IIT, and the robustness of empirical results obtained in tests of these predictions.

Empirical studies have shown that the simultaneous export and import of products within the same industry, intra-industry trade (IIT), constitutes an important part of total world trade. IIT was identified empirically in the late 1960s and early 1970s and its importance was documented comprehensively by Grubel and Lloyd (1975). Subsequently, theoretical models that could explain IIT were constructed (Krugman, 1979). Later, traditional models of trade were generalized to incorporate the modelling of concepts such as scale economies and product differentiation (see for example Dixit and Norman, 1980;

13

Helpman, 1981). These models of the 'new trade theory' offered a theoretical underpinning for IIT and some testable hypotheses on the determinants of IIT (see Helpman and Krugman, 1985, chapters 7 and 8). Following on from this, a large number of empirical studies were carried out to study determinants of IIT econometrically, but these studies have more often than not, used intuitive generalizations of several theoretical models to generate testable hypotheses. As a result, there has been a gap between the theoretical models and empirical work.[1]

In the second section of the chapter I discuss the theoretical advances generated by the emergence of IIT. This should help close the gap between the theoretical and the empirical work. I introduce a simple model in which the standard assumptions of the 'new trade theory', scale economies and product differentiation, are complemented by the (realistic) assumption that trade is restricted by impediments.[2] I begin with an investigation of the link between theory and IIT with this traditional model and show that the degree of scale economies, in fact, is *negatively related to IIT*, although scale economies are a necessary condition for IIT in this analysis.

In Section 2.3, some empirical results are presented. First, I test the implications of the specific model of Section 2.2. Then, I examine hypotheses derived from a variety of models. I focus on the sensitivity of empirical results to changes in the set of control variables and to errors of measurement in the independent variables arising from the use of proxies. Some recent empirical results are presented in Section 2.4. The final section of the chapter makes a projection of the future prospects for IIT in Europe. I discuss whether IIT will stagnate or fall, or whether it will increase as it did in the 1960s and 1970s. The chapter closes with some concluding comments.

2.2   THEORETICAL UNDERPINNINGS

This section identifies determinants of IIT through the standard model of the 'new trade theory'. Although IIT models have been used for various purposes, such as the explanation of the very existence of IIT and to offer normative conclusions (for example arguments for strategic trade policy), surprisingly few economists have used them to derive firm theoretical hypotheses on the determinants of IIT. This is the objective of the current section. For completeness, I begin with a brief presentation of other models used to explain IIT.

Background

IIT has been explained theoretically in various ways. The majority of models assume that production functions exhibit increasing returns and that products do not differ in their quality but are differentiated horizontally (see Dixit and Norman, 1980; Helpman and Krugman, 1985, Chapters 6 to 9). I shall return to these types of models in the next subsection.

There are also models that generate IIT with oligopolistic market structures and homogeneous products (Brander, 1981). In these models, IIT occurs as a result of so-called 'reciprocal dumping'. Another type of model deals with IIT in vertically differentiated products. The most acclaimed of these is the model by Falvey (1981), further developed by Falvey and Kierzkowski (1987). Here, vertical IIT occurs in a model with perfect competition, between countries with differences in factor endowments, since high-quality products are assumed to require higher capital intensity in their production than low-quality products. Thus, we expect capital-abundant countries to export high-quality products in exchange for low-quality products from labour-abundant countries. In one sense, Falvey and Kierzkowski (1987) explain IIT in a neo-Heckscher-Ohlin (H-O) model, but the stated aim of the Falvey approach is to explain one type of IIT (rather than to argue that all IIT can be explained within this model), and to take an important empirical phenomenon such as vertical differentiation into consideration by *modifying* the traditional H-O theory.

There have also been attempts to explain (implicitly, all) IIT without even modifying traditional trade models. This tradition dates back to Finger (1975) and others. This has recently been taken a step further by Davis (1995) and Bhagwati and Davis (1994) who show that IIT can occur in traditional trade models with technical differences between countries. The basic intuition is quite simple. Consider a model with two countries, two goods and only one factor, so that factor intensities by definition are equal and the two goods are in the same industry. In this way the model is compatible with the convention of thinking of IIT as occurring in goods with identical factor intensities. Clearly, then, even small technical differences will generate complete specialization in production. As long as there is demand for both goods in both countries, there will be trade, and this trade will be of an IIT type.

The models of Davis and Bhagwati are clearly interesting. They show that IIT can be explained in a very simple framework. It is probably also quite realistic to say that technical differences within industries and between countries are an important cause of IIT. There are relatively large technical differences at the industry level even between highly industrialized countries (see Dollar and Wolff, 1993; Torstensson, 1996c). Yet, it seems somewhat far-fetched to think of all or even most IIT being caused by technical differences, particularly as we know that scale economies and product differentiation, the cause of IIT in monopolistically competitive models, are of considerable empirical importance.

The Model

For the purposes of this chapter, I use the 'workhorse' of the new trade theory, the monopolistically competitive model. Consider a world with one factor of production, labour, and two countries, A and B. There are two industries, X and Y. Industry Y produces homogeneous products under constant returns to scale (CRS). For the sake of simplicity, it is assumed that free trade prevails in this industry. The other industry, X, produces differentiated products under increasing returns (IRS-industry). Let us follow Helpman and Krugman (1985) in assuming trade impediments of the 'iceberg type' in industry X. This means that only a certain part $(1/\tau, \tau > 1)$ of each exported unit is received by the importer.[3]

We assume that all individuals have identical utility functions given by:

$$U_x = \left(\sum_{i=1}^{n} x_i^{\varepsilon}\right)^{\gamma/\varepsilon} Y^{1-\gamma}, \ 0 < \varepsilon < 1, \ \varepsilon = 1 - (1/\sigma) \qquad \ldots (2.1)$$

where x_i is consumption of variety i in industry X, Y is consumption of the homogeneous product, σ is the constant elasticity of substitution, and γ is the share of expenditure devoted to industry X.

Without loss of generality, we can choose units so that there is one unit of labour in country A and L units in country B. It then follows that the aggregate demand for products produced in the two countries will be equal to (see Helpman and Krugman, 1985, p. 206):

$$D_A = n_A x_A = \left[\left[n_A p_A^{-\sigma}\gamma\right]/\left[n_A p_A^{1-\sigma} + n_B(p_B\tau)^{1-\sigma}\right]\right]$$
$$+ \left[\left[n_A(p_A\tau)^{-\sigma}\tau\gamma L\right]/\left[n_A(p_A\tau)^{1-\sigma} + n_B p_B\right]\right] \ \ldots (2.2)$$

$$D_B = n_B x_B = \left[\left[n_B (p_B \tau)^{-\sigma} \gamma \right] / \left[n_A p_A^{1-\sigma} + n_B (p_B \tau)^{1-\sigma} \right] \right]$$
$$+ \left[\left[n_B p_B^{-\sigma} \tau \gamma L \right] / \left[n_A (p_A \tau)^{1-\sigma} + n_B p_B \right] \right] \qquad \dots (2.3)$$

where the first term in each expression represents demand from country A and the second term demand from country B.

The cost functions are the same for all firms. Production of each variety of the IRS-good incurs a fixed cost and a constant marginal cost. In this context, output per firm (x) will be constant. Since I assume that both countries produce the CRS-good and that technologies are identical, the wage rate and the price of the IRS-products will also be equal.

Consider then the demand equations 2.2 and 2.3 and let us divide both sides of the two equations with n_A and n_B, respectively. Furthermore, I choose units so that $w = p = 1$ and define $\rho = \tau^{1-\sigma} < 1$. In this model it is easy to show that the elasticity of demand, σ, is positively related to equilibrium economies of scale (measured by the ratio of average to marginal cost). It is also useful to note that ρ decreases with trade impediments and increases with the degree of scale economies. Rewriting then yields:

$$x/\gamma = \left[1/(n_A + n_B \rho) \right] + \left[(\rho L)/(n_A \rho + n_B) \right] \qquad \dots (2.4)$$

$$x/\gamma = \left[\rho/(n_A + n_B \rho) \right] + \left[L/(n_A \rho + n_B) \right] \qquad \dots (2.5)$$

Equations 2.4 and 2.5 can be solved to yield the equilibrium number of firms in each country. Each country can either have positive or zero production. Solving the equations, we have:

$$n_A = \left[\gamma (1 - \rho L) \right] / \left[(1 - \rho) x \right] \qquad \dots (2.6)$$

$$n_B = \left[\gamma (L - \rho) \right] / \left[(1 - \rho) x \right] \qquad \dots (2.7)$$

Equations 2.6 and 2.7 can be used to solve for zero production in each country. Then, we have:

$$n_A = 0 \rightarrow \rho = 1/L$$

$$n_B = 0 \rightarrow \rho = L$$

I assume that A is the larger country $(L < 1)$, and that it will always have positive production in the IRS good. The smaller country will also produce in the IRS-industry when $\rho < (1/L)$. When both countries produce in the IRS-industry, there will be IIT.

I can refine this analysis by examining the share of IIT when both countries have some IRS industry. The Grubel-Lloyd (GL) index is equal to:

$$GL_i = 1 - [|X_i - M_i|/(X_i + M_i)] \equiv [2\min(X_i, M_i)]/[X_i + M_i]$$
$$\ldots (2.8)$$

Let us examine IIT from the point of view of country A. Since I have assumed that country A is the larger country $(L < 1)$, it is a net exporter of IRS-products. From equations 2.2 and 2.3, and 2.6 and 2.7 IIT in industry i can, therefore, be expressed as:

$$GL_i = 2D_{21}/(D_{21} + D_{12}) = 2(L - \rho)/((L+1)(1-\rho)) \quad \ldots (2.8^*)$$

In order to derive testable hypotheses, let us take the partial derivative of 2.8* with respect to ρ, to arrive at:

$$\partial GL_i/\partial\rho = 2(L - 1)/((L+1)(\rho - 1)^2) < 0 \qquad \ldots (2.8^{**})$$

Since $L < 1$, this expression is always negative, hence IIT decreases in ρ. This implies that IIT decreases in scale economies and increases in trade costs.[4] The negative relationship between IIT and scale economies is an important and somewhat counterintuitive prediction rarely recognized in the IIT literature. The underlying intuition is as follows. Without scale economies there would be no IIT, as all possible varieties of the IRS good could be produced domestically. If I assume some degree of increasing returns, some potential arises for IIT. However, we have to remember that net trade is determined by the interaction of scale economies and market size. The country with the larger domestic market will be the net exporter in the industry characterized by scale economies, and the more scale economies matter the more important this tendency will be. Since net exports from the larger country increase in scale economies, IIT will decrease in the degree of scale economies.

One might ask whether this result is specific to the model used here, or whether it could be derived also in a more general framework where net trade is not only caused by differences in country size. The most obvious alternative explanation of net trade is differences in comparative costs, arising, for example, when countries differ in their technology in industry X while sharing production in industry Y.[5] It has been shown in Torstensson (1996b) that these predictions also hold when the cause of net trade is differences in comparative costs. In such a model, IIT also decreases with scale economies and increases with trade costs, and it can be shown furthermore that IIT decreases with differences in comparative costs.

2.3 EMPIRICAL EVIDENCE

Having derived some theoretical predictions, this section presents empirical evidence in two stages. First, I test the model presented in Section 2.2. To be more precise, I apply the generalization of the model to differences in comparative costs as outlined above. Second, I examine the econometric characteristics of earlier, more general, econometric tests of IIT that are not based on any specific theoretical model.

Data Sources

In the evaluation of the specific model, I have used figures for trade among the Nordic countries in 1985.[6] This study relies on two different types of data collected by the OECD; industrial statistics presented in the *OECD Industrial Structure Statistics 1989/90* at the 3- or 4-digit level of ISIC (International Standard Industrial Classification) and foreign trade statistics collected from the *COMTAP* database at the 4-digit level of ISIC. Our data set identifies 52 industries.

The expanded model needs empirical proxies for four variables: scale economies, technical differences, market size and trade impediments. I measure *scale economies* by a variable closely related to the theoretical variable: a proxy for the ratio of average to marginal costs in various industries.[7] *Technical differences* are measured by inter-country differences in labour productivity, that is differences in value added per employee, TECHDIFF.[8] *Market size* is measured by total GDP. Data on trade impediments are somewhat harder to come by. However, I use a dummy-variable that takes the value of 1 in industries where non-tariff barriers (as perceived by major firms) affect trade barriers considerably and 0 otherwise (Hansson, 1993).

It is also appropriate to account for the fact that real-world industries are often more heterogeneous than suggested in the theoretical analysis. When the phenomenon of IIT started to appear in empirical studies, some observers argued that this trade was simply a statistical artefact, *categorical aggregation*, resulting from the fact that products with different factor intensities were classified as belonging to the same 'industry'. Therefore, I introduce the variable CATAGG that is the number of basic tariff headings within each ISIC product group.

Test of the specific model

Based on the model of Section 2.2 and its extension to technical differences, I test the following equation.

$$IIT_{ijk} = \mathbf{D} + DIFFMS_{jk}^* SCALE_i + TECHDIFF_{ijk}^* SCALE_i$$
$$+ (TRIMP_i^*(1/SCALE_i)) + CATAGG_i \qquad \ldots (2.9)$$

where
$$IIT_{ijk} = \ln(IIT_{ijk}^*/(1 - IIT_{ijk}^*);$$
$$IIT_{ijk}^* = 1 - (|X_{ijk} - M_{ijk}|/(X_{ijk} + M_{ijk})$$

X_{ijk} and M_{ijk} are exports and imports, respectively, in industry i in trade between countries j and k. The transformation of the dependent variable is undertaken in order to obtain predicted values in a range without bounds. $DIFFMS_{jk}$ is difference in country size between countries j and k; $SCALE_i$ is the degree of scale economies in industry i; $TECHDIFF_{ijk}$ is meant to capture technical differences between countries j and k in industry i. The country dummies are included to capture factors such as unbalanced bilateral trade and omitted variables.

It can be seen that in equation 2.9 market size, technical differences and trade impediments all interact with scale economies. As shown in the theoretical model, a given degree of technical differences gives rise to a higher share of IIT, the lower the degree of scale economies, other things being equal. Finally, the combination of scale economies and trade impediments is expected to affect the share of IIT. Note, that we use the inverse of scale and expect a positive sign for this interaction variable, since the expected effect of trade impediments on IIT is positive and that of scale economies is negative.

Equation 2.9 is estimated with ordinary least squares (OLS) but corrected for heteroscedasticity by the method introduced by White (1980). The results are presented in Table 2.1. All coefficients of interest have the expected signs, but, with the exception of the variable capturing categorical aggregation, they are insignificant. Furthermore,

Table 2.1   Determinants of intra-industry trade

Variable	(1)	(2)	(3)
TECHDIFF* SCALE	−0.168 (−1.17)	−0.156 (−1.06)	−0.167 (1.16)
DIFFMS* SCALE	−1.67 (−1.27)	−1.51 (−1.13)	−1.59 (−1.26)
TIMP* SCALE	0.410 (1.13)	0.385 (1.06)	0.404 (1.11)
CATAGG	0.003* (2.69)	0.003* (2.68)	0.003* (2.69)
PCAPDIFF* SCALE		−2.93 (−0.68)	
PCAPDIFF			−3.45 (−0.08)
n	310	310	310
R^2	0.10	0.10	0.10

t-values according to heteroscedastic-consistent estimates of standard errors are presented within parentheses.
* = coefficient significant at the 1 per cent level.
n = number of observations

the coefficient of determination is fairly low, only 0.10. Thus, our attempt to explain IIT empirically from the starting point of one specific model was not particularly successful.

Test of an eclectic approach

It may be, of course, that I simply used inadequate proxy-variables to capture the empirical variables. However, it may also be that IIT is what Gray (1988) defined as an 'untidy' phenomenon, and that several different models are needed to explain IIT. Thus, I may need to choose a different strategy, a strategy chosen by most empirical researchers of IIT: namely to combine hypotheses from various theoretical models of IIT into one empirical model. However, this approach involves econometric complications, since partial correlations based on *ad hoc* controls can, as pointed out by Leamer (1994), be difficult to interpret. Is a significant positive correlation merely due to the choice of specific control variables? Moreover, the built-in need to use control variables that are crude (to say the least), may give rise to errors of measurement.

These two issues are dealt with in Torstensson (1996a), using data for Sweden's bilateral trade with all partner countries. I will summarize the results here. I first use extreme-bounds analysis (EBA), following Leamer (1983), Leamer and Leonard (1983) and Levine and Renelt (1992), to study whether estimated coefficients are sensitive to the choice of control variables. Then, I introduce methods to deal with measurement errors.

We can employ a linear regression of the following type:

$$\ln(IIT_i/(1 - IIT_i)) = \mathbf{B_i}\mathbf{I} + B_m M + \mathbf{B_z}\mathbf{Z} \qquad \ldots (2.10)$$

where IIT_i is the GL index, $\mathbf{I}$ is the set of 'necessary' variables; M is the variable we are primarily interested in; $\mathbf{Z}$, finally, is the set of 'doubtful' variables that is varied in order to examine whether the estimate B_m is robust.

The extreme lower and upper bounds of the variable in question are defined by the combination of 'doubtful' variables that yield the lowest and highest sum, respectively, of the estimated coefficients plus two standard deviations. A partial correlation is defined as robust if the regression coefficients are significant and of the same sign at the extreme bounds.

In deciding which variables to use, I have simply included those used in earlier empirical studies. The empirical results are presented in Table 2.2 which shows that most variables can be considered 'fragile' using

Table 2.2　EBA results

Variable	Coefficient B/U/L	Percentage Significance	Robust / Fragile
MS(83)	+/+*/+	26	Fragile
MS(89)	+/ + /−	0	Fragile
TB1(83)	+/ + /−	0	Fragile
TB1(89)	−*/ − /−*	96	Fragile
TB2(83)	+/+*/+	9	Fragile
TB2(89)	+/ + /−	0	Fragile
TB3(83)	−/ + /−	0	Fragile
TB3(89)	+*/+*/+*	100	Robust
PE(83)	−*/−*/−*	100	Robust
PE(89)	−*/−*/−*	100	Robust

HE(83)	+/ + /−	0	Fragile
HE(89)	+/ + /−	0	Fragile
MF1(83)	+/+*/+	5	Fragile
MF1(89)	+/ + /−	0	Fragile
MF2(83)	+/ + /−	0	Fragile
MF2(89)	+/ + /+	0	Fragile
SE1a(83)	+/ + /−	0	Fragile
SE1a(89)	+/ + /+	0	Fragile
SE1b(83)	+/ + /−	0	Fragile
SE1b(89)	+/ + /−	0	Fragile
SE2(83)	−/ + /−	0	Fragile
SE2(89)	−/ + /−	0	Fragile
SE4(83)	+*/+*/+	36	Fragile
SE4(89)	−/ − /−	0	Fragile
PD1(83)	+/ + /−	0	Fragile
PD1(89)	−/ + /−*	12	Fragile
PD2(83)	+/+*/+	4	Fragile
PD2(89)	+*/+*/−	48	Fragile
PD3(83)	+/ + /+	0	Fragile
PD3(89)	−/ − /−	0	Fragile
PD4(83)	+/ + /−	0	Fragile
PD4(89)	+/ + /+	0	Fragile
TF(83)	+/+*/+	1	Fragile
TF(89)	+*/+*/+	55	Fragile

+ indicates a coefficient that is positive but insignificant;
+* indicates a coefficient that is positive and significant at the 5% level;
− indicates a coefficient that is negative but insignificant;
−* indicates a coefficient that is negative and significant at the 5% level;
Coefficient B/U/L presents first the coefficient in the base regression, then the coefficients at the extreme and upper and lower bounds, respectively. For example; +/+*/− means that the coefficient is positive but insignificant in the base regression, positive and significant at the upper extreme bound but negative and insignificant at the lower extreme bound. Thus, the relationship is fragile.
Percentage significance indicates the proportion of significant regression coefficients.

the EBA-method. For definitions of the variables see the Appendix at the end of this chapter. However, the variable for extreme physical capital-intensity is robust in both years. Moreover, some variables are significant in a number of regressions but still technically fragile (see Torstensson, 1996a). The results of this study suggest that caution should be exercised in interpreting cross-sectional tests of IIT, and they add to the insights on the limitations of cross-sectional studies of IIT put forward by Greenaway and Milner (1986, Chapters 9 and 12).

Nevertheless, I managed to identify one variable, capital intensity, which was robust even to the (perhaps too) demanding test of EBA-analysis. This variable is also well founded theoretically (see Hansson and Lundberg, 1989). Moreover, the variable capturing transportation costs is robust in 1993, and other variables are significant in a substantial proportion of the regressions.

Measurement errors

Measurement errors can also be expected to be a serious problem in tests of IIT. There can be two types of errors: most of the theoretical concepts are captured by potentially inadequate proxies when they are used as explanatory variables, and data can be recorded inaccurately.

This sub-section, therefore, deals with measurement errors, following Torstensson (1996a). I use the results in the previous section and include only variables that were shown to be relatively robust according to EBA. It is easy to show that, since the covariance between the explanatory variables differs from zero with measurement errors in the independent variables, estimations with OLS will lead to biased estimates (see Maddala, 1989). There are two standard ways of handling such errors, the instrumental variables method (IV) and reverse regressions, both of which were used in Torstensson (1996a).

The results of the IV estimations show that the coefficients of most of the variables increase in magnitude with IV, which suggests that OLS underestimates the true coefficients. However, the standard errors have also increased, as might be expected with the technique of IV, but all variables are significant at the 1 per cent level.

On the assumption that measurement errors are orthogonal to the true unobserved variables, reversed regressions can be performed by using all the independent, right-hand-side, variables expected to have measurement errors as dependent, left-hand-side, variables. Klepper and Leamer (1984) showed that the coefficient of the 'true' maximum likelihood estimate is bounded by the minimum and maximum estimate when direct and reverse regressions are carried out. Thus, if there are no changes in sign when estimating the reversed regressions, this suggests that the estimates are robust to measurement errors. If, however, the estimates change sign, they are unbounded and I cannot draw inferences about the coefficient of a correctly measured, 'true', variable unless I have prior information on how much R^2 would increase with the removal of the measurement errors.

The results of the reverse and the direct regressions show that all coefficients have the same sign throughout and are thus bounded if we are very strict in including variables for the 'correct model'. This suggests that if this is the 'correct' model, errors of measurement do not prevent us drawing inferences from the data. When including other variables, on the other hand, the estimates are unbounded, since in a number of cases they change sign in the reverse regressions.[9]

So far, I have presented some theoretical implications derived from a specific model, then tested the empirical relevance of the model, after which I undertook a more general econometric analysis. What can be concluded from these exercises? First, it was possible to derive testable hypotheses from a simple model. Second, these hypotheses did not seem to fit well with the empirical observations. Third, empirical conclusions drawn from more general empirical modelling are sensitive to various econometric problems. My reading of these exercises is, therefore, that we perhaps know less about IIT than we thought we did. Although some hypotheses stand up fairly well to sensitivity analysis, there is clearly a need to advance towards new empirical approaches to IIT.

2.4 NEW EMPIRICAL APPROACHES TO INTRA-INDUSTRY TRADE

The main breakthrough to a theoretical explanation of IIT occurred in the late 1970s. However, more recent research has produced interesting developments in empirical approaches to IIT. These include attempts to distinguish between IIT caused by vertical differentiation and horizontal differentiation; studies of determinants of quality in vertical IIT; new methods of analysing the country pattern of IIT, and, finally, case studies of different industries.[10] I will look at each of these issues.

Interesting attempts to distinguish between horizontal and vertical IIT have been made by Greenaway, Hine and Milner (GHM) (1994, 1995). They use the approach taken by Torstensson (1991, 1996d) where quality of vertically differentiated products is assumed to be measured by price. Some of their main results need to be looked at carefully. First, it seems surprising that a large part of IIT is caused by vertical rather than horizontal product differentiation. Second, the determinants of vertical and horizontal IIT seem to differ, which may explain why econometric exercises have led to differing conclusions. In other words, if the dependent variable in a regression is heterogeneous, it is not surprising that the coefficients for the explanatory variables are unstable. The studies by GHM have been useful in presenting unresolved puzzles rather than in presenting solutions to these issues. In particular, their results suggest that determinants of vertical and horizontal IIT differ sometimes in counterintuitive ways.

Previously, Torstensson (1991) used price indices to examine whether vertical IIT can be explained by differences in factor proportions. A relationship was found between the quality of trade in vertically differentiated products and the factor endowment of the exporting country. In Torstensson (1996d), it was found that it is primarily human capital and not physical capital that determines the quality of production.

In Section 2.3, I presented studies of the industry pattern of IIT and the results were somewhat disappointing. It is often thought that we know much more about the country pattern of IIT. However, Hummels and Levinsohn (1995) have undertaken an empirical study, based on the Helpman-Krugman model of monopolistic competition, the results of which appear to match those of Helpman (1987), that is to offer support for the theoretical predictions. However, the explanatory power of the model diminishes over time. While the initial coefficients for differences in relative factor endowments are significant at the beginning of the period (1960s and 1970s), they are not significant in the 1980s. Hummels and Levinsohn (1995) also use panel data, and the most important conclusion from this exercise is that country-pair dummies explain a large proportion of the variation in IIT, thereby casting doubt on general models of IIT.

Finally, it deserves to be mentioned that case studies of IIT have come to some important conclusions. These case studies include Tharakan (1989) for various product groups exhibiting IIT between developed and developing countries; Jordan (1993) in a study of liquid pumps; and Tharakan and Kerstens (1994) in a study of IIT in toys. Whereas the results in Tharakan (1989) suggest that the neo-Heckscher-Ohlin theory is an important explanation of IIT between developed and developing countries, the analysis of the toy industry in Tharakan and Kerstens (1994) suggest the opposite: it is horizontal and not vertical differentiation that is the main cause of IIT between countries at widely different levels of development. Finally, Jordan (1993) suggests that there is a variety of causes of IIT in the pump industry, but that product differentiation is not among the important factors.

What conclusions can be drawn from these new empirical approaches to IIT? It has become hard to refute that we need to distinguish between various types of IIT. The pattern of vertical IIT is predicted fairly well by the theoretical models, whereas horizontal IIT seems to be determined by a more heterogeneous array of causes.

2.5 THE FUTURE OF INTRA-INDUSTRY TRADE IN EUROPE

This book deals with IIT in the EU. Let us, therefore, extend the model outlined in Section 2.2 to three countries and ask what can then be said about the effects of regional integration. Without loss of generality, we can choose units so that there is one unit of labour in country I. In country II, there are β units of labour, and the endowment of labour in country III equals α units. The other assumptions from section 2.2 are retained.

I define $1/\tau_i$ ($\tau_i > 1$) as the fraction of manufacturing products that 'arrive' at the importers in bilateral trade flows between countries I to II and I to III in industry X_i, whereas $1/\zeta_i$, ($\tau_i > \zeta_i > 1$) is the fraction of products that arrive at the importers in trade flows between countries II and III in industry X_i. A CU is conventionally defined as an absence of tariffs and quotas among member countries that also apply a common external tariff. In our model, there is a common external trade barrier, but positive internal trade barriers persist even after formation of the CU between the 'centre' and the 'periphery'. I also define $\rho = \tau^{1-\sigma} < 1$, $\delta = \zeta^{1-\sigma} < 1$. Note that ρ and δ decrease in trade impediments (since $\sigma > 1$) and increase in the degree of equilibrium scale economies.

I can then solve for the equilibrium number of firms as (see Torstensson, 1996b).

$$n_1 = \gamma[[2\rho - \delta - 1)\rho(\alpha + \beta)]$$
$$- (\rho - 1)(\delta + 1)]/[x(\rho - 1)(2\rho - \delta - 1)] \qquad \ldots (2.11)$$

$$n_2 = \gamma[\alpha(\rho^2 - \delta)(2\rho - \delta - 1) + (1 - \rho)(\beta(2\rho^2 + \rho(1 - \delta)$$
$$- \delta - 1) + \rho(1 - \delta))]/[x(\rho - 1)(\delta - 1)(2\rho - \delta - 1)] \ldots (2.12)$$

$$n_3 = \gamma[\alpha(2\rho^3 - \rho^2(\delta + 1) - 2\rho + \delta + 1) + \beta(\delta - \rho^2)(2\rho - \delta - 1)$$
$$+ \rho(1 - \delta)(\rho - 1)]/[x(1 - \delta)(\rho - 1)(2\rho - \delta - 1)] \qquad \ldots (2.13)$$

From 2.11 to 2.13, we can solve for equilibrium IIT between countries II and III. Note, first, that the negative relationship between scale

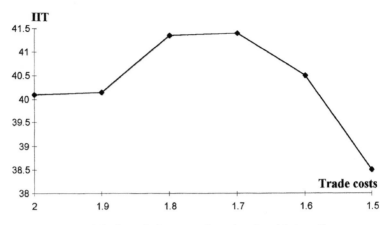

Figure 2.1   Intra-industry trade and regional integration

economies and IIT also holds in this setting. More interestingly, in the general case I derive a hump-shaped relationship between intra-union trade barriers and IIT. Figure 2.1 illustrates equilibrium intra-CU IIT shares, based on the following initial parameter values; $\beta = 0.2$, $\alpha = 0.15$, $\tau = \zeta = 2$, $\sigma = 4$. In this scenario, the share of IIT in the bilateral trade flows between the CU countries is 40.1 per cent. Then, I gradually reduce trade impediments within the CU but keep the other parameter values unchanged. IIT first increases to 41.4 per cent but, with further trade liberalization within the CU, the share of IIT decreases to 38.3 per cent. This non-monotonic equilibrium path generally emerges when scale economies are important.

There is some empirical evidence confirming that such a non-monotonic change in IIT levels may occur in reality. This evidence is of two types. First, some results suggest that a long period of growth in the share of IIT was followed by a period of stagnation or even a decline in the share of IIT. This was first suggested by Greenaway and Hine (1991), Globerman and Dean (1990), and later evidence has been provided by Brülhart and Torstensson (1996).[11] Nevertheless, it still appears premature on the basis of this evidence to conclude that shares of IIT are set to decrease in the long run.

Second, the implications of the particular model presented above have been tested in Brülhart and Torstensson (1996). We find that increasing-returns industries tend to be highly localized, concentrated in central EU countries and subject to relatively low IIT. These industries have also been subject to a reversal of intra-EU IIT growth in the 1980s. We find, furthermore, that concentration of manufacturing production has increased somewhat in the 1980s.

A third type of (indirect) evidence has been provided by Krugman (1991) who argues that concentration of manufacturing production, and thus inter-industry specialization, is much more important in the United States than it is in Europe. Thus, further liberalization of trade in Europe bringing it closer in style to trade in the USA could be expected to lead to a European production 'landscape' more like that of the USA, in other words, involving a considerably higher concentration of manufacturing production and less IIT.

However, it is questionable whether we will, in fact, reach a situation comparable to that in the USA. As argued by Krugman (1991), there may be multiple equilibria in a model with scale economies. Hence, different degrees of concentration of production in the USA and in Europe may simply be reflections of two different equilibria where historical accidents have caused production in the USA to be relatively more concentrated than in Europe. Furthermore, one could question whether the *countries* of Europe could ever be compared to the *states* of the USA. In the foreseeable future it is, for example, quite likely that preferences in favour of domestically produced varieties will continue to act as 'preference barriers' to intra-European trade for quite some time. Trade costs in the form of costs related to gathering information about foreign markets, due to such factors as cultural differences, are likely to remain. Therefore, it is doubtful that trade impediments in Europe will ever fall as low as those in the USA, and we probably will not see the same degree of concentration of production on the two sides of the Atlantic. However, it is likely that production will become more concentrated than it is today, and we can, therefore, anticipate a certain decrease in the average share of IIT in intra-European trade flows.

2.6 CONCLUDING REMARKS

After two decades of theoretical and empirical studies of IIT, numerous issues remain unresolved. The first generation of empirical tests were probably somewhat deceptive in the sense that they indicated a more deterministic relationship than could later be upheld in empirical work. The current generation of empirical studies points to serious deficiencies in the results of the first generation.

Future research might solve some of the remaining puzzles. We have been able to document the extent to which IIT occurs, and this forms a major part of this book. Furthermore, it seems that we have robust knowledge of the country pattern of IIT. However, we need to gain a better understanding of IIT determinants across industries. One promising clarification comes from the disaggregation of IIT into horizontal and vertical IIT and a separate testing of their determinants.

Finally, one might ask what has the theoretical and empirical research on IIT contributed to the general understanding of the causes and effects of international trade? The sensitivity of certain empirical results should not hide the fact that there is a robust stock of empirical knowledge of IIT. It is undeniable that this has affected trade theory at large. For example, it is now well understood that analyses of trade and trade policies need to take scale economies and imperfect competition into consideration.

Furthermore, *theories* initially designed to explain IIT have been instrumental in two of the presently most vibrant areas in economics: endogenous growth and economic geography. Endogenous growth models have drawn heavily on static IIT models, and models of economic geography are even more closely related to the first wave of IIT models (see Greenaway and Torstensson, 1997, for a discussion).

Models of the new growth theories have been tested empirically in a number of settings and using state-of-the-art econometric methods. However, in the field of economic geography, little empirical analysis has been undertaken. Therefore, the future research agenda ought to focus on subjecting the new theoretical tools of IIT and economic geography theories to serious empirical evaluation. One important lesson from the first decades of empirical analysis of IIT is that advanced methods of econometric analysis need to be used, rather than the rudimentary tools frequently utilized in early studies.

Notes

* The research that forms the basis for this chapter has been presented and discussed at various locations, in particular the SPES-Workshops on 'Trade Specialization and Market Structure in the European Community After 1992' in Antwerp, October 1993, Athens, April 1994, Nottingham, September 1994 and Coimbra, November 1995. Important stimulus was also given by seminars at the conference on 'Trade and Technology', Oslo, October 1995 at Trinity

College, Dublin, and at CREDIT, University of Nottingham, November 1995. In particular, I want to thank David Greenaway, Bob Hine, Dermot McAleese, Chris Milner, Victor Norman and Matthew Tharakan. I have also received comments and other help from Karolina Ekholm, Pär Hansson, Lars Lundberg. Lena Dahl has provided excellent research assistance. Marius Brülhart deserves special gratitude for carefully commenting on various drafts of the chapter. The *Crafoordska stiftelsen* and the Swedish Council for Research in the Humanities and Social Sciences (HSFR) have provided financial support.

1. Only a small number of empirical studies have derived their hypotheses from a specific theoretical model (see Bergstrand, 1983, 1990; Hansson and Lundberg, 1989).
2. This model has previously been used by Krugman (1980) and Helpman and Krugman (1985, chapter 10) to examine the role of market size in determining net trade.
3. Note that as long as both countries have production in industry Y, the analysis could also be extended to more than one industry. When we examine changes in the degree of scale economies/product differentiation, this could, therefore, be interpreted as a comparison between different IRS-industries with various degrees of product differentiation/ scale economies.
4. Moreover, the partial derivate of 2.8* with respect to L is equal to: $2(\rho + 1)/((1 - \rho)(L + 1)^2) > 0$ (since $L < 1$). Thus, the share of IIT is higher, the lower are the differences in country size. We will not, however, pursue this hypothesis empirically (see instead e.g. Hummels and Levinsohn, 1995).
5. Note that we then need to assume that costs differ in the same proportion as the activities that generate fixed and marginal costs.
6. For a test of the net trade pattern on the same sample, see Torstensson (1996c).
7. For a fuller discussion of the empirical variables, see Torstensson (1996b).
8. For a critical discussion of this variable, see Torstensson (1996c).
9. See Klepper and Leamer (1984) and Torstensson (1996a) for a further discussion.
10. Another important development has been the introduction of measures to capture marginal IIT. Since this is dealt with extensively in Chapter 3, it is not discussed here.
11. For the most comprehensive survey, see Chapter 5.
12. For data on the variables, see Torstensson (1996a)

References and Further Reading

Bergstrand, Jeffrey H. (1983) 'Measurement and Determinants of Intra-Industry Trade', in: Tharakan P.K.M. (ed.) 'Intra-Industry Trade: Empirical and Methodological Aspects', Amsterdam, North-Holland.

Bergstrand, Jeffrey H. (1990) 'The Heckscher-Ohlin-Samuelson Model, the Linder Hypothesis and the Determinants of Bilateral Intra-Industry Trade'. *Economic Journal*, 100, 1216–29.

Bhagwati, J. and Davis, D.R. (1994) 'Intraindustry Trade Issues and Theory', Discussion Paper 1695, Harvard Institute of Economic Research.

Brander, J.A. (1981) 'Intra-Industry Trade in Identical Commodities', *Journal of International Economics*, 11, 1–14.

Brülhart, M. (1994), 'Marginal Intra-Industry Trade: Measurement and Relevance for the Pattern of Industrial Adjustment', *Weltwirtschaftliches Archiv*, 130, 600–13.

Brülhart, M. and Torstensson, J. (1996) 'Regional Integration, Scale Economies and Industry Location in the European Union', CEPR Discussion Paper 1435.

Caves, Richard E. (1981) 'Intra-Industry Trade and Market Structure in the Industrial Countries', Oxford Economic Papers, vol. 33, 203–223.

Davis, D.R. (1995) 'Intra-Industry Trade: A Heckscher-Ohlin-Ricardo Approach', *Journal of International Economics*, 39, 201–26.

Dixit A.K. and Norman, V. (1980) *Theory of International Trade*, Cambridge: Cambridge University Press.

Dollar, D. and Wolff, E.N. (1993) *Competitiveness, Convergence, and International Specialisation*, MIT Press.

Falvey, R.E. (1981) 'Commercial Policy and Intra-Industry Trade', *Journal of International Economics*, 11, 495–511.

Falvey, R.E. and Kierzkowski, H. (1987) 'Product Quality, Intra-Industry Trade and (Im)perfect Competition', in Kierzkowski, H. (ed.), *Protection and Competition in International Trade*, Oxford: Blackwell.

Finger, J.M. (1975) 'Trade Overlap and Intra-Industry Trade', *Economic Inquiry*, 13, 143–61.

Globerman, S. and Dean, J.W. (1990) 'Recent Trends in Intra-Industry Trade and Their Implications for Future Trade Liberalization', *Weltwirtschaftliches Archiv*, 126, 25–49.

Gray, H.P. (1988) 'Intra-Industry Trade: An "Untidy Phenomenon"', *Weltwirtschaftliches Archiv*, 124, 211–29.

Greenaway, D. and Hine, R.C. (1991) 'Intra-Industry Specialization, Trade Expansion and Adjustment in the European Economic Space', *Journal of Common Market Studies*, 24, 603–22.

Greenaway, D. and Milner, C. (1986) *The Economics of Intra-Industry Trade*, Oxford: Blackwell.

Greenaway, D. and Milner, C. (1987) 'Intra-Industry Trade: Current Perspectives', *Weltwirtschaftliches Archiv*, 123, 39–48.

Greenaway, D. and Torstensson, J. (1997) 'Back to the Future: Taking Stock on Intra-Industry Trade', *Weltwirtschaftliches Archiv*, 133, 249–65.

Greenaway, D., Hine, R.C. and Milner, C. (1994) 'Country-Specific Factors and the Pattern of Horizontal and Vertical Intra-Industry Trade in the UK', *Weltwirtschaftliches Archiv*, 130, 78–100.

Greenaway, D., Hine, R.C. and Milner, C. (1995) 'Vertical and Horizontal Intra-Industry Trade: A Cross-Industry Analysis for the United Kingdom', *Economic Journal*, 105, 1505–18.

Grubel, H. and Lloyd, P. (1975) *Intra-Industry Trade*, London: MacMillan.

Hansson, P. (1991) 'Determinants of Intra-Industry Specialisation in Swedish Foreign Trade', *Scandinavian Journal of Economics*, 93, 391–406.

Hansson, P. (1993) 'The Effects of Trade Barriers on Domestic Market Performance-Evidence from the Swedish and Norwegian Manufacturing Industries', in Fagerberg, J. and Lundberg, L. (eds), *European Economic Integration: A Nordic Perspective*, Aldershot: Averbury.

Hansson, P. and Lundberg, L. (1989). 'The Role of Comparative Costs and Elasticities of Substitution as Determinants of Inter-and Intra-Industry Trade', in Tharakan, P.K.M. and Kol, J. (eds), *Intra-Industry Trade: Theory, Evidence and Extensions*, London: Macmillan.

Harrigan, J. (1994) 'Scale Economies and the Volume of Trade', *Review of Economics and Statistics*, 76, 321–8.

Helpman, E. (1981) 'International Trade in the Presence of Product Differentiation, Economies of Scale and Product Differentiation', *Journal of International Economics*, 11, 305–40.

Helpman, E. (1987) 'Imperfect Competition and International Trade: Evidence from Fourteen Industrial Countries', *Journal of the Japanese and International Economies*, 1, 62–81.

Helpman, E. and Krugman, P.R. (1985) *Market Structure and Foreign Trade: Increasing Returns, Imperfect Competition and the International Economy*, Cambridge, Mass: MIT Press.

Hummels, David and Levinsohn, James (1995) 'Monopolistic Competition and International Trade: Reconsidering the Evidence', *Quarterly Journal of Economics*, 110, 799–836.

Jordan, T. (1993) 'Intra-Industry Trade: An In-Depth Study of Swedish Liquid Pump Trade', *Weltwirtschaftliches Archiv*, 129, 752–76.

Klepper, S. and Leamer, E.E. (1984) 'Consistent Sets of Estimates for Regressions with Errors in All Variables', *Econometrica*, 52, 163–83.

Krasker, W.S. and Pratt, J.W. (1986) 'Bounding the Effects of Proxy Variables on Regression Coefficients', *Econometrica*, 54, 641–55.

Krugman, P. (1979) 'Increasing Returns, Monopolistic Competition and International Trade', *Journal of International Economics*, 9, 469–79.

Krugman, P. (1980) 'Scale Economies, Product Differentiation and the Pattern of Trade', *American Economic Review*, 70, 950–9.

Krugman, P. (1991) *Geography and Trade*, Cambridge, Mass: MIT Press.

Leamer, E.E. (1983) 'Let's Take the Con Out of Econometrics', *American Economic Review*, 73, 31–43.

Leamer, E.E. (1984) *Sources of International Comparative Advantage*, Cambridge, Mass: MIT Press.

Leamer, E.E. (1986) 'Sensitivity Analyses Would Help', *American Economic Review*, 75, 308–13.

Leamer, E.E. (1994) 'Testing Trade Theory', in Greenaway, D. and Winters, A.L. (eds), *Surveys in International Trade*, Oxford: Blackwell.

Leamer, E.E. and Leonard, H. (1983) 'Reporting the Fragility of Regression Estimates', *Review of Economics and Statistics*, 65, 306–17.

Levine, R. and Renelt, D. (1992) 'A Sensitivity Analysis of Cross-Country Growth Regressions', *American Economic Review*, 82, 942–63.

Lundberg, Lars (1982) 'Intra-Industry Trade: The Case of Sweden', *Weltwirtschaftliches Archiv*, 118, 302–316.

Maddala, G.S. (1989) *Introduction to Econometrics*, New York: Macmillan.

Tharakan, P.K.M. (1989) 'Bilateral Intra-Industry Trade between Countries with Different Factor Endowment Patterns', in Tharakan, P.K.M. and Kol, J. (eds), *Intra-Industry Trade: Theory, Evidence and Extensions*, London: Macmillan.

Tharakan, P.K.M. and Kerstens, B. (1994) 'Does North-South Horizontal Intra-Industry Trade Really Exist? An Analysis of the Toy Industry', *Weltwirtschaftliches Archiv*, 131, 86–105.

Torstensson, J. (1991) 'Quality Differentiation and Factor Proportions in International Trade', *Weltwirtschaftliches Archiv*, 127, 183–94.

Torstensson, J. (1996a) 'Determinants of Intra-Industry Trade: A Sensitivity Analysis', *Oxford Bulletin of Economics and Statistics*, 58, 507–24.

Torstensson, J. (1996b) 'Intra-Industry Trade Under Monopolistic Competition: Some Theoretical Results', mimeo, Lund University.

Torstensson, J. (1996c) 'Technical Differences and Inter-Industry Trade in the Nordic Countries', *Scandinavian Journal of Economics*, 98, 93–110.

Torstensson, J. (1996d) 'Can Factor Proportions Explain Vertical Intra-Industry Trade', *Applied Economics Letters*, 3, 307–9.

White, H. (1980) 'A Heteroscedasticity-Consistent Covariance Matrix Estimator and a Direct Test for Heteroscedasticity', *Econometrica*, 48, 817–38.

APPENDIX: VARIABLES AND RESULTS IN THE EBA-TEST

This appendix describes the variables in the EBA-test and Table 2.2 presents the empirical results (for further discussion, see Torstensson (1996a)). PD1 is the number of tariff groups on the lowest level of CCCN within each 6-digit SNI product group.[12] The variable PD2 measures the coefficient of variation in export unit prices whereas the variable PD3 captures the proportion of sales personnel in the labour force. The variable PD4 aims to measure the elasticity of demand (see Hansson, 1991). Hansson and Lundberg (1989) suggest including variables capturing comparative costs. I include two variables: the deviation in absolute terms from the average proportion of technicians in the labour force as a measure of 'extreme' human capital-intensity, HE. As a measure of physical capital-intensity, I follow Hansson and Lundberg (1989) in measuring it by a *stock* variable, the power of installed machinery per employee, PCAP. Consequently, the absolute deviation from the installed power of machinery per employee is used as a measure of 'extreme' physical capital-intensity, PE. Caves (1981) proposed including the extent of activities of multinational firms (MF) as a determinant of IIT. Data on output of MFs is not available, so I have used employment data. The variable MF1 measures the ratio of employment in Swedish-owned MFs abroad to total domestic employment while MF2 measures the proportion of employment in foreign-owned MFs. The variable SE1a measures employment per establishment whereas SE1b measures value added per establishment as proxy-variables for scale economies. The variable SE2 captures the proportion of the labour force employed in plants with more than 500 employees (see Lundberg, 1982). Finally, SE4 aims to capture the ratio of average to marginal cost by defining marginal costs as wages for employees involved in direct production (manual labour), costs of raw material, packaging and transportation, and costs of energy and fuel. All other costs are defined as fixed costs (a similar measure of price-cost margins is used by Harrigan, 1994). The variable TB1 is the nominal tariff rate whereas TB2 is a dummy-variable that takes the value of 1 in industries where non-tariff barriers (as perceived by major firms) affect trade barriers considerably and 0 otherwise (Hansson, 1993). Finally, the variable TB3 measures the unit weight assuming that products with a high unit value can be transported at lower cost than products with low unit values. As suggested by, for example Greenaway and Milner (1986), to capture market structure I also use the variable MS that measures the four-firm concentration ratio. Finally, I use the variable TF to measure the proportion of technical personnel in the labour force. This variable has previously been used by, for example, Hansson and Lundberg (1989).

3. Marginal Intra-Industry Trade and Trade-Induced Adjustment: a Survey

Marius Brülhart

3.1 INTRODUCTION

Probably the greatest source of interest in intra-industry trade (IIT) has been its link with factor-market adjustment. Policy-oriented economists readily grasped the opportunity of an index which was simple to calculate and presumed to indicate relatively frictionless adjustment to trade liberalization.

Trade theorists had been demonstrating the superiority of free trade since Adam Smith. The observation of pervasive IIT led to the 'new trade theory' which identified additional sources of gains from trade, through scale economies and product differentiation. However, policy makers often find the obstacle of short-term adjustment costs, frequently borne by well-organized groups, in the way of the long-term gains of trade liberalization. Here too, IIT appeared to help the case of free-traders. Simple intuition suggests that IIT expansion is concomitant with factor reallocation within rather than between industries. To redeploy workers or machinery in another firm within the same sector is likely to be considerably easier than to adapt them for production in an entirely different industry. The liberalization of trade between countries with high or growing IIT was seen therefore to entail relatively low adjustment costs. We refer to this assumption as the 'smooth-adjustment hypothesis'. This argument has been invoked in the discussion of the EU enlargement to Central and Eastern Europe, the '1992' Single Market, the NAFTA agreement in North America and global trade liberalization under successive GATT rounds.

We proceed as follows. Section 3.2 illustrates the pervasive impact of the smooth adjustment hypothesis on the applied trade literature and reveals the comparative weakness of its theoretical and empirical underpinnings. In Section 3.3, we provide a rigorous formulation of the hypothesis. Section 3.4 surveys the literature on marginal IIT, which has proposed a number of measures of relevance to adjustment, Section 3.5 examines the theoretical foundations of these measures, and Section 3.6 discusses the empirical evidence on the subject. We conclude with a brief summary in Section 3.7.

3.2 WEIGHTY HYPOTHESIS – WOBBLY FOUNDATIONS

An article of faith: The smooth-adjustment hypothesis in the literature

The supposition that IIT entails lower costs of factor-market adjustment than inter-industry trade, referred to here as the 'smooth-adjustment hypothesis' (SAH), is as old as the study of IIT. Balassa (1966, p. 472), opened the debate by writing that 'the difficulties of adjustment to freer trade have been generally overestimated', because 'it is apparent that the increased (intra-industry) exchange of consumer goods is compatible with unchanged production in every country'. Over the following three decades the SAH has become firmly established. The degree of acceptance is well captured by Grant *et al.* (1993, pp. 32f.): 'A (···) purported characteristic of intraindustry trade is its allegedly low adjustment costs in the face of trade liberalization. It has become an article of faith that the European Community's early liberalization succeeded because of intraindustry trade'.

We have compiled Table 3.1 in order to illustrate the pervasive use economists have made of the SAH. Reported are only studies published during the last decade. Even though this list is certainly not exhaustive, and not all the included studies accept the hypothesis uncritically, we can note that the SAH has been invoked in the academic analysis of most recent episodes of trade liberalization.

Grounds for scepticism

The SAH has been absorbed into the canon of international economics with an astonishing lack of critical scrutiny. It has neither been formalized in a rigorous model, nor has it been subjected to much empirical testing.

Let us first consider theory. Sceptics, on theoretical grounds, of the SAH have been rare. The most celebrated model of IIT, based on large firm numbers, horizontal product differentiation and monopolistic competition, has generally been invoked as the main underpinning of the SAH. Krugman's (1981, p. 970) model, for instance, yields the

Table 3.1   Recent empirical studies with reference to the smooth-adjustment
hypothesis

Region	Episode	Studies
World	Global integration	Fischer and Serra (1996)
	Regional integration	Hoekman and Kostecki (1995)
European Union	Iberian enlargement	Greenaway (1987); Krugman (1987); Hine (1989)
	Single Market	CEC (1996), CEPII (1988); Greenaway and Hine (1991); Balasubramanyam and Greenaway (1993); Sapir (1992)
	EU Eastward enlargement	Cadot *et al.* (1995); Drábek and Smith (1995); Hoekman and Djankov (1996); Lemoine (1995); Neven (1995)
	Swedish trade with EU	Lundberg (1992)
North America	NAFTA	Globerman (1992); Gonzalez and Velez (1993); Little (1996); Shelburne (1993)
Latin America	Regional integration	Primo Braga *et al.* (1994)
Asia	Trade expansion by Japan and NICs	Grant *et al.* (1993); Lincoln (1990); OECD (1994); Noland (1990); Rajan (1996)
	Regional integration	Drysdale and Garnaut (1993); Khalifah (1996)
Australia	Regional integration	Hamilton and Kniest (1991); Menon and Dixon (1995)
South Africa	Regional integration	Parr (1994)

hypothesis that IIT 'poses fewer adjustment problems than inter-industry trade'. However, use of the term 'adjustment' in the interpretation of such a model is misleading. The welfare effects Krugman alluded to did not relate to transition costs but to end-state utility distributions before and after trade liberalization. This result, valid in its own right but not to be confused with the SAH, has been expressed succinctly by Rodrik (1994, p. 7): 'intra-industry trade will make everyone better off: it will increase the number of varieties available for consumption without reducing anyone's real income'. The mainstream large-number models of horizontal IIT assume the products of an industry to be perfectly homogenous in terms of quantitative and qualitative factor requirements and thus eliminate transitional costs by assumption.

The second body of theory explaining horizontal IIT is constituted by small-number oligopoly models of 'reciprocal dumping'. There is some empirical evidence that the pricing and purchasing behaviour of international oligopolies or oligopsonies and differentiation of inter-mediate products might be the main explanations of horizontal IIT.[1] Having surveyed the literature on oligopolies in international trade, Richardson (1989, p. 15) pointed out that 'trade liberalization under imperfect competition...can cause much more dramatic, discontinuous changes in trade, production and market structure than under perfect competition'. Intuitively, adjustment seems likely to be more disruptive in homogenous industries with concentrated market structures than in sectors with differentiated products and large firm numbers.[2] However, these issues have been formally explored neither in terms of their implications for real factor rewards nor in terms of transitional adjustment costs. The main theories capable of explaining IIT, therefore, do not provide a coherent underpinning for the SAH.

While we look in vain for a rigorous theoretical foundation to the SAH, it might be the case that empirical work has produced support-ive evidence. However, explicit empirical verification of the SAH has also been scant. A mere handful of studies have been devoted to this topic, and they all explored the issue in an indirect fashion. The main approach was to examine whether factor intensities are less hetero-geneous within than between industries. Considerable heterogeneity has been found within industries, but differentials between industries tend also to be significant.[3] The persuasiveness of such factor-ratio analyses, however, is constrained by the crude measures of produc-tion factors. These measures are unable to distinguish, for instance, between industry-specific and transferable factors.

The SAH has also been examined through industry case-studies. Adler (1970) analysed data on the European steel industry and found that high IIT in that sector subsequent to the formation of the Euro-pean Coal and Steel Community was accompanied by relatively fric-tionless adjustment.[4] Reker (1994) has explored IIT and adjustment patterns in European machine tool manufacturing. He found that this industry is very heterogeneous and that high levels of IIT masked considerable adjustment processes within this sector.

A third empirical approach to the SAH was taken via political-economy considerations. Lundberg and Hansson (1986) conjectured that the fast trade liberalization of Swedish sectors subject to high initial IIT levels resulted from a lower demand for protection in these industries, which in turn suggests that IIT has relatively benign welfare effects.[5] In a study of Australian trade liberalization, however, Ratnayake and Jayasuriya (1991) argued that previous single-equation estimations had suffered from simultaneity bias, and they detected no effect of IIT on tariff reduction when estimated through a simultaneous-equation model.

The available empirical evidence on the SAH therefore appears as inconclusive as the relevant theoretical work. Furthermore, there is an even more fundamental issue which needs to be clarified, namely the precise meaning of the SAH. The two core variables, trade-induced adjustment costs and IIT, have never been clearly defined and have, therefore, been subject to differing implicit interpretations. In Section 3.4 we provide a precise formulation of the SAH. Section 3.5 surveys the recent literature on marginal IIT (MIIT), which proposes the relevant measures of IIT in the context of adjustment issues.

3.3   CLEARING THE MIST: WHAT THE HYPOTHESIS REALLY MEANS

The SAH propounds a link between trade and adjustment. These two variables need to be clarified. This section therefore provides a definition of the SAH which can serve as a basis for rigorous theoretical and empirical treatment.

Trade as a cause for adjustment

What do we mean when we say a certain change is 'trade-induced'? Trade flows are an endogenous variable in all open-economy models, and cannot *per se* be a source of adjustment. Rather, trade flows and factor allocations are determined jointly given certain parameter values on the exogenous variables.

There are two principal conceptions of trade as a source of adjustment. In partial-equilibrium, small-open-economy (SOE) models adjustment is traditionally analysed by departing from a change in world market prices. Such price changes are exogenous to the SOE, and can originate in a multitude of sources, such as changes in demand, factor endowments or trade policies of trading partners. These changes can be labelled 'trade-induced', since they would not affect the SOE in autarky. Trade costs are generally ignored in this modelling framework. The second concept of trade as a source of adjustment centres on changes in these trade costs, holding everything else constant in multi-country general-equilibrium models. Under that definition, 'trade-induced' means sparked by a change in the level of barriers to international trade. These barriers can take the form of policy measures, such as tariffs, non-tariff barriers or monetary transaction costs, or they can come in the form of natural obstacles, through topographical features or through the bulkiness of traded goods. We refer to a reduction in any of these barriers as 'economic integration'. In a nutshell, domestic adjustment is trade-induced either if caused by a reduction in trade barriers, holding everything else constant; or if caused by any relevant changes in foreign markets, holding trade costs constant.[6]

The definition of adjustment costs

Adjustment costs can also be divided into two categories. First, they can arise even in perfectly competitive markets with flexible prices. If factors are subject to any degree of heterogeneity and product specificity, then trade-induced reallocation will inevitably divert resources to make the transition possible. Hence, production will occur inside the long-run production possibility frontier for the duration of adjustment, as resources are used to retrain, move and match labour, and to adapt the capital stock. Temporary factor-price disparities are needed to incite resource use on such *adjustment services*. This is why intersectoral wage differentials can be taken as an indicator for labour specificity (that is, costly adjustment services in the labour market).

When arising from a fall in the relative price of importables (for example through integration), adjustment costs of this nature do not lead to an aggregate welfare loss, and their impact is purely distributional.[7] In theory, lump-sum transfers can be designed so as to compensate all individuals for transitional income losses.[8] In practice, however, transitional wage and income disparities often go uncompensated, thus producing net losers and feeding protectionist pressures.

The second class of adjustment costs arises in the presence of market imperfections. The most commonly analysed imperfection is that of downwardly rigid nominal wages. Under such a configuration, adjustment costs might outweigh the gains from trade, hence trade liberalization might be Pareto inferior.[9] The cost–benefit balance depends on the magnitude of adjustment costs and trade gains as well as on the social discount rate.

Labour specificity and wage rigidity both give rise to unemployment if a trade shock upsets the initial labour–market equilibrium. Most trade models suggest that adjustment problems result in *temporary* unemployment. While the duration of the adjustment process cannot be determined *a priori*, the underlying expectation is that market forces tend towards full employment. In practice, however, market rigidities combined with hysteresis effects may extend the duration of trade-induced unemployment. Hence, trade-induced unemployment could conceivably be long-term. The theory of adjustment, however, is firmly rooted in neo-classical thinking, where the market-based price mechanism is driving the economy relentlessly towards full employment.[10]

The Smooth-Adjustment Hypothesis rigorously defined

Having defined its constituent parts, we can now formulate the SAH with greater precision. The fully specified hypothesis can be spelt out in four steps.

1. Define *adjustment costs* as the sum of resources utilized in adapting factors to alternative uses and the resources left unemployed because of sticky factor prices.
2. Assume that *industries* are defined in such a way that adjustment costs from a shift in production between sub-industries are lower than the adjustment costs from an equiproportional shift in production between industries.
3. Define *intra-industry trade* in such a way that changes in world market prices or in trade barriers result in greater changes of relative demand between sub-industries than between industries, and inter-industry trade as the opposite configuration.
4. Given 1. to 3., intra-industry trade will entail lower adjustment costs than inter-industry trade, *ceteris paribus*.

With this clarified formulation of the SAH, the hypothesis can be examined meaningfully and coherently through theory and empirical work. As a by-product, our formulation reveals additional limitations of previous empirical explorations. Each of the four steps is necessary but not sufficient for the hypothesis to hold. Yet, factor-content analyses were concerned solely with Step 2. Industry case studies did not isolate various determinants of structural change and therefore fail the *ceteris paribus* test of Step 4. Finally, inferences drawn from tariff levels are based on the implicit assumption that adjustment costs, as identified in Step 1, translate directly into protection. This ignores the fact that adjustment costs are only one of several welfare effects of trade policy, and should thus not be treated as the sole determinant of an industry's demand for (and policy makers' supply of) protection.

One aspect that was ignored by all previous empirical studies of the SAH is Step 3, the relevant definition of IIT in the adjustment context. This question is addressed by the literature on marginal IIT, to which we turn in the next section.

3.4 MEASURING MARGINAL INTRA-INDUSTRY TRADE: A TOOLKIT

The Concept

In mentioning the SAH different commentators have implicitly held different conceptions of IIT. The standard IIT measure is the Grubel-Lloyd (GL) index. This leaves room for at least two interpretations of 'IIT' in the adjustment context. IIT could refer to either the GL index at the start or end of the relevant period (GL_t), or to the growth of the GL index over that period (ΔGL). The GL index is a static measure, in the sense that it captures IIT for one particular year.[11] However, adjustment is a dynamic phenomenon. By suggesting the concept of marginal IIT (MIIT), Hamilton and Kniest (1991) have opened a dimension to the empirical study of IIT which for the first time acknowledged this problem and endeavoured to define IIT in a sense that is compatible with Step 3 of the SAH. They showed that the observation of a high proportion of IIT in one particular time period does not justify *a priori* any prediction of the likely pattern of *change* in trade flows. Even an observed increase in static IIT levels between two periods (positive ΔGL) could 'hide' a very uneven change in trade flows, concomitant with *inter*- rather than *intra*-industry adjustment.

In order to infer conclusions on adjustment from the measurement of IIT, it is necessary, therefore, to analyse the pattern of *change* in trade flows rather than comparing the composition of trade at different points in time. Several methods for the dynamic analysis of IIT have been suggested to date. This section summarizes the main measures. A simple numerical illustration of these measures is given in the Appendix.

Comparing Grubel-Lloyd indices

Prior to the introduction of the MIIT concept, the evaluation of IIT changes over time was confined to the comparison of GL indices for different time periods, where

$$\Delta GL = GL_t - GL_{t-n} = \left(1 - \frac{|M - X|}{(M + X)}\right)_t - \left(1 - \frac{|M - X|}{(M + X)}\right)_{t-n},$$
$$\ldots (3.1)$$

where M stands for imports, X represents exports, t is the end year, and n is the number of years separating the base and end years.

Hamilton and Kniest (1991, p. 360) revealed that this method was flawed, pointing out that 'an increase in inter-industry trade flows will show up as an increase in the GL index of IIT when the increase in inter-industry trade acts to reduce the trade imbalance in the sector being measured'. Thus, the juxtaposition of corresponding GL indices for different periods conveys some information on the structure of trade in each of these time periods, but it does not allow conclusions on the structure of the *change* in trade flows.[12] These theoretical considerations are backed up by empirical evidence in Little (1996), where a *rise* in GL indices in inter-regional trade between Canada and the United States was generally accompanied by *above-average* degrees of structural change.

The Hamilton-Kniest index

The first measure of MIIT was proposed by Hamilton and Kniest (1991) according to which:

$$MIIT_{HK} = \begin{cases} \frac{X_t - X_{t-n}}{M_t - M_{t-n}} & \text{for } M_t - M_{t-n} > X_t - X_{t-n} > 0 \\ \frac{M_t - M_{t-n}}{X_t - X_{t-n}} & \text{for } X_t - X_{t-n} > M_t - M_{t-n} > 0 \\ \text{undefined} & \text{for } X_t < X_{t-n} \text{ or } M_t < M_{t-n} \end{cases}$$
$$\ldots (3.2)$$

where $X_t(M_t)$ and $X_{t-n}(M_{t-n})$ are exports (imports) of a particular industry in years t and $t - n$, and n represents the number of years separating the two years of measurement. This measure eliminates the first shortcoming of simple GL-index comparison by examining the structure of the *change* in trading patterns. However, Greenaway *et al.* (1994b) have highlighted the fact that the HK index, being undefined when either X or M has decreased, can lead to a non-random omission of a significant number of statistical observations and, therefore, to potentially misleading results.[13]

Furthermore, Hamilton and Kniest (1991) have interpreted any situation where their index is undefined as representing 'an increase in exports and a decrease in imports (or vice versa), which indicates inter-industry trade'. Yet, the HK index is also undefined where both imports and exports have decreased, a situation in which the matched decreases should be recorded as MIIT. In contrast to the interpretation by its inventors, the HK index does therefore not convey any information as to the structure of MIIT for the sectors where the index is undefined.

The Greenaway-Hine-Milner-Elliott measure

Greenaway *et al.* (1994b) have suggested an alternative measure of MIIT:

$$MIIT_{GHME} = [(X + M) - |X - M|]_t - [(X + M) - |X - M|]_{t-n},$$
$$\ldots (3.3)$$

or:

$$MIIT_{GHME} = \Delta[(X + M) - |X - M|]. \qquad \ldots (3.4)$$

This measure, unlike the HK index, is always defined. However, the GHME measure resembles the juxtaposition of GL indices in that it corresponds to the difference in IIT levels of two periods, and therefore shares the latter method's inaccuracy for the assessment of the structure of *change* in trading patterns. Hamilton and Kniest's criticism of the GL-comparison method thus also applies to the GHME measure. Assume, for instance, that over the period of investigation a particular sector experiences a shift from a trade surplus to balanced trade while exports remain unchanged. The GHME measure will show a positive value of twice the increase in imports, even though this is an obvious case of *inter*-industry adjustment, because the increase in imports is not matched by any corresponding increase in exports.

The GHME measure fundamentally differs from the GL and HK indices in that it reports IIT in absolute values rather than as a ratio. This feature is desirable mainly because it facilitates the scaling of MIIT relative to gross trade levels, production or sales in a particular industry, which in turn is crucial for the assessment of specialization and adjustment pressures. The GHME measure in itself is unscaled. It is inferior to traditional indices in that it says nothing about the proportion of (marginal) intra-relative to inter-industry trade, and it lacks the presentational appeal of a simple index contained between, say, 0 and 1. Hence, its *raison d'être* rests upon the fact that 'it can be related to corresponding levels of gross trade or real output in the context of any analysis of adjustment problems' (Greenaway *et al.*, 1994b, p. 424).

A Grubel-Lloyd style measure of MIIT: the 'A' index

Brülhart (1994) has suggested the following MIIT index.[14]

$$MIIT = A = 1 - \frac{|(X_t - X_{t-n}) - (M_t - M_{t-n})|}{|X_t - X_{t-n}| + |M_t - M_{t-n}|} \qquad \ldots (3.5)$$

which can also be written as:

$$A = 1 - \frac{|\Delta X - \Delta M|}{|\Delta X| + |\Delta M|}. \qquad \ldots (3.6)$$

This index, like the GL coefficient, varies between 0 and 1, where 0 indicates marginal trade in the particular industry to be completely of the *inter*-industry type, and 1 represents marginal trade to be entirely of the *intra*-industry type. The index A shares most of the statistical properties of the GL index, of which a comprehensive description is provided in Greenaway and Milner (1986).[15]

Note that A can be summed, like the GL index, across industries of the same level of statistical disaggregation by applying the following formula for a weighted average:

$$A_{tot} = \sum_{i=1}^{k} w_i A_i, \qquad \text{where } w_i = \frac{|\Delta X|_i + |\Delta M|_i}{\sum_{i=1}^{k}(|\Delta X|_i + |\Delta M|_i)} \qquad \ldots (3.7)$$

and where A_{tot} is the weighted average of MIIT over all industries of the economy or over all the sub-industries of an industry, denoted by $i \ldots, k$.

The main appeal of the A index lies in the fact that it reveals the structure of the *change* in import and export flows, similar to the HK index. Yet, unlike the latter measure, the A coefficient is defined in all cases and shares many familiar statistical properties of the GL index.

The A index relates absolute values of import and export changes to each other, irrespective of the initial levels of imports or exports. When this index is equal to one, both imports and exports have grown (or shrunk) to an equal extent, hence neither the domestic nor the competing foreign industry has achieved a superior trade performance in absolute terms. However, this could conceal different *relative* performances. It could be the case, for instance, that the domestic industry started off from a considerably lower level of exports than its foreign counterpart, hence the initial trade balance for this sector was strongly negative. If, after *n* years, both imports and exports have expanded by equal amounts, then the *A* index is equal to one, which we interpret as a purely *intra*-industry change in trade patterns. Yet, relative to its initial trade performance, the home country's industry has achieved a greater increase in exports than its foreign competitor, since the sectoral trade deficit has narrowed. A narrowing sectoral deficit (or surplus), in turn, is equivalent to a rise in the GL index.

It might thus be useful to construct a measure which takes account of the sectoral trade balance in the initial year, and defines as MIIT any change in trade flows which does not affect the industry's trade balance. The following coefficient ('A for relative trade changes') could be applied:

$$A^r = 1 - \frac{\left| \frac{\Delta X}{X_{t-n}} - \frac{\Delta M}{M_{t-n}} \right|}{\left| \frac{\Delta X}{X_{t-n}} \right| + \left| \frac{\Delta M}{M_{t-n}} \right|}, \qquad \text{for all} (X, M)_{t-n} > 0. \qquad \ldots (3.8)$$

Whether *A* or A^r should be used is a matter of judgement. Preferring A^r implies that fixed trade shares for each country in each sector, concomitant with unchanged GL indices in each industry, are regarded as the 'pure' MIIT scenario. If the *A* index is chosen, equal absolute amounts of trade changes on the import and export sides are seen as 'pure' MIIT. In purely conceptual terms, A^r is the superior measure, since it reflects symmetrical proportionate trade changes across countries, thus not affecting the relative size of industries in terms of imports and exports. One way of choosing is to establish empirically which of the two coefficients is a better indicator of trade-induced adjustment costs. We can also note that the higher the GL index in the initial year $(t - n)$, the smaller – and the less important – is the difference between *A* and A^r.

Linking MIIT with the analysis of sectoral trade performance: the 'B' index

The *A* index (like the GL index) can provide results which are relevant for multilateral studies by relating to overall adjustment pressures.

Yet, it is of limited usefulness for one-country studies, since it does not contain any information as to the *distribution* of trade-induced gains and losses among countries or sectors.

Hence, Brülhart (1994) suggested the following index:

$$B = \frac{\Delta X - \Delta M}{|\Delta X| + |\Delta M|},\qquad\qquad\qquad\qquad \ldots(3.9)$$

where $\quad |B| = 1 - A.$ $\qquad\qquad\qquad\qquad\qquad\qquad$ ...(3.10)

The B coefficient can take values ranging between -1 and 1. It is two-dimensional, containing information about both the proportion of MIIT and country-specific sectoral performance. First, the closer B is to zero, the higher is MIIT. B is equal to zero where marginal trade in the particular industry is entirely of the *intra*-industry type, whereas at both -1 and 1 it represents marginal trade to be entirely of the *inter*-industry type. Second, sectoral performance is defined as the change in exports and imports in relation to each other, with exports representing good domestic performance and imports reflecting weak domestic performance in a particular sector. Thus defined, B is directly related to sectoral performance. When $B > 0, \Delta X$ was $> \Delta M$. The opposite holds for $B < 0$.

Unlike the A index, B cannot be aggregated meaningfully across industries.[16] Since high marginal inter-industry trade is expressed by values close to either -1 or 1, the weighted average of two sub-industries might yield a value close to zero (high MIIT) even where high marginal *inter*-industry trade prevails in both of them. Therefore, B cannot be used for summary statistics resulting from calculations on a disaggregated level. Its applicability is thus confined to the industry-by-industry assessment of MIIT and performance.

Analogous to the A^r index, we can define a coefficient B^r, which weights trade changes relative to their initial levels:

$$B^r = \frac{\frac{\Delta X}{X_{t-n}} - \frac{\Delta M}{M_{t-n}}}{\left|\frac{\Delta X}{X_{t-n}}\right| + \left|\frac{\Delta M}{M_{t-n}}\right|},\qquad \text{for all}(X, M)_{t-n} > 0,\qquad \ldots(3.11)$$

where $\quad |B^r| = 1 - A^r.$ $\qquad\qquad\qquad\qquad\qquad\qquad$ ...(3.12)

The distinction between B and B^r is the same as that between A and A^r outlined above.

The interpretation of trade flows which underlies the above measure is somewhat mercantilistic in nature. Obviously, the relation between a sector's export performance and its import penetration does not convey the full information on competitiveness and adjustment costs. Nevertheless, this analysis provides some indication of the sectors a country specialized '*into*', the sectors it specialized '*out of*' and the sectors in which increased (or reduced) trade flows did not affect the international pattern of adjustment and inter-industry specialization.

Scaling MIIT measures: the 'C' index

As Greenaway *et al.* (1994b, p. 423) have noted, 'when we think about adjustment we are thinking about the implications of changes in the pattern of specialization, *not* changes in the shares of exports and imports in increased trade'. It is only by relating measures of the composition of trade to variables such as initial gross trade or production that they can be interpreted as valid indicators of structural change. Therefore, a third method has been suggested by Brülhart (1994), where the *absolute* values of MIIT, representing matching *changes* in trade flows, yield the following measure.[17]

$$C = (|\Delta X| + |\Delta M|) - |\Delta X - \Delta M|, \qquad \ldots (3.13)$$

which can be scaled even at the disaggregated industry level, like the GHME measure:

$$C_V = \frac{C}{V}, \qquad \ldots (3.14)$$

where V is any relevant scaling variable.

Menon and Dixon (1997) have proposed a very similar measure. Instead of capturing absolute values of sectorally matched trade changes, like C, theirs is a 'measure of unmatched changes in trade' ($UMCIT = |\Delta X - \Delta M|$). The two measures are closely related, as C shows the absolute magnitude of MIIT and $UMCIT$ shows the absolute magnitude of marginal *inter*-industry trade.

Absolute values of MIIT, such as C and $UMCIT$, are difficult to interpret in isolation, since they give no indication of the proportion between intra- and inter-industry trade, which, after all, is central to the definition of the very concept of IIT. Therefore, it seems most appropriate for studies investigating MIIT and adjustment to use a two stage approach, where MIIT is expressed first in relation to marginal *inter*-industry trade and second in relation to structural variables.

3.5   WHY WE EXPECT MARGINAL INTRA-INDUSTRY TRADE TO MATTER: THEORETICAL UNDERPINNINGS

Measures of MIIT have been developed because they are thought to relate more directly to adjustment than traditional IIT indices. This relationship, however, has not yet been demonstrated formally. Therefore, we present a simple algebraic framework which formalizes the intuition behind the proposed measures of MIIT.

A two-industry, four-goods open economy

Assume an economy consisting of two industries $i = 1, 2$. Each of these industries produces two homogeneous product varieties $j = 1, 2$. Labour is the only production factor, and $\bar{L}$ is the given stock of labour in our reference economy. This labour is allocated to the production of some or all of the four varieties, and no labour is unemployed, so that $L_{ij} \geq 0, \sum_i \sum_j L_{ij} = \bar{L}$.

The total quantity of output is $\bar{P}$. We assume constant returns to scale and uniform technologies, so that each unit of labour produces one unit of output, and $L_{ij} = P_{ij}$. We denominate aggregate domestic demand by $\bar{D}$; hence, with a balanced current account, $\bar{L} = \bar{P} = \bar{D}$.

Consumers share equal preferences and purchase fixed shares of the four available product varieties, so that $D_{ij} \geq 0, \sum_i \sum_j D_{ij} = \bar{D}$.

Through trade with the rest of the world the structure of domestic production is not necessarily equal to that of domestic consumption; hence D_{ij} can differ from P_{ij}, this difference being composed of exports (X) or imports $(M = -X)$, so that $X_{ij} = P_{ij} - D_{ij}$ and $M_{ij} = D_{ij} - P_{ij}$.[18] Current-account balance requires that $\sum_i \sum_j (P - D)_{ij} = 0$.

So much for the basic framework. Without consideration for the causes of change, we now look at some simple relationships if an initial configuration of demand, production and trade is altered. Since, according to step 4 of the SAH, we are interested in the link between trade changes and production changes, *ceteris paribus*, we assume that the structure of demand remains unaltered by changes in trade and domestic production. Therefore, any increase in imports will necessitate a decrease in domestic production of the same magnitude, a redeployment of the free workers in the production of other varieties and a corresponding import reduction or export expansion of those varieties. If we denote changes between two points in time by Δ, we can express these relationships as follows:[19]

$$\Delta X_{kl} = \Delta P_{kl} = \Delta L_{kl} = \sum_i \sum_j -\Delta X_{ij \neq kl}$$
$$= \sum_i \sum_j -\Delta P_{ij \neq kl} = \sum_i \sum_j -\Delta L_{ij \neq kl}, \qquad \dots (3.15)$$

where $k \in 1, 2; l \in 1, 2$.

Let us first define our trade variables. IIT by industry is given by:

$$GL_t = 1 - \frac{|X_{i1} + X_{i2}|}{|X_{i1}| + |X_{i2}|}. \qquad \dots (3.16)$$

The economy-wide IIT average is:

$$GL = \sum_i \left(\frac{|X_{i1}| + |X_{i2}|}{\sum_i \sum_j |X_{ij}|} * GL_i \right) = 1 - \frac{\sum_i |X_{i1} + X_{i2}|}{\sum_i \sum_j |X_{ij}|}. \qquad \dots (3.17)$$

MIIT by industry can be written as follows:

$$A_i = 1 - \frac{|\Delta X_{i1} + \Delta X_{i2}|}{|\Delta X_{i1}| + |\Delta X_{i2}|}, \text{ and } B_i = \frac{\Delta X_{i1} + \Delta X_{i2}}{|\Delta X_{i1}| + |\Delta X_{i2}|}, \qquad \dots (3.18)$$

where the economy-wide average for the A index is:

$$A = 1 - \frac{\sum_i |\Delta X_{i1} + \Delta X_{i2}|}{\sum_i \sum_j |\Delta X_{ij}|}. \qquad \dots (3.19)$$

Let us now identify variables relating to intra- and inter-industry factor movements. Even though our simple framework does not model factor specificity, we can assume that what defines our two industries is that factors move more easily to the production of another variety in the same industry than to the production of a variety in the other industry. Labour freed from the production of a variety in industry 1 will therefore only move to the production of a variety in industry 2 if production of the other variety in industry 1 does not expand sufficiently to absorb all the freed labour. Therefore, there will be intra-industry factor movement to the extent that the contraction in the production of one variety is matched by expansion in the production of the other variety, whereas net changes in the production of entire industries will lead to inter-industry factor shifts.

The corresponding measure of intra-industry labour movements (IILM) is:

$$IILM = 1 - \frac{\sum_i |\Delta L_{i1} + \Delta L_{i2}|}{\sum_i \sum_j |\Delta L_{ij}|}. \qquad \dots (3.20)$$

This measure, constructed analogously to the A index, reports the proportion of *intra-industry labour movements* in total net inter-variety labour shifts. The IILM index takes values between 0, where all labour movements are between the two industries, and 1, where all labour remains occupied in their original industry, but some labour moves between varieties.

Like A, the IILM index reports the proportion of intra-industry changes relative to all changes, but it conveys no information on the absolute size of intra- and inter-industry changes. This information can be reported with measures constructed in analogy to the C measure of MIIT. The *absolute size of intra-industry labour movements* (IILMA) is then given by:

$$IILMA = \left(\left[\sum_i \sum_j (|\Delta L_{ij}|) \right] - \sum_i |\Delta L_{i1} + \Delta L_{i2}| \right) * \frac{1}{2}, \quad \dots (3.21)$$

and the corresponding absolute measure of *inter*-industry labour movements (IILMA⁻) is:

$$IILMA^- = \left(\sum_i |\Delta L_{i1} + \Delta L_{i2}| \right) * \frac{1}{2}. \qquad \dots (3.22)$$

The relationship between (M)IIT and factor movements

We are now in a position to explore the relationship between (M)IIT and labour shifts. First, we investigate the link between IIT, measured by the GL index, and labour movements. Compare equations (3.17), defining the GL index, and 3.20, indicating the proportion of labour movements which occur within industries. It becomes immediately apparent that there must be a functional relationship between X_{ij} and ΔL_{ij} if there is to be a link between the two concepts. Our model identifies no such relationship. Since $\Delta L_{ij} = \Delta X_{ij}$ (equation 3.15), we could also find a link between IIT and factor movements if there were a relationship between X_{ij} and ΔX_{ij}. Again, our framework suggests no such relationship. The same reasoning applies to ΔGL and the GHME measure: equations (3.1) and (3.3) cannot be expressed purely in first differences, hence the relevance of ΔGL and GHME for adjustment also hinges on a relationship between X and ΔX.

Note, however, that we have not identified any determinants of trade changes, and that we cannot, therefore, rule out a link between

X_{ij} (base or end year) and ΔX_{ij}. Nevertheless, it appears far-fetched that a country's export or import volume of a certain good should be related systematically to the change in that volume prior or subsequent to the reference period. This is why doubt has been cast over the relevance of IIT for adjustment issues.

It is now straightforward to identify the correspondence between MIIT, measured by the A index, and labour movements. Combining equations (3.15), (3.19) and (3.20), we find that:

$$A = IILM. \qquad \qquad \ldots (3.23)$$

In our simple framework, the relative size of intra- and inter-industry trade changes is exactly equal to the *relative* size of intra- and inter-industry movements of labour.

What about the relationship between A and the *absolute* size of labour movements? Combining equations (3.14), (3.19), (3.21) and (3.22), we find that

$$A = \left(\frac{2}{\sum_i \sum_j |\Delta X_{ij}|}\right) IILMA, \qquad \ldots (3.24)$$

and

$$1 - A = \left(\frac{2}{\sum_i \sum_j |\Delta X_{ij}|}\right) IILMA^-. \qquad \ldots (3.25)$$

There is thus a positive/negative relationship between MIIT and the absolute size of intra-/inter-industry labour shifts. It is the fact that this relationship is not constant (but depends on the sum of absolute trade changes) which motivated the development of measures such as C and $UMCIT$ to complement the A index.

If we make the assumption that inter-industry labour shifts are more costly than intra-industry movements, then equations (3.23 to 3.25) suggest a strictly negative relationship between the A index and adjustment costs. This is the rationale for using measures of MIIT rather than the traditional GL index.

Beyond accounting

Our algebraic exercise formalizes the intuition behind MIIT. It is not, however, an economic model, and it does not amount to a theoretical foundation of the SAH. We have constructed a set of accounting identities, ignoring causal relationships. Let us explore the limitations of this analysis in the order of the four steps constituting the SAH, and discuss how an extension of our framework in each case would affect the results.

Our exercise is clearly remote from the SAH in terms of Step 1. We have not modelled adjustment costs explicitly. We merely assume that there is a one-to-one relationship between net aggregate factor movements and adjustment costs. This ignores the fact that, in the real world, sector specificity varies across factors and factor price rigidity differs across sectors. The one-to-one nature of the relationship therefore amounts to strong oversimplification, but a positive correlation between net intersectoral factor shifts and adjustment costs nevertheless seems plausible, and is ultimately an issue for empirical verification.[20]

Step 2 of the SAH relates to the much discussed 'categorical aggregation question' of IIT. Our algebraic analysis resembles the conventional IIT models in so far as it circumvents the empirical obstacles simply by assuming them away. We assume that factor shifts within industries give rise to lower adjustment costs than movements between industries. Whether this is realistic for the industries as defined in statistical nomenclatures is an old empirical question. Note, however, that the answer to this question should be sought not only in the similarity of factor requirements within and between industries (which has been the sole focus of previous studies), but also in the flexibility of factor prices within and between industries.

The main purpose of our algebraic exercise was to show that MIIT is the relevant concept in terms of Step 3 in the SAH, since there is a one-to-one relationship between MIIT and net factor movements. Again, this is an obvious oversimplification. Even if we hold domestic demand constant in quantity terms, an increase (decrease) in the net exports of an industry will not stimulate (crowd out) a perfectly proportional quantity of domestic production. Real-world products are heterogeneous and can be complementary rather than competing, factors are not fully employed, and price effects can offset some of the quantity effects. As above, therefore, real-world elasticities are likely to be lower than unity. As long as export (import) elasticities of domestic output are positive (negative), however, our assertion that MIIT is the relevant concept in terms of the SAH remains valid.

The limiting element of step 4 lies in its *ceteris paribus* assumption. This implies that, for an empirically testable model of adjustment costs, we need to know which other factors to control for and how to link them to MIIT. The specification of such a model will have to be decided on the basis of a theory about factor-market adjustment and trade, to which we now turn.

Trade theory and MIIT

If we want to test the SAH empirically, the most serious challenge arises from the fact that the hypothesis says nothing about causation. This does not deprive it of meaning or usefulness. We might ask whether the relative magnitude of intra- or inter-industry trade change relates in some systematic way to adjustment, irrespective of the causal nexus. If we found robust evidence for, say, a negative relationship between MIIT and adjustment costs across a number of samples, then we could interpret high/low MIIT levels in other samples as indicators of low/high adjustment costs. This evidence could be gathered through bivariate correlation analysis between (M)IIT and a measure of adjustment costs.

If we did find significant correlations we would have detected a statistical regularity, but we would be agnostic about its economic explanation and policy implications; it would be measurement without theory. The main problem is that we do not avail of a model encompassing determinants of MIIT and of adjustment.

One may look at, for instance, the monopolistic–competition model of horizontal IIT. This model succeeds in predicting IIT at intermediate levels of trade costs, but it cannot generate MIIT. Any variation in trade barriers results in pure inter-industry adjustment. IIT falls monotonically with trade costs, and inter-industry specialization is complete where trade costs are zero.[21] MIIT is thus always zero.[22]

Small-number oligopoly models, however, do generate MIIT. In the stylized symmetric monopoly version of Brander (1981), all trade is IIT, and all trade change is MIIT. Krugman and Venables (1990) have presented a two-country model with fixed positive firm numbers interacting as Cournot competitors in a horizontally differentiated industry. In that scenario, trade liberalization can spur imports and exports of the differentiated sector simultaneously and hence generate MIIT. One stylized and testable hypothesis we can retain from the small-number models is that MIIT will be most pronounced in sectors subject to oligopolistic market structure.

Most models explaining IIT completely abstract from factor markets. Indeed, their *raison d'être* lies in their ability to predict trade in goods with very similar factor requirements between countries with very similar factor endowments. There is a rich literature on trade-induced adjustment (see, for example, Neary (1982) and Mussa (1982)), but it is firmly rooted in the tradition of H-O-S trade models with constant returns to scale and perfect competition in two homogeneous product sectors. (M)IIT does, therefore, not feature in these models. Hence, while we have some models that are able to generate MIIT, we have no integrated theory of MIIT and factor markets.

3.6   PREDICTIONS TO BE TESTED: EMPIRICAL STUDIES

The way forward: linking trade and industry data

An uninitiated commentator would probably be puzzled by the dearth of empirical evidence on the SAH, as discussed in Section 3.2. It is likely that she would also be bewildered by the roundabout methodology employed by the few existing studies. She would presumably recommend as the common-sense research strategy that a comparison be made between, on the one hand, adjustment costs across industries (measured, say, by frictional unemployment, labour turnover or wage dispersion) and, on the other hand, a relevant measure of IIT in these same industries. To support the SAH, a negative correlation should emerge between IIT and adjustment costs, *ceteris paribus*. Such an analysis has so far been prevented by data limitations, but there is no reason to believe that this is an insurmountable obstacle.

Chapters 6 to 13 report preliminary correlation and regression results on this topic. These pilot studies generally show that MIIT does matter for adjustment and that it is superior in this context than static IIT.

Why has it taken so long for a direct and intuitively sensible method of elucidating the IIT-adjustment issue to be applied? The principal answer probably lies in data limitations. IIT is normally calculated at the 3, 4 or 5-digit level of the SITC classification. The 3-digit level of the current SITC code distinguishes 261 product groups, and 3118 products are identified at the 5-digit level. Data for sectoral employment, wages or output are generally available only at a much higher level of aggregation. Another problem has resided in the definition of IIT in the context of adjustment. The development of MIIT measures has occurred only recently.

Limitations of correlation and regression analyses

Two problems of specification limit the usefulness of the empirical studies reported in this volume. First, a single correct and theoretically founded specification of the exogenous variables has not yet been developed. Therefore, the existing regression studies use very different model specifications without much concern for the causal nexus between the various regressors.

Second, the dependent variable also needs to be specified more adequately. Most correlation and regression analyses use percentage employment changes as an inverse proxy for adjustment costs. This is not consistent with the theoretical definition of adjustment, which encompasses frictional unemployment and wage differentials, not net increases or decreases in total sectoral employment. Percentage employment changes are a measure of net employment performance rather than of adjustment costs. One solution might be to use absolute changes in sectoral employment ($|\Delta Empl.|$) as an alternative proxy for adjustment costs, presuming that frictional unemployment is related to the magnitude of change in the number of jobs provided by a certain industry. The optimum, however, would be to obtain data on intra- and inter-sectoral employment *flows*, as well as information on intra- and inter-sectoral wage dispersion. One promising avenue is the growth in statistical coverage of firm-level creation and destruction of jobs.[23] The net difference between the numbers of jobs created and destroyed within an industry is a sensible proxy for inter-industry labour re-allocation, while the residual of gross job creation and destruction of an industry after subtraction of the net flows could be a useful approximation of intra-industry reallocation of workers.

3.7 CONCLUSION: WEIGHTY HYPOTHESIS – HARDENING FOUNDATIONS

The hypothesis that intra-industry trade relates negatively to factor-market adjustment costs (SAH) has found widespread acceptance in the literature. We have shown that this piece of conventional wisdom suffers from a considerable lack of theoretical and empirical support. First, it was highlighted that the hypothesis has not been defined rigorously, and is, therefore, subject to varying implicit interpretations. Hence, we have provided an explicit four-step formulation of the SAH.

Second, we found that conventional IIT measures are inappropriate for the analysis of adjustment questions. We provided a first stock-taking exercise of the emerging literature on marginal IIT (MIIT), which still concentrates on developing empirical measures. The intuition underlying MIIT is illustrated in a simple algebraic multisectoral open-economy framework.

Third, we referred to the preliminary empirical tests of the SAH reported in the country studies of this volume. Some support is found for the proposition that MIIT is the more relevant concept for adjustment than traditional Grubel-Lloyd measures of IIT. However, we also find that empirical analysis of this issue provides ample scope for elaboration in terms of methodology, specification and coverage. The most important items on this research agenda are the development of an economic model integrating (M)IIT and factor-market adjustment, and the testing of the SAH on more refined data for labour flows and wages.

APPENDIX: A HYPOTHETICAL NUMERICAL EXAMPLE ILLUSTRATING MIIT MEASURES

Three scenarios

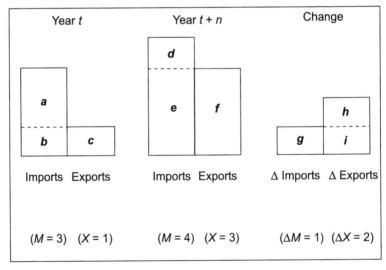

SCENARIO II

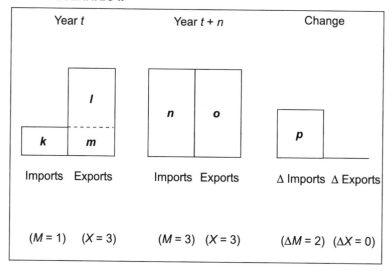

SCENARIO III

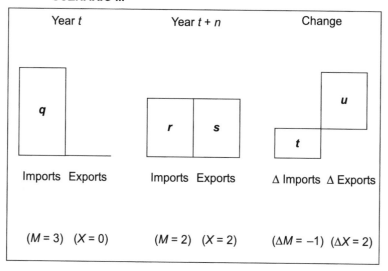

Figure 3.1 Three hypothetical trade-change scenarios

Explaining the differences between the various measures is made simpler by a hypothetical numerical example. We therefore set out three scenarios, I, II and III, each representing a different trade configuration. These scenarios can be thought of as representing three different industrial sectors in a particular country. The hypothetical import and export figures for each of these sectors can stand for trade with the rest of the world, or they could represent bilateral flows with only one or several partner countries. This distinction is irrelevant for the description of various measurement methods. Since we want to illustrate measures of MIIT, each scenario includes the trade configuration in some initial year and in the end year of the considered period, t and $t + n$, as well as the representation of the change in trade flows between the two benchmark years, denoted by Δ.

The three scenarios are given in Figure 3.1, and the derived values of the various (M)IIT measures are reported in Table 3.2. In each scenario trade within the particular industry has become more balanced over time, hence all three scenarios represent a rise in IIT as measured by the GL index. In Scenario I, a large sectoral deficit has shrunk to a small deficit, while in Scenarios II and III strongly unbalanced trade (surplus in II, deficit in III) has become perfectly balanced over the analysed period.

Table 3.2   IIT measures calculated from the three scenarios

Measures	Scenario I	Scenario II	Scenario III
GL_t	0.5	0.5	0
GL_{t+n}	0.86	1	1
ΔGL	0.36	0.5	1
HK	2	undefined	undefined
GHME	4	4	4
A	0.67	0	0
B	0.33	−1	1
C	2	0	0

The Grubel-Lloyd index

To start, we use this representation to illustrate the computation of GL indices. In terms of the sectoral trade flows in year t of Scenario I, IIT can be expressed as follows:

$$GL_{1t} = 1 - \frac{|(a + b) - c|}{(a + b + c)} = \frac{(b + c)}{(a + b + c)},$$

which shows clearly that this index represents the proportion of matched trade $(b + c)$ in total trade $(a + b + c)$.

All three scenarios resemble each other by displaying a rise in the GL index, which has been interpreted by many commentators as implying modest trade-induced adjustment costs.[24] The limitations of such an analysis become obvious when we take into consideration the third bar chart for each scenario, depicting the *changes* in imports and exports between t and $t + n$. A glance at Figure 3.1 should suffice to visualize that the IIT rises in the three Scenarios are based on fundamentally different patterns of change in trade flows. It is this ambiguity left by the observations of changes in static IIT that led to the development of alternative measures.

Early MIIT measures

The principal shortcoming of the HK index is that it is only defined where neither imports nor exports have fallen over the period of investigation. This is not the case in Scenario III, where $\Delta M < 0$, hence the HK index is undefined. In the case of Scenario III one could contend that the opposing changes in imports and exports reflect *inter*-industry trade changes, and conjecture with Hamilton and Kniest (1991) that the undefined range of their index represents marginal *inter*-industry trade. This, however, is erroneous, since HK is not defined either where imports and exports have decreased simultaneously, which is a situation of *intra*-industry trade change. This 'grey area' of the HK index motivated the work of Greenaway *et al.* (1994b) in search of a MIIT measure covering all possible trade configurations.

In terms of the trade flows of Scenario I, the GHME measure can be expressed as follows:

$$GHME_1 = (\{d+e+f\} - |f-(d+e)|) - (\{a+b+c\} - |c-(a+b)|),$$

hence

$$GHME_1 = (e+f) - (b+c) = 6 - 2 = 4.$$

Unlike the HK index, this measure is always defined. However, it is subject to two important drawbacks, one being that the measure is unbounded (hence it is not an index), and the other being that the GHME measure is not really an indicator of MIIT. The second point can be illustrated easily with our hypothetical example. It can be shown that GHME is a 'comparative static' measure of the differences between the trade structures in two years. In this respect, GHME is of the same nature as ΔGL. This is illustrated by the variables used in our calculation of the GHME measure for Scenario I. We calculate GHME with the variables a to f, which define static IIT patterns, while g, h and i, representing the change in trade flows, do not enter the calculation. Although g, h and i define MIIT, GHME measures cannot be calculated on their basis. The GHME measure simply indicates the increase or decrease in matched trade (static IIT) between the initial year and the end year, but it does not indicate whether this change was brought about by matched or unmatched changes in imports and exports. In Scenario III, for instance, the GHME measure suggests that IIT has increased by 4, even though the changes in imports and exports point in opposite directions, which should be defined as marginal *inter*-industry trade. Like ΔGL, Table 3.2 reports positive GHME measures for all three Scenarios, even though a glance at the third column of bar charts suffices to show that they differ considerably in terms of the underlying trade changes.

The *A* index

We attempt to eliminate the shortcomings of the existing MIIT measures by providing an index which:

- is defined in all cases;
- is related to the structure of changes in imports and exports; and
- is contained between two easily interpretable bounds.

These are the features of the '*A*' index. For Scenario I the index is calculated as follows:

$$A_{\mathrm{I}} = 1 - \frac{|(h+i)-g|}{|h+i|+|g|} = \frac{(g+i)}{(g+h+i)}.$$

Since $g = h = i = 1, A = 2/3 = 0.67$. The *A* index thus expresses the proportion of matched trade change relative to total trade change.

Note that the *A* index is also defined in Scenario III, where the change in imports is negative:

$$A_{\mathrm{III}} = 1 - \frac{|u-t|}{|u|+|t|} = 1 - \frac{|2-(-1)|}{|2|+|-1|} = 1 - \frac{3}{3} = 0.$$

All situations where either exports or imports have remained unchanged, or where these changes have opposite signs, are defined as marginal *inter*-industry trade, hence *A* equals zero. This is the case in our Scenarios II and III.

The *C* measure

The idea of expressing MIIT not as a proportion of total trade change within the relevant industry but in money or quantity terms underlies the '*C*' measure, which is defined as follows for Scenario I:

$$C_{\mathrm{I}} = (|h+i|+|g|) - |h+i-g| = (2+1) - |1| = 2.$$

It should now be easy to verify that *C* equals zero in Scenarios II and III. Wherever *A* equals zero, *C* is also zero (since there is no MIIT), and when $A > 0$, then $C > 0$ (since there is some MIIT). *C* can thus take values between zero and infinity.

The difference between *C* and GHME can be shown with reference to the graphical representation of our three scenarios. While the GHME measure is calculated from the figures underlying the first two columns (*a* to *f* in I, *k* to *o* in II and *q* to *s* in III), *C* can be obtained by looking merely at the changes in trade flows, that is the last column of bar charts (*g* to *i* in I, *p* in II and *t* and *u* in III). We therefore say that *C* is a dynamic measure, while GHME is comparative static.

The *B* index

As suggested above, it often matters little from a one-country perspective whether trade expansion (or contraction) is matched on the export and import sides within each industry. What matters more is whether exports grow relative to imports or vice versa. In other words, the aspect of trade *structure*, scrutinized by IIT and MIIT analyses ought to be complemented by an analysis of trade *performance*. Trade performance is particularly relevant where MIIT is low, that is where *inter*-industry trade changes dominate. We say that marginal inter-industry trade can reflect a country's specialization *into* or *out of* a particular industry. If, in a certain industry, exports expand faster (or contract more slowly) than imports, we say that the country is specializing *into* this particular activity. Accordingly, a country is specialising *out of* industries with the opposite composition of trade change.

This distinction is illustrated by our Scenarios II and III. Both represent situations of zero MIIT ($A = C = 0$). Yet, in a mercantilist sense, Scenario III is preferable for the home country to Scenario II. Scenario III reflects a 'catching up' of the domestic industry relative to its foreign competitors, while Scenario II testifies an erosion of the domestic industry's net trade surplus through a 'catching up' by its foreign competitors.

We can illustrate this by comparing the B indices of Scenarios II and III:

$$B_{II} = \frac{0 - p}{|p|} = \frac{-2}{2} = -1,$$

$$B_{III} = \frac{u - t}{|u| + |t|} = \frac{2 - (-1)}{2 + 1} = 1.$$

The changes in exports and imports are totally unmatched in both scenarios, hence MIIT is zero. This is expressed by the extreme values of B, -1 and 1. In Scenario II the domestic industry has lost ground relative to its foreign competitors, as competing imports trebled while exports remained unchanged. This specialization out of the particular sector is represented by the negative value of B. Scenario III depicts the opposite situation, exports shot up while competing imports were reduced. The home country specialized into this industry, hence B is positive.

Notes

1. For a revealing industry case study, see Jordan (1993). A cross-industry study for the United States by Marvel and Ray (1987, p. 1279) concludes that 'models that focus on product differentiation of consumer goods and scale economies in production as stimulants of intraindustry trade are strongly contradicted by the data'.
2. Grant *et al.* (1993, p. 33) put it as follows. 'the basic mechanism of trade liberalization in the face of scale economies tends to concentrate production in some regions and extinguish it in others. There is no guarantee that each region will retain comparative advantage in at least one or two varieties of every industry group. And regions are able by policy to prey on each others' perceived strategic niches. Thus

adjustment costs may be unusually high, not low, in regions whose pattern of intraindustry trade leads to widespread industry closure after liberalization.'

3. See Lundberg and Hansson (1986), Tharakan and Calfat (1994). It would also be appropriate to consider the empirical literature on vertical IIT as part of the effort to gauge the heterogeneity of industries (see Chapter 4). Vertical differentiation within industries is likely to be accompanied by substantial intra-industry variance of factor requirements.

4. Since the early 1970s, the European steel industry has suffered considerably in terms of job losses. Elliott (1994) has shown that, nevertheless, IIT in steel products among European countries has remained high. This might thus be taken as an example where adjustment is not primarily trade-induced, since it affects countries symmetrically, but caused by factors such as a technology-induced increase in productivity and stagnating demand for steel.

5. A similar finding was obtained by Marvel and Ray (1987) for Kennedy-Round tariff concessions by the USA.

6. Actual economies, of course, are subject to continuous changes in demand and production structures. Therefore, integration occurs simultaneously with other changes, and the two types of trade-induced adjustment, while separable in theory, are difficult to disentangle empirically.

7. see Baldwin *et al.* (1980, p. 408).

8. see Feenstra and Lewis (1994, p. 202). Dixit and Norman (1986) have proposed an incentive-compatible taxation scheme which ensures Pareto gains.

9. see Baldwin *et al.* (1980, pp. 408ff.). Brecher and Choudhri (1994) have formalized this proposition in an efficiency-wage model.

10. see Greenaway and Milner (1986, pp. 161f.).

11. Even though the GL index relates to *flows* of goods and is thus not a static measure in the strict sense, it will be referred to in this work as being of a 'static' nature. Thus, IIT contrasts with measures of MIIT, which are 'dynamic' since they relate to the *change* in these flows between defined time periods.

12. This, however, is not to say that time-series analysis of corresponding GL indices is misleading or flawed *per se*. If the aim of the analysis is 'comparative static', meaning that what is sought is a comparison of the structure of trade at different points (years) in time, then the comparison of GL indices is adequate. It is only when the aim of the analysis is 'dynamic' in nature, meaning that the structure of the *change* in trading patterns is to be scrutinized, that the comparison of GL indices is inadequate. Since the costs of adjustment depend on the latter rather than on the former, an alternative measurement method is warranted.

13. Greenaway *et al.* (1994b) have also pointed to the fact that the use of nominal rather than inflation-adjusted trade data biases the MIIT measure upward. While this is a valid point, it is applicable to any measure of MIIT and not just to the HK index. For the remainder of this survey we will thus assume all import and export data to be adjusted for inflation.

14. Hamilton and Kniest (1991, p. 360) have mentioned consideration of a very similar measure, a 'modified Grubel-Lloyd index', where $MIIT = 1 - \{|\Delta X - \Delta M|/(\Delta X + \Delta M)\}$. They subsequently refuted this index because it 'calculates the degree of IIT in total new trade rather than comparing new bilateral trade flows'. But the degree of IIT in new trade is precisely what we strive to measure, and any 'modified GL index' can be applied to a country's trade with either one or several partners, just as the GL index itself. Furthermore, their failure to use absolute values for ΔX and ΔM in the denominator makes the measure meaningless where either of the two values is negative. Shelburne (1993) has applied the formula suggested here, omitting, however, to consider only *real* changes in trade values. Dixon and Menon (1995) have developed a similar measure, termed 'dynamic IIT' (DIIT), but they committed the same error as Hamilton and Kniest (1991), by failing to use absolute values for ΔX and ΔM for the calculation of matched trade change (equation 12, p. 4), and they have scaled MIIT to total base-year trade and not to total trade change.

15. The statistical properties of the A index differ from those of the GL index in two respects. First, Murshed and Noonan (1994) have shown empirically that the A index is not subject to an increasing downward bias as the level of statistical disaggregation is increased. The formal proof for this property was given by Oliveras and Terra (1996). Second, Olivera and Terra (1996) also showed that there is no functional relationship between the A index for a certain period and the A indices of constituent sub-periods.

16. The exception to this is where the Bs of all sub-industries have the same sign.

17. Unlike the GHME measure, C is never negative.

18. Henceforth, we shall refer to imports as $-X$, instead of M.

19. Since all our variables are flows, Δ does not, strictly speaking, refer to changes between to *points* in time, but to changes between two non-overlapping time periods (for example, years).

20. One piece of empirical support for the intuition can be found in Baldwin *et al.* (1980, pp. 419f.). In a carefully calibrated simulation of tariff-reduction effects on US industrial sectors, a significant positive correlation appears between 'percentage employment loss' and 'labour adjustment costs' per sector.

21. For a formal proof, see Brülhart (1995).

22. An extension of the traditional two-country setting to three countries can produce a non-monotonic relationship between IIT and integration and hence MIIT (Brülhart and Torstensson, 1996). However, MIIT thus generated is multilateral, meaning that a country may increase its net exports of a particular industry to one partner and see them decreased towards another. Bilateral trade changes are always inter-industry in this setting as well.

23. See Brülhart *et al.* (1998).

24. We could, of course, also consider scenarios with falling IIT levels (negative ΔGL). This would alter none of our insights.

References and Further Reading

Adler, Michael (1970) 'Specialization in the European Coal and Steel Community'. Journal of Common Market Studies, vol. 8, 175–191.

Balassa, B. (1966) 'Tariff Reductions and Trade in Manufactures among the Industrial Countries', *American Economic Review*, 56, 466–73.

Balasubramanyam, V.N. and Greenaway, D. (1993) 'Regional Integration Agreements and Foreign Direct Investment', in Anderson, K. and Blackhurst, R. (eds), *Regional Integration and the Global Trading System*, Hemel Hempstead: Harvester Wheatsheaf.

Baldwin, R.E., Mutti, J.H. and Richardson, J.D. (1980) 'Welfare Effects on the United States of a Significant Multilateral Tariff Reduction', *Journal of International Economics*, 36, 405–23.

Bhagwati, J.N. (ed.) (1982) *Import Competition and Response*, Chicago and London: The University of Chicago Press.

Brander, J. (1981) 'Intra-Industry Trade in Identical Commodities', *Journal of International Economics*, 11, 1–14.

Brecher, R.A. and Choudhri, E.U. (1994) 'Pareto Gains from Trade Reconsidered: Compensating for Jobs Lost', *Journal of International Economics*, 36, 223–38.

Brülhart, M. (1994) 'Marginal Intra-Industry Trade: Measurement and Relevance for the Pattern of Industrial Adjustment', *Weltwirtschaftliches Archiv*, 130, 600–13.

Brülhart, M. (1995) 'Scale Economics, Intra-Industry Trade and Industry Location in the New Trade Theory', *Trinity Economic Papers*, Technical Paper No. 4, Trinity College Dublin.

Brülhart, M., Murphy, A. and Strobl, E. (1998) 'Intra-Industry Trade and Job Turnover: A Panel Analysis Using Plant-Level Data', mimeo, University of Manchester.

Brülhart, M. and Torstensson, J. (1996) 'Regional Integration, Scale Economies and Industry Location in the European Union', *CEPR Discussion Paper*, 1435, Centre for Economic Policy Research, London.

Cadot, O., Faini, R. and de Melo, J. (1995) 'Early Trade Patterns under the Europe Agreements: France, Germany and Italy', *European Economic Review* (Papers and Proceedings), 39, 601–10.

Centre d'Études Prospectives et d'Informations Internationales (CEPII) (1988) 'Commerce intra-branche: Performance des firmes et analyse des échanges commerciaux dans la Communauté européenne', in Commission of the European Communities, *Studies on the 'Cost of Non-Europe'* 2, Luxembourg.

Commission of the European Communities (CEC) (1996) 'The 1996 Single Market Review', Commission Staff Working Paper SEC (96) 2378, Brussels.

Dixit, A. and Norman, V. (1986) 'Gains from Trade Without Lump-Sum Compensation', *Journal of International Economics*, 21, 111–22.

Dixon, P.B. and Menon, J. (1995) 'Measures of Intra-Industry Trade as Indicators of Factor Market Disruption' *CREDIT Research Paper*, 95/15, University of Nottingham.

Drábek, Z. and Smith, A. (1995) 'Trade Performance and Trade Policy in Central and Eastern Europe', *CEPR Discussion Paper*, 1182, Centre for Economic Policy Research, London.

Drysdale, P. and Garnaut, R. (1993) 'The Pacific: An Application of a General Theory of Economic Integration', in Bergsten, C.F. and Noland, M. (eds), *Pacific Dynamism and the International Economic System*, Washington, DC: Institute for International Economics.

Elliott, R. (1994) 'Adjustment, Changing Intra-Industry Trade and Special-isation – A Case Study Analysis of the Steel Industry', *mimeo*, University of Nottingham.

Feenstra, R.C. and Lewis, T.R. (1994) 'Trade Adjustment Assistance and Pareto Gains from Trade', *Journal of International Economics*, 36, 201–22.

Finger, J.M. (1975) 'Trade Overlap and Intra-Industry Trade', *Economic Inquiry*, 13, 581–9.

Fischer, R.D. and Serra, P. (1996) 'Income Inequality and Choice of Free Trade in a Model of Intraindustry Trade', *Quarterly Journal of Economics*, 111, 41–64.

Globerman, S. (1992) 'North American Trade Liberalization and Intra-Industry Trade', *Weltwirtschaftliches Archiv*, 128, 487–97.

Globerman, S. and Dean, J.W. (1990) 'Recent Trends in Intra-Industry Trade and Their Implications for Future Trade Liberalization', *Weltwirtschaftliches Archiv*, 126, 25–49.

Gonzalez, J.G. and Velez, A. (1993) 'An Empirical Estimation of the Level of Intra-Industry Trade between Mexico and the United States', in Fatemi, K. *North American Free Trade Agreement*, New York: St. Martin's Press.

Grant, R.J., Papadakis, M.C. and Richardson, J.D. (1993) 'Global Trade Flows: Old Structures, New Issues, Empirical Evidence', in Bergsten, C.F. and Noland, M. (eds), *Pacific Dynamism and the International Economic System*. Washington, DC: Institute for International Economics.

Greenaway, D. (1987) 'Intra-Industry Trade, Intra Firm Trade and European Integration', *Journal of Common Market Studies*, 26, 153–72.

Greenaway, D. and Hine, R.C. (1991) 'Intra-Industry Specialization, Trade Expansion and Adjustment in the European Economic Space', *Journal of Common Market Studies*, 29, pp. 603–22.

Greenaway, D. and Milner, C. (1986) *The Economics of Intra-Industry Trade*, Oxford: Blackwell.

Greenaway, D. Hine, R.C. and Milner, C. (1994a) 'Country-Specific Factors and the Pattern of Horizontal and Vertical Intra-Industry Trade in the UK', *Weltwirtschaftliches Archiv*, 130, 77–100.

Greenaway, D. Hine, R.C., Milner, C. and Elliott, R. (1994b) 'Adjustment and the Measurement of Marginal Intra-Industry Trade', *Weltwirtschaftliches Archiv*, 130, 418–27.

Grubel, H. and Lloyd, P.J. (1975) *Intra-Industry Trade*, London: Macmillan.

Hamilton, C. and Kniest, P. (1991) 'Trade Liberalization, Structural Adjustment and Intra-Industry Trade: A Note', *Weltwirtschaftliches Archiv*, 127, 356–67.

Hine, R.C. (1989) 'Customs Union Enlargement and Adjustment: Spain's Accession to the European Community', *Journal of Common Market Studies*, 28, 1–27.

Hoekman, B. and Djankov, S. (1996) 'Intra-Industry Trade, Foreign Direct Investment and the Reorientation of East European Exports', *CEPR Discussion Paper*, 1377, London: Centre for Economic Policy Research.

Hoekman, B. and Kostecki, M. (1995) *The Political Economy of the World Trading System*, Oxford: Oxford University Press.

Jordan, T. (1993) 'Intra-Industry Trade – An In-Depth Study of Swedish Liquid Pump Trade', *Weltwirtschaftliches Archiv*, 129, 752–76.

Khalifah, N.A. (1996) 'AFTA and Intra-Industry Trade', *ASEAN Economic Bulletin*, 12, 351–68.

Krugman, P. (1980) 'Scale Economies, Product Differentiation, and the Pattern of Trade', *American Economic Review*, 70, 950–9.

Krugman, P. (1981) 'Intraindustry Specialization and the Gains from Trade', *Journal of Political Economy*, 89, 959–73.

Krugman, P. (1983) 'New Theories of Trade Among Industrial Countries', *American Economic Review* (Papers and Proceedings), 73, 343–7.

Krugman, P. (1987) 'Economic Integration in Europe: Some Conceptual Issues', reprinted in Jacquemin, A. and Sapir, A. (eds) (1989) *The European Internal Market*, Oxford: Oxford University Press.

Krugman, P. (1994) 'Empirical Evidence on the New Trade Theories: The Current State of Play', in CEPR Conference Report, *New Trade Theories*, London.

Krugman, P. and Venables, A.J. (1990) 'Integration and the Competitiveness of Peripheral Industry', in Bliss, C. and de Macedo, J. (eds) *Unity with Diversity in the European Community*, Cambridge: Cambridge University Press, pp. 56–75.

Lemoine, F. (1995) 'La dynamique des exportations des PECO vers l'Union Européenne', *Économie Internationale*, 62, 145–72.

Lincoln, Edward J. (1990) 'Japan's Unequal Trade', Washington D.C., Brookings Institute.

Little, J.S. (1996) 'U.S. Regional Trade with Canada during the Transition to Free Trade', *New England Economic Review*, January 3–22.

Lundberg, L. (1992) 'Economic Integration, Inter- and Intra-Industry Trade: The Case of Sweden', *Scandinavian Journal of Economics*, 94, 393–408.

Lundberg, L. and Hansson, P. (1986) 'Intra-Industry Trade and its Consequences for Adjustment', in Greenaway, D. and Tharakan, P.K.M. (eds), *Imperfect Competition and International Trade*, Brighton, Wheatsheaf.

Marvel, H.P. and Ray, E.J. (1987) 'Intraindustry Trade: Sources and Effects on Protection', *Journal of Political Economy*, 95, 1278–91.

Menon, J. and Dixon, P.B. (1995) 'Regional Trading Agreements and Intra-Industry Trade', *CREDIT Research Paper*, 95/14, University of Nottingham.

Menon, J. and Dixon, P.B. (1997) 'Intra-Industry versus Inter-Industry Trade: Relevance for Adjustment Costs'. *Weltwirtschaftliches Archiv*, 133, 164–169.

Mussa, M. (1982) 'Government Policy and the Adjustment Process', in Bhagwati, pp. 73–120.

Murshed, M. and Noonan, D. (1994) 'Measures of Marginal Intra-Industry Trade: A Comment on the Brülhart Index', *mimeo*, University of Bradford.

Neary, J.P. (1982) 'Intersectoral Capital Mobility, Wage Stickiness, and the Case for Adjustment Assistance', in Bhagwati, pp. 39–69.

Neven, D. (1995) 'Trade Liberalisation with Eastern Nations: Some Distribution Issues', *European Economic Review* (Papers and Proceedings), 39, 622–32.

Noland, M. (1990) *Pacific Basin Developing Countries: Prospects for the Future*, Washington, DC: Institute for International Economics.

OECD (1994) *The OECD Jobs Study: Evidence and Explanations*, Paris: OECD.

Oliveras, J. and Terra, I. (1996) ' "A" Marginal-Intra-Trade Index: A Comment', *mimeo*, Universidad de la República, Uruguay.

Parr, R.G. (1994) 'Intra-Industry Trade and the Prospect of Trade Liberalisation in South Africa', *South African Journal of Economics*, 62, 393–405.

Primo Braga, C.A., Safadi, R. and Yeats, A. (1994) 'Regional Integration in the Americas: *Déjà Vu* All Over Again?', *World Economy*, 17, 577–601.

Rajan, R.S. (1996) 'Measures of Intra-Industry Trade Reconsidered with Reference to Singapore's Bilateral Trade with Japan and the United States', *Weltwirtschaftliches Archiv*, 132, 378–89.

Ratnayake, R. and Jayasuriya, S. (1991) 'Intra-Industry Trade and Protection: Which Way Does the Causation Go?', *Economics Letters*, 35, 71–6.

Reker, C. (1994) 'Adjustment Pressures and Adjustment Processes in the Machine Tool Industry: The Role of Intra-Industry Trade', *mimeo*, University of Düsseldorf, Germany.

Richardson, J.D. (1989) 'Empirical Research on Trade Liberalisation with Imperfect Competition: A Survey', *OECD Economic Studies*, 12, 7–50.

Rodrik, D. (1994) 'What Does the Political Economy Literature on Trade Policy (Not) Tell Us That We Ought to Know?', *NBER Working Paper*, 4870, Cambridge, MA: National Bureau of Economic Research.

Sapir, A. (1992) 'Regional Integration in Europe', *The Economic Journal*, 102, 1491–1506.

Shelburne, R.L. (1993) 'Changing Trade Patterns and the Intra-Industry Trade Index: A Note', *Weltwirtschaftliches Archiv*, 129, 829–33.

Tharakan, P.K.M. and Calfat, German (1994) 'Adjustment and Intra-Industry Trade: A factor-Heterogeneity Test using Firm-Level Data' mimeo, University of Antwerp.

4. Vertical and Horizontal Intra-Industry Trade: An Analysis of Country- and Industry-Specific Determinants*

Robert C. Hine, David Greenaway and
Chris Milner

INTRODUCTION

As discussed in Chapter 2 of this book, much theoretical effort has been expended in explaining the circumstances in which intra-industry trade (IIT) will arise. Besides a range of country-specific determinants this work has shown that scale economies, product differentiation and imperfect competition are typically important. Although the empirical work also confirms that IIT levels vary with market, production and product characteristics across industries, the results show a degree of inconsistency across studies.

One important distinction which arises out of the theoretical literature is that between horizontal and vertical product differentiation. The former arises when different varieties of a product are characterized by different attributes (in a Lancastrian sense); the latter arises when different varieties offer different levels of service.[1] The importance of the distinction derives from the fact that different industry and country characteristics are likely to be associated with trade in the two types of product. Moreover, there are good reasons for believing that the adjustment implications of a given trade expansion will differ between the two. All of this is well known, but empirically under-researched due to the difficulties of disentangling horizontal and vertical intra-industry trade in the data.

In this chapter we deploy a new methodology, which builds upon the work of Abd-el-Rahman (1991), to identify vertical and horizontal intra-industry trade in the UK and estimate a model which is aimed at establishing whether country-specific factors are important in explaining the relative importance of vertical and horizontal IIT in the UK's trade. The chapter is organized as follows: in Section 4.1 we briefly review the theoretical literature on vertical and horizontal IIT; Section 4.2 describes the methodology used for disentangling vertical and horizontal IIT; Section 4.3 sets out the methodology for our analysis of country-specific determinants of IIT and Section 4.4 reports our results; Section 4.5 deals with the methodology for the industry-specific analysis and Section 4.6 presents the results of this; Section 4.7 discusses the implications of our results and concludes.

4.1 PRODUCT DIFFERENTIATION AND INTRA-INDUSTRY TRADE

From the earliest work on IIT, product differentiation was seen as an important ingredient in its explanation (see for example Balassa 1967, Grubel and Lloyd 1975). It is only really following the contributions of Dixit and Stiglitz (1977) and Lancaster (1979) that it has become explicitly modelled in formal analyses of IIT. Dixit and Stiglitz and Lancaster offer alternative representations of *horizontal* differentiation – the first, the 'love of variety approach', the second the 'favourite variety' approach. Both were explicitly incorporated in models of IIT in Krugman (1979) and Lancaster (1979).

Although at the level of the individual agent these two approaches are quite different, with appropriate assumptions regarding the distribution of preferences in the Lancaster case, they yield similar representations in the aggregate. Both demonstrate that horizontal IIT can be expected to be associated with preference diversity and decreasing costs. From an empirical standpoint, however, what is important is the interaction of IIT with non-IIT and the factors which explain the relative importance of the two. Here the key contribution is Helpman and Krugman (1985). This can be thought of as a Chamberlin-Heckscher-Ohlin (CHO) model. It incorporates factor endowments, decreasing costs and horizontal product differentiation in a model which generates both intra- and inter-industry trade. In the process it generates several testable hypotheses based on the deterministic role of country and industry specific factors.

To illustrate, take a standard $2 \times 2 \times 2$ structure. Of the two products one is differentiated and the other homogenous; the former is produced using relatively capital-intensive techniques, the latter using relatively labour-intensive technology. Assume that the home country is relatively capital-abundant and the foreign country relatively labour-abundant. What Helpman and Krugman show is that only the foreign country will export the homogenous good, while both countries will export differentiated products. Clearly, the requirement that trade be balanced results in the capital abundant country running a surplus in differentiated goods. The greater the difference in initial factor endowments the less important will IIT be in their bilateral trade. If relative capital abundance is reflected in relative income per capita one generates the following hypotheses: the greater the similarity in per capita incomes between the two countries, the greater the share of IIT in their bilateral trade volume; the smaller the difference in market size between the two countries, the greater the share of IIT in their bilateral trade; the greater the average market size of the countries (in terms of total income), the greater the share of IIT in their total trade.

Models of vertical IIT date from Falvey (1981), Falvey and Kierzkowski (1987) and Shaked and Sutton (1984). In these models, vertical differentiation is explicitly modelled as differences in quality between similar products. Falvey (1981) demonstrates that, again using a simple $2 \times 2 \times 2$ structure, one can explain the simultaneous existence of vertical IIT and inter-industry trade. Specifically he takes a case where two countries have differential endowments of capital and labour, and the higher quality variety of the differentiated good is produced using relatively capital-intensive techniques. As a result, the higher income, relatively capital-abundant country specializes in, and exports, relatively high quality manufactures, while the lower income, relatively labour-abundant country specializes in low quality manufactures. Falvey's model does not have an explicit demand side. This however is added in Falvey and Kierzkowski (1985). The results suggest that, as with horizontal IIT, the share of vertical IIT will be correlated with the average market size of the two countries, albeit with a distinctly different pattern of specialization. In addition however, it predicts from a supply side perspective that the share of vertical IIT in the bilateral trade of a pair of countries will be greater, the greater the difference in the capital–labour endowment of the two countries and, therefore, the greater the difference in per capita income.

A number of studies have tested for country-specific and industry-specific determinants of IIT of the type discussed above. For example, Loertscher and Wolter (1980), Havrylyshyn and Civan (1983) and

Balassa (1986a, 1986b) all include income per capita and market size as explanatory variables. Loertscher and Wolter (1980) and Tharakan (1984) also include a proxy for taste overlap which is an important ingredient in the analysis. Helpman (1987) explicitly tests the CHO model, including as variables the average of joint market sizes, per capita income differences and so on. It is fair to say that these studies find stronger support for country-specific than industry-specific factors as determinants of the relative importance of inter and intra-industry trade. However, not all of the studies implement these tests on bilateral trade flows. More importantly, however, all of them focus on the links between IIT in general and country-specific and industry-specific factors, without attempting to disentangle horizontal and vertical IIT. Thus their results pertain to *aggregate* IIT. In this chapter, we separate out the two in the trade of the UK, and test for the role of country-specific and industry-specific factors for each.

4.2 MEASURING VERTICAL AND HORIZONTAL IIT

If the relative importance of vertical and horizontal IIT is to be assessed, a satisfactory means has to be found for measuring quality differences in trade. Hedonic regression has been used to determine the relative importance of a range of product attributes in influencing price (for example Cooper *et al.*, 1993). The approach is, however, very data-intensive and is more appropriate for the analysis of individual product markets rather than a multiproduct analysis. Another possibility is to infer quality differences from measurements of demand elasticities among products from different sources. Thus Brenton and Winters (1992) interpret the low elasticities of demand for domestically produced manufactures in Germany compared with the elasticities for imports as reflecting their higher quality.

In the evaluation of trade flows, quality analysis has been undertaken principally with the use of unit value (UV) indexes which measure the average price of a bundle of items from the same general product grouping. The rationale for using UVs as an indicator of quality is that, assuming perfect information, a variety sold at a higher price must be of higher quality than a variety sold more cheaply. Even with imperfect information, prices will reflect quality (Stiglitz 1987). In the short run, however, consumers may buy a more expensive product out of ignorance, or inertia or because it is costly to switch suppliers (Oulton 1990). Price is then an (imperfect) indicator of quality, and is certainly the most accessible source of information about consumer assessments of products. In one way or another, all studies of quality in international trade start from the position that, at least at a very disaggregated level, relative prices reflect relative qualities.

Unit values themselves may be computed in several ways, for example per tonne, per square metre or per item. One problem with using unit values per item as a measure of quality is that unit prices may be a function of size as well as other characteristics which are more narrowly related to quality (for example durability, finish, reliability) and in some cases the latter may be inversely related to size. Thus, in one sense, a more expensive, large but poorly-finished car could be regarded as of lower 'quality' than a smaller, cheaper but well-finished car. Torstensson (1991) has successfully used unit values per item to analyse the pattern of Swedish vertical intra-industry trade in relation to factor endowments. However, a drawback of this measure is that unit values per item are available for only a limited range of products.

Unit values per tonne are similarly problematic. For example, a higher quality (in the sense, say, of more durable) product, may be made out of heavier material so that its value per tonne is lower than that of an inferior quality item. It is not clear how serious a problem this is in practice. Moreover, sample investigations of UK data suggest that the unit values per item and the unit values per tonne among different source or destination countries tend to be highly correlated, that is the variance of average weights per item is relatively low. Oulton (1991) has used unit values per tonne for an extensive survey of quality in UK trade 1978–87 and Abd-el-Rahman (1991) has also employed this measure in a study of French trade. Using data disaggregated at the six digit level, an (arbitrary) spread of more than 15 per cent between import and export prices was used to identify vertical IIT. On this basis about a third of French trade in 1985–87 was vertical IIT, compared with just under a half for horizontal IIT.

A further possible criticism of the unit value approach is that the unit values of two bundles of goods may differ for two reasons: (a) prices of individual products may differ between the two bundles, and (b) the mix of products may differ so that one bundle contains a higher proportion of high unit value items than the other. In much of the literature, especially that relating to the quality upgrading effects of quantitative import restrictions, the latter component – the product mix – is taken to be the indicator of quality (for example Feenstra (1984), Aw and Roberts (1988), Faini and Heimler (1991)). To measure quality in this sense, requires that the unit values of two product bundles be adjusted for price differences in individual items in the bundle. Any difference in unit values between two bundles of goods not accounted for by relative prices is then considered to reflect differences in the product mix of the two bundles in other words quality as in (b) above.

In this study, IIT in UK trade with individual partner countries and with all partner countries combined has been calculated at the 5 digit SITC level using the unadjusted Grubel-Lloyd index. IIT has then been divided into horizontal and vertical components using relative unit values of exports and imports, unit values being calculated per tonne. Horizontal IIT was defined as the simultaneous export and import of a 5 digit SITC product where the unit value of exports (measured f.o.b.) relative to the unit value imports (measured c.i.f.) was within a range of ± 15 per cent. Where relative unit values were outside that range, any IIT was considered to be vertical. Abd-el-Rahman (1991) also used this range to distinguish horizontally and vertically differentiated products. Matched trade in each 5 digit SITC product (SITC sections 5 to 8) was thus categorized as either vertical or horizontal IIT and the amounts of each were summed over all the five digit categories comprising a particular industry.[2] Although ± 15 per cent gives us a 'wedge' of 30 per cent, it could be argued that with imperfect information, this is too narrow. In addition, therefore, we have also calculated vertical and horizontal components for a spread of ± 25 per cent in unit values. This provides a useful basis for evaluating the robustness of our results.

Thus, intra-industry trade at the third digit SIC level is measured as follows:

$$IIT_j(3) = 1 - \frac{|X_j - M_j|}{(X_j + M_j)} \qquad \ldots (4.1)$$

where j refers to a the jth (SIC) industry. This is the standard Grubel and Lloyd index.

$$B_j = \frac{\sum IIT_{ij}^p}{\sum (X_{ij}^p + M_{ij}^p)} \qquad \ldots (4.2)$$

where p denotes horizontally (H) or vertically (V) differentiated products, i refers to fifth digit SITC products in a given third digit industry, and, as Greenaway and Milner (1983) show, $0 \leq B_j \leq IIT_j(3) \leq 1$. In disentangling total IIT (B_j) into vertical (VB_j) and horizontal (HB_j) IIT, we use unit value information, calculated at the fifth digit as follows:

$$B_j = HB_j + VB_j \qquad \qquad \dots (4.3)$$

where HB_j is given by (4.2) for those products (i) in j where unit values of imports (UV_{ij}^m) and exports (UV_{ij}^x) for a particular dispersion factor (α) satisfy the condition,

$$1 - \alpha \leq \frac{UV_{ij}^x}{UV_{ij}^m} \leq 1 + \alpha$$

and VB_j is given by (4.2) for those products (i) in j where,

$$\frac{UV_{ij}^x}{UV_{ij}^m} < 1 - \alpha \text{ or } \frac{UV_{ij}^x}{UV_{ij}^m} > 1 + \alpha$$

where $\alpha = 0.15$ or 0.25.

An industry is represented in this work by the third digit level of aggregation of the UK SIC (Standard Industrial Classification), which permits use of available data on a comparable basis for industry and market characteristics. Table 4.1 summarizes the evidence on levels[3] of total IIT (B_j), vertical IIT (VB_j) and horizontal IIT (HB_j) in UK trade with all its partner countries, i, combined for a sample of 77 industries for which comprehensive information was available. In the case of total IIT alternative summary measures are reported; $B_j(3)$ measures IIT directly at the 3rd digit level, while B_j is a weighted average of the levels of IIT at the 5 digit level.

The average for B_j for all SIC industry groups (2 to 4) in the sample is high at 60.3 per cent. Aggregation effects are not expected to be serious therefore, and there appears to be a fairly consistent relationship between the B_j and $B_j(3)$ indices. We use B_j indices in the empirical analysis, because of the consistency that this permits when computing the results for B_j, VB_j and HB_j.

The striking feature of the descriptive information in Table 4.1 is the fact that VB_j is consistently higher than HB_j for all sub-groups when we use the ± 15 per cent criterion. For the sample as a whole, vertical IIT accounts on average for about two-thirds of total IIT ($\overline{VB_j}$ equals 40.6 per cent and $\bar{B}_j$ equals 60.3 per cent). In only 19 out of the 77 industries in the sample is the HB_j index greater than the corresponding VB_j index.

Of course this result may be fashioned by the size of the unit value dispersion criterion used to distinguish between vertical and horizontal IIT. Thus we also report results for ± 25 per cent. Predictably the relative importance of vertical IIT declines in some sub-groups.

Table 4.1 Average level of total, vertical and horizontal intra-industry trade by manufacturing industry group, UK 1988

SIC Industry group	Grubel Lloyd indices (%) Total (%)				Type of Differentiation			
	3rd Digit $B_j(3)$	no. of industries	5th Digit B_j	no. of subgroups	(±15%)	VB_j (±25%)	HB_j (±15%)	(±25%)
2: Extraction of minerals and ores, manufacture of metals, mineral products and chemicals	80.0	15	56.2	738	35.0	23.1	21.2	33.1
3: Metal goods, engineering and vehicle industries	81.4	34	68.6	935	42.7	29.0	25.9	39.6
4: Other manufacturing industries	63.0	28	52.3	674	41.2	33.8	11.2	18.5
Total (2–4)	74.4	77	60.3	2347	40.6	29.6	19.6	30.6

Crucially, however, the average levels of horizontal and vertical are almost the same (29.6 and 30.6 per cent) and vertical still dominates horizontal in other manufactures. Thus, the dominance of vertical over horizontal IIT in the United Kingdom's multilateral trade applies for fairly generous definitions of horizontal IIT.[4]

In addition to measuring the incidence of vertical and horizontal IIT multilaterally by industry, we have also computed the bilateral coverage of UK IIT by partner country. Table 4.2 reveals some interesting differences across trading partners. The incidence of horizontal IIT is highest where EC Member States are concerned and lowest in the case of geographically distant trading partners. This may be a consequence of the influence of transport costs. Trade is dominated by vertical IIT,

Table 4.2   Product coverage of UK IIT by partner country, 1988

Partner country	no of SITC 5-digit products[1]			% of Total		
	all IIT	horizontal	vertical[2]		horizontal	vertical[2]
			I	II		I	II
Germany	1881	423	634	824	22	34	44
France	1749	366	620	763	21	35	44
United States	1610	258	590	762	16	37	47
Netherlands	1572	334	570	668	21	36	42
Italy	1491	244	412	835	16	28	56
Ireland	1338	306	525	507	23	39	38
Belgium	1326	205	455	666	16	34	50
Sweden	1093	184	435	474	17	40	43
Switzerland	1015	184	436	395	18	43	39
Spain	1002	157	284	561	16	28	56
Denmark	898	149	362	387	17	40	43
Japan	855	98	258	499	11	30	58
Canada	640	94	231	315	15	36	49
Austria	618	107	210	301	17	34	49
Norway	555	98	206	251	18	34	45
Finland	504	75	183	246	15	36	49
Australia	381	45	164	172	12	43	45
Portugal	360	46	92	222	13	26	62
Singapore	327	34	117	176	10	36	54
South Africa	304	42	70	192	14	23	63
Israel	280	40	102	138	14	36	49
Korea,	232	22	35	175	9	15	75
Republic of India	192	15	52	125	8	27	65

Greece	186	21	50	115	11	27	62
Turkey	123	18	29	76	15	24	62
New Zealand	117	9	58	50	8	50	43
Yugoslavia	107	8	23	76	7	21	71
Brazil	104	14	23	67	13	22	64
China	102	7	22	73	7	22	72
Poland	82	4	13	65	5	16	79
Malaysia	81	5	27	49	6	33	60
Czechoslovakia	65	7	10	48	11	15	74
Hungary	63	5	5	53	8	8	84
Malta	60	6	36	18	10	60	30
Cyprus	59	8	15	36	14	25	61
Thailand	58	5	18	35	9	31	60
Egypt	45	2	14	29	4	31	64
Kuwait	33	4	18	11	12	55	33
Pakistan	32	3	11	18	9	34	56
Mexico	28	5	6	17	18	21	61
Nigeria	27	3	14	10	11	52	37
Iceland	23	5	8	10	22	35	43
Jordan	23	1	17	5	4	74	22
Philippines	18	1	4	13	6	22	72
Morocco	16	3	3	10	19	19	63
Kenya	14	3	5	6	21	36	43
Bulgaria	13	1	5	7	8	38	54
Indonesia	11	3	1	7	27	9	64
Libya	11	2	5	4	18	45	36
Algeria	9	2	1	6	22	11	67
Ghana	9	2	2	5	22	22	56
Sri Lanka	8	1	2	5	13	25	63
Cote D'Ivoire	7	1	3	3	14	43	43
Iran	6	0	2	4	0	33	67
Chile	6	1	2	3	17	33	50
Mauritius	5	0	2	3	0	40	60
Zimbabwe	5	1	2	2	20	40	40
Panama	5	1	2	2	20	40	40
Zambia	4	1	1	2	25	25	50
Sudan	3	0	1	2	0	33	67
Papua New Guinea	3	0	1	2	0	33	67
Tanzania	2	0	1	1	0	50	50
Total					**17**	**35**	**48**

[1] Since for very small amounts of trade unit values may be unreliable IIT has been measured only where exports and imports each exceed $50 million.
[2] Category I where the export unit value of a product is below 0.85 of the import value, category II where this ratio exceeds 1.15.

although the pattern does not vary markedly from one partner to another. Table 4.2 also distinguishes between vertical IIT where the UK exports have high unit values relative to those of imports ('high-quality' exports) and where relative unit values are low ('low-quality' exports). What is most striking is the fact that the incidence of 'high-quality' vertical IIT exceeds 'low-quality' vertical trade for the great majority of trading partners. In other words, in a higher proportion of cases exports appear to be predominantly of higher quality than imports.

Although the descriptive data presented in Tables 4.1 and 4.2 indicate that IIT in the UK tends overall to take a vertical rather than horizontal form, there is considerable variation in their relative shares across industries and also across trade with different partner countries. The following sections attempt to explain these variations first in relation to partner country characteristics and then in relation to industry characteristics.

4.3   METHODOLOGY: COUNTRY-SPECIFIC ANALYSIS

The hypotheses formulated in Section II were tested with the following equations:

$$VB_{j(ik)} = \alpha_0 + \alpha_1 \left| \frac{Y_i}{N_i} - \frac{Y_k}{N_k} \right| + \alpha_2 \left(\frac{Y_i + Y_k}{2} \right) + e_{ik} \qquad \dots (4.4)$$

where $VB_{j(ik)}$ = average share of vertical IIT in gross bilateral trade in commodity j between country i and UK (k). $Y_{i(k)}$ = national income of country $i(k)$ $N_{i(k)}$ = population of country $i(k)$
(The expected signs are $\alpha_1 > 0$, $\alpha_2 > 0$).

$$HB_{j(ik)} = \alpha_0 + \alpha_1 \left| \frac{Y_i}{N_i} - \frac{Y_k}{N_k} \right| + \alpha_2 \left(\frac{Y_i + Y_k}{2} \right) + \alpha_3 |Y_i - Y_k| + e_{ik}$$

$$\dots (4.5)$$

where $HB_{j(ik)}$ = average share of (horizontal) total IIT in gross, bilateral trade in commodity j between country i and UK (k) (The expected signs are $\alpha_1 < 0$, $\alpha_2 > 0$, and $\alpha_3 < 0$).

In previous work, the same formula has been assumed to hold for $B_{j(ik)}$ as dependent variable, defined as the average share of total IIT in gross bilateral trade in commodity j between country i and UK (k).

The data definitions and sources for the dependent and independent variables are set out in Appendix 4.1. The alternative criteria for separating the total share of IIT in gross trade (B_j) into the share of vertical IIT (VB_j) and horizontal IIT (HB_j) in gross trade were discussed in some detail in Section 4.2. In the results tables the dependent variable may be followed by $\pm 15\%$ or $\pm 25\%$ in brackets or (3); the former refers to the per unit value deviation used to separate horizontal from vertical IIT; the latter refers to measurement at an alternative 3-digit level of aggregation of the trade data. (In all other cases where the dependent variable is not followed by the term (3), IIT is measured at the 5th digit level of the SITC, and average levels of HB_j and VB_j at the 3-digit level are identified.)

All the equations were initially estimated using ordinary least squares (OLS) for a sample of 62 countries. The sample size is substantially smaller than the total number of the UK's trading partners for several reasons. First, it was necessary to cleanse the data for the effects of small scale or special transactions, in order to reduce the effects of reporting errors and idiosyncratic influences. Second, some countries had to be excluded because information for the independent variables was not available. Finally Oman, Saudi Arabia and Bahrain were excluded from the sample because of idiosyncratic factors.[5] The final country coverage for the sample is reported in Table 4.2.

The measured levels of IIT relate to the year 1988, derived from import and export value and quantity data taken from OECD data tapes and classified according the SITC.[6] All the data for right-hand side variables apply also to 1988. All the OLS equations and the diagnostic tests were estimated with MICROFIT.

4.4 RESULTS: COUNTRY-SPECIFIC ANALYSIS

The results for the regressions testing the hypotheses about vertical intra-industry trade are set out in Table 4.3. The equation has an overall explanatory power of over 70 per cent and it is possible to accept the null hypotheses of homoscedasticity, normality and linear functional form. Note, however, that this robustness was assisted by use of the country dummy for Switzerland (SWIDUM), which eliminated the statistical problems caused by this (large) positive outlier in the initial regressions.

The signs on most of variables in (4.4) and (4.5) are as expected and the estimated coefficients significant at the 1 per cent level. The signs on the market size variable $(Y_i + Y_k)/2$ and integration dummy

Table 4.3   OLS results for vertical intra-industry trade

Independent variable	Dependent variable		
	(1) $VB_j(\pm 15\%)$	(2) $VB_{jH}(\pm 15\%)$	(3) $VB_{jL}(\pm 15\%)$
Constant	.1727	.0877	.0851
	(7.3349)***	(5.1009)	(6.4888)
$\|Y_i/N_i - Y_k/N_k\|$	−.0131	−.0058	−.0072
	(−6.3597)***	(−3.8838)	(−6.3323)
$(Y_i + Y_k)/2$	.00008	.00004	.00003
	(4.2055)***	(3.2743)	(3.2621)
ECDUM	.0980	.00567	.0413
	(4.8906)***	(3.8795)	(3.6995)
SWIDUM	.2722	.1155	.1567
	(5.2347)***	(3.0448)	(5.4114)
Statistics			
N	62	62	62
$\bar{R}^2$	.7351	.5641	.6895
F(4, 57)	43.3176	20.7323	34.8579
Diagnostics			
A. Functional form	chi-sq (1) .4847	.2967	.1164
	F(1,56) .4412	.2692	.1053
B. Normality	chi-sq(2) 4.003	15.2696	17.7526
C. Heteroscedasticity	chi-sq(1) .0435	.6553	2.5589
	F(1,60) .0421	.6410	2.5830

Notes: Diagnostics are A: Ramsey's reset test, B: test of skewness and kurtosis of residuals,
C: based on regression of squared residuals on squared fitted values. Significance levels ***(1%), **(5%), *(10%) The dependent variable is differentiated for the per unit value deviation used to separate horizontal from vertical IIT (15% or 25%) and for the level of aggregation of the trade data (usually at the 5-digit level of the SITC, but sometimes at the 3-digit level and the explicitly shown by (3).
Independent variables:
$\|Y_i/N_t - Y_k/N_k\|$ = the absolute difference in income per head between country i and the UK (k)
$(Y_i + Y_k)/2$ = average national income in country i and the UK (k)
ECDUM, SWIDUM = dummy variables for the EC Countries and Switzerland.

(ECDUM) are in line with expectations. The sign on the factor endowment difference proxy $|Y_i/N_i - Y_k/N_k|$ is, however, contrary to expectations. We do not find support for the hypotheses suggested by the neo-factor proportions models of vertical IIT. To the extent that per-capita income differences adequately proxy endowment differences, we find that the share of vertical IIT in gross trade decreases as the difference in (relative) capital abundance increases.[7]

Rather we find evidence in support of the Linder-type demand similarity hypothesis. This type of result has been consistently found in econometric work on testing country-specific hypotheses of IIT. But it has invariably been found where *total* (vertical and horizontal combined) intra-industry trade has been used to test the hypothesis. Although the Linder thesis is not explicitly a model of monopolistic competition, it does relate quality range or taste overlap to per capita income levels. In any case much of the econometric work has also explicitly or implicitly derived the per capita income similarity hypothesis from the CHO model. In which case total IIT has been interpreted as a proxy for horizontal IIT, in so much as it has been assumed that intra-industry trade was typically of a horizontal form. As discussed earlier, this assumption was probably not justified.

Before turning to the results which directly test the hypotheses derived from the CHO model (by using the share of horizontal IIT in gross trade (HB_j) as the dependent variable), let us consider some alternative testing of the neo-factor proportions model of vertical IIT. In equation (1) of Table 4.3, the dependent variable, VB_j, measures the share of all vertical IIT in gross trade irrespective of whether the UK is the relatively high or low unit value (higher or lower quality) exporter in the two-way exchange. The robustness of the conclusions drawn from the results of equation (1) may be investigated, using revised measures of the share of vertical IIT in gross trade; in equation (2) VB_{jH} measures the share of vertical IIT where the UK is the 'high-quality' exporter and VB_{jL} measures the share of vertical IIT where the UK is the 'low-quality' exporter. The non-normality of the residuals in (2) and (3) means that we cannot strictly comment on the significance of the estimated coefficients. The results do not however, encourage one to contradict the earlier conclusions drawn from equation 1. The sign on the per capita income differential variable is negative throughout, and not as expected where a neo-factor proportions explanation of vertical IIT was influential.

Table 4.4 seeks to test the hypotheses relating to horizontal IIT directly. Equation (1) gives similar results as the earlier ones for VB_j the same signs on the right-hand variables albeit with somewhat lower levels of apparent significance. However, this equation fails the (linear) functional form, normality and homoscedasticity tests, and there are again some collinearity problems with the market size, income

Table 4.4 OLS results for horizontal intra-industry trade

Independent variable	Dependent variable			
	(1) $HB_j(\pm15\%)$	(2) $HB_j(\pm25\%)$	(1) B_j	(2) B_j
Constant	.0206	.0328	.1983	.0970
	(1.4442)	(2.7207)	(6.2143)	(6.1651)
$\lvert Y_i/N_i - Y_k/N_k \rvert$	−.0032	−.0041	−.0163	−.0169
	(−2.5624)	(−3.7535)	(−5.7099)	(−6.0741)
$(Y_i + Y_k)/2$	.00007	.00016	.0002	.0001
	(3.0699)	(7.1848)	(3.6164)	(5.5758)
$\lvert Y_i - Y_k \rvert$	−.00001	−.00006	−.00004	
	(−.4832)	(−3.8763)	(−1.1004)	
ECDUM	.0679		.1555	.1668
	(5.1866)		(5.356)	(6.1359)
SWIDUM			.3304	.3414
			(4.6455)	(4.8399)
IREDUM		.1441		
		(4.9496)		
JAPDUM		−.1424		
		(−4.4412)		
Statistics				
N	62	62	62	62
$\bar{R}^2$	.6535	.7062	.7739	.7731
F(4,57)	29.7564	30.3295	42.7585	52.9497
Diagnostics				
A. Functional Form	chi-sq(1) 8.3180	.0093	2.0223	3.9566
	F(1,56) 8.6771	.0083	1.8545	3.8173
B. Normality	chi-sq(2) 9.7913	46.2674	1.1942	1.3388
C. Hetero-scedasticity	chi-sq(1) 11.8413	1.1710	1.4424	1.2316
	F(1,60) 14.1646	1.1550	1.4291	1.2160

Note: IREDUM, JAPDUM, SWIDUM = dummy variables for Ireland, Japan and Switzerland.
All other notes as in Table 4.3.

differential variables and the integration dummy included together. The diagnostics are improved with the inclusion of two country dummies (IREDUM and JAPDUM). The exceptionally high levels of HB_j for Ireland and the exceptionally low levels for Japan, are not too surprising given f.o.b. and c.i.f. measurement of export and import values and the differences in 'distance' involved in the two cases, the structural surplus on the Japanese current account and the long-standing free trade arrangements between the UK and Ireland (The inclusion of a distance/transport cost variable in the equation may reduce the extent of these effects. It is not inevitably so, however, since the model is explaining the *share* of horizontal IIT in gross trade, not the absolute amount of such trade).

For comparison, Table 4.4 also shows results where the dependent variable is total IIT (B_j). They follow the pattern already established for horizontal IIT treated separately, but with a somewhat higher explanatory power. We conclude, therefore, that the horizontal IIT hypotheses are at least no more strongly supported with HB_j rather than B_j as the dependent variable.

4.5 METHODOLOGY: INDUSTRY-SPECIFIC ANALYSIS

Thus far empirical testing of industry-specific hypotheses about IIT has related to total IIT (B_j). Many of the models tested have been of the form:

$$B_j = \alpha_0 + \alpha_1 PD_j + \alpha_2 SE_j + \alpha_3 MS_j + \alpha_4 MNE_j + e_j \qquad \ldots (4.6)$$

where PD_j = proxy variable for attribute product differentiation in industry j, SE_j = proxy variable for scale economies in industry j; MS_j = measure of market structure competitiveness of industry j and MNE_j = measure of the importance of multinational enterprises in industry j.

Following on from the discussion in Section 4.1, PD, SE and MS are included to test for industry-specific factors suggested by models of both horizontal and vertical differentiation. MNE is often included because many multiproduct firms are also multinational firms and, as Helpman and Krugman (1985) show, there are a number of models where multinational firms are an important deterministic factor where both horizontally and vertically differentiated products are concerned. The expected sign on MNE is, therefore, positive. Note, however, that the expected signs on α_1, α_2 and $\alpha_3 \gtrless 0$. These ambiguities arise because the data do not distinguish between horizontal and vertical product differentiation and because, as we have seen, either may be associated with large or small numbers cases.

Thus, although the presence of scale economies of some form is a necessary condition for IIT in most of the theoretical work, it does not follow that IIT in a particular industry is (continuously) positively related to decreasing unit costs. In the present study we relate SE_j to the MES of production. Our preferred hypothesis is that the smaller the MES in an industry the greater the scope for firm entry and product differentiation (that is that $\alpha_2 < 0$). Some authors, however, expect plant size to be *positively* related to IIT. To the extent that the minimum efficient scale of production is small relative to the total size of the industry's market and that the large number model is the dominant paradigm, then we would expect that $\alpha_3 > 0$. If, however, market structures with small numbers of firms are the dominant source of IIT then we would expect $\alpha_3 < 0$.

Some of this ambiguity about expected signs disappears if we can separate total IIT into vertical and horizontal IIT. Then we can test the hypotheses presented in Section 4.1 with the following equations:

$$VB_j = \alpha_0 + \alpha_1 PD_j + \alpha_2 SE_j + \alpha_3 MS_j + \alpha_4 MNE_j + e_j \qquad \ldots (4.7)$$

(The expected signs are $\alpha_1 < 0$, $\alpha_2 \gtrless 0$, $\alpha_3 \gtrless 0$, $\alpha_4 > 0$).
and

$$HB_j = \alpha_0 + \alpha_1 PD_j + \alpha_2 SE_j + \alpha_3 MS_j + \alpha_4 MNE_j + e_j \qquad \ldots (4.8)$$

(The expected signs are $\alpha_1 > 0$, $\alpha_2 < 0$, $\alpha_3 > 0$, $\alpha_4 > 0$).

Thus separation of horizontal and vertical differentiation is not only of interest in itself, it facilitates empirical analysis with clearer priors, and allows us to test one theoretical structure against another. In the case of horizontal IIT the ambiguity on the expected signs present in equation (4.6) disappears. In the context of large numbers of models of IIT we would expect HB_j to be positively related to the extent of attribute differentiation and the lack of concentration of markets and inversely related to the MES. By contrast the ambiguity remains in explaining VB_j (equation (4.7)); α_2 and α_3 have positive or negative signs according to whether a 'large' or 'small' numbers model applies.

Using a SIC/SITC concordance for UK data we are able to estimate these equations. The data definitions and sources for the dependent and independent variables are set out in Appendix 4.1. The measured levels of IIT relate to the year 1988, using import and export value data taken from OECD data tapes (classified according to the SITC) and measured on a SIC 3 digit basis. The data for the independent variables in equations 4.5, 4.6, 4.7 or 4.8 also apply to 1988. All the regression results reported are for a sample of 77 industries and the descriptive statistics for the variables in the sample are given in Appendix 4.2. In the case of two of the explanatory variables, alternative proxies were investigated. A measure of market concentration

($CONC_j$) was substituted in some cases for the number of firms measure of market structure (MS_j); opposite signs being expected on these two variables. In the case of (4.7) a proxy for the degree of vertical product differentiation (VPD_j) was investigated as a replacement for PD_j; again opposite signs are expected on these.

All of the equations and diagnostics were estimated with SHAZAM. Least squares estimation was used in the equations for B_j, VB_j, and HB_j and Tobit estimation was also used for the equation for HB_j (where a number of zero or near zero values for the dependent variable applied). In all cases weighted regressions are reported, to remedy evident heteroscedasticity problems. Net output by each industry (in 1988) was used as the weights; each observation of the dependent and independent variable being multiplied by the square root of the weight variable.

4.6   RESULTS: INDUSTRY-SPECIFIC ANALYSIS

The estimated equations for *total IIT* (B_j) are set out in Table 4.5. Three equations are reported; (1) using number of firms (MS_j) to capture market structure, (2) using sales concentration ($CONC_j$) as the market structure variable and (3) which includes both MS_j and $CONC_j$ but excludes SE_j. They produce consistent results and reasonably stable estimated coefficients. The overall explanatory power of both equations is between 0.25 and 0.33 per cent, not unsatisfactory for cross sectional work. Except for the alternative specification in (1) which just fails the normality test at the 5 per cent level, diagnostic tests indicate that we can accept the null hypotheses of homoscedasticity, normality and linearity (at the 5 per cent level at least).[8]

The results confirm the consensus that has emerged from previous testing of total IIT, namely that large numbers models seem most appropriate in explaining IIT. The sign on MS_j is positive (1) and on $CONC_j$ is negative (2); in both cases with significance at the 5 per cent level. Similarly the negative sign for α_2, again with strong significance, supports the hypothesis that a relatively small MES permits greater firm entry. The somewhat surprising result is that the sign on PD_j (the attribute diversity proxy) is negative (and with significance at the 1 per cent level in (2)). This is contrary to earlier evidence including some for the UK (Greenaway and Milner 1984), which may suggest that the composition of total IIT (that is the relative importance of horizontal and vertical IIT) has changed over time. A growth in the relative

Table 4.5   Estimated WLS[1] regressions for total intra-industry trade

Independent variables	Expected sign	Dependent variable		
		(1) B_j	(2) B_j	(3) B_j
(α_0) Constant		64.086	71.342	70.820
		(20.59)***	(20.69)***	(15.88)***
(α_1)PD_j	+/−	−0.0748	−0.0759	−0.0728
		(−3.435)***	(−3.444)***	(−3.160)***
(α_2)SE_j	−/+	−0.3532	−0.2762	
		(−4.502)***	(−2.816)***	
(α_3)MS_j	+/−	0.0006		0.0003
		(2.350)**		(1.072)
(α_3)$CONC_j$	−/+		−0.1480	−0.2397
			(−1.922)**	(−3.233)***
(α_4)MNE_j	+	0.1412	0.1451	0.1778
		(1.334)*	(1.343)*	(1.577)*
N		77	77	77
$\bar{R}^2$		0.326	0.310	0.246
Diagnostics				
Ramsey Reset test	$F(3, 69)$	8.530	8.611	7.056
Normality test	(χ^2, 2df)	7.548	6.340	3.442
Heteroscedasticity	(χ^2, 4df)	5.349	6.154	7.651

[1] Weighted least square using net output in each industry (j) as weights.
***1% level of significance, **5% and *10%

importance in vertical IIT in the last decade could account for a switch in the sign on α_1, (from positive to negative). This is not inconsistent with the findings of Oulton (1990) who also uses unit value information and concludes that UK exports in manufactures are predominantly high quality.

What happens when we estimate equations with VB_j and HB_j as dependent variables? In fact we generate results for PD_j which accord with our priors: VB_j and PD_j are inversely related (Table 4.6) and HB_j and PD_j are positively related (but without significance in the latter case). Moreover, these findings are consistent with both a ±15 per cent and ±25 per cent unit value criterion. We also introduce a proxy for vertical product differentiation (VPD_j), namely the share of non-manual employment in total employment. In other words we are assuming that product quality is systematically related to skill intensity. VPD_j also comes out with a highly significant positive sign in (3) and (4) in Table 4.6. These are important results which may give us a clue

Table 4.6 Estimated WLS[1] regressions for intra-industry trade in vertically differentiated goods

Independent variables	Expected sign	Dependent variable			
		(1) VB_j (±15%)	(2) VB_j (±25%)	(3) VB_j (±15%)	(4) VB_j (±25%)
(α_0) Constant		45.039 (12.12)***	36.282 (9.239)***	30.736 (5.438)***	22.295 (3.973)***
$(\alpha_1)PD_j$	−	−0.0848 (−3.264)***	−0.0439 (−1.597)*		
$(\alpha_1)VPD_j$	+			0.4009 (2.577)***	0.4460 (2.887)***
$(\alpha_2)SE_j$	+/−	−0.1487 (−1.587)*	0.0048 (0.0490)	−0.1090 (−1.2137)	0.0344 (0.3615)
$(\alpha_3)MS_j$	−/+	0.0013 (4.231)***	0.0017 (5.230)***	0.0011 (3.463)***	0.0015 (4.683)***
$(\alpha_4)MNE_j$	+	0.0040 (0.0317)	−0.3315 (−2.483)***	−0.1807 (−1.299)	−0.5032 (−3.643)***
N		77	77	77	77
$\bar{R}^2$		0.287	0.339	0.251	0.387
Diagnostics					
Ramsey Reset test	$F(3, 69)$	3.271	0.340	0.418	0.266
Normality	$(\chi^2, 2df)$	1.536	6.714	2.987	7.993
Hetero-scedasticity	$(\chi^2, 4df)$	6.473	1.810	2.324	8.100

[1] Weighted least squares using net output in each industry (j) as weights.
*** 1% level of significance, ** 5% and * 10%

as to why much previous work on IIT and product differentiation appears to have generated such inconsistent results. That inconsistency may reflect the fact that vertical and horizontal IIT differ in their relative importance across different samples.

The separate equations for vertical and horizontal IIT do produce some surprising results, however, for some of the other explanatory variables. Consider first the results in Table 4.6 for vertical IIT. Note that the arrangement of signs on MS_j (in both equations with a 1 per cent level of significance) on SE_j and on MNE_j (albeit without significance in several cases). Vertical IIT is directly related to the number of firms in the industry; vertical IIT appears to predominate in the large numbers case rather than oligopolistic market structures. The result for SE_j is also consistent with this interpretation of the market structure influences on vertical IIT; a lower MES permitting larger entry and being positively related, therefore, with vertical IIT. Thus referring back to the classification in Section 4.1 the combined evidence for MS_j and SE_j does not support the small numbers interpretation of vertical IIT. Finally we find a negative sign with a statistically significant coefficient on MNE_j in (2) and (4) in Table 4.6. We would have expected a positive relationship, if IIT of all types was positively related to the scope for intra-firm trade or if vertical IIT in oligopolistic conditions provided greater scope for rents which attracted greater multinational involvement.

By contrast we turn to the results for horizontal IIT in Table 4.7 we find a positive and highly significant sign on MNE_j in (2) and (4). Of course transfer pricing behaviour may distort the 'true' dispersion between import and export values in the case of intra-firm IIT by multinationals. In which case we must interpret the results on the MNE_j variable in both Tables 4.6 and 4.7 with some caution. With respect to the remaining results in Table 4.7, mixed signs are obtained for attribute differentiation $(\hat{\alpha}_1 \gtrless 0)$ but without significance in all cases. The estimated coefficient on SE_j is, as expected, negative (and significant at the 5 per cent level in both equations). This result appears to be consistent with the 'large numbers' model, that is with monopolistically competitive market structures including IIT in horizontally differentiated goods. In contrast, however, the sign on MS_j is negative and significant and is not, therefore, consistent with the 'large numbers' model of IIT. Indeed one may be inclined to attach greater importance to the result for MS_j than for SE_j, since MS_j is likely to be a more reliable indicator of market structure than SE_j. It is of some interest that the estimated model for horizontal IIT is rather less robust than those for total IIT and vertical IIT; its explanatory power is much lower and there are some problems with the diagnostics in the WLS regressions. The dominant explanation of IIT (the 'large numbers' model) seems to fit vertical IIT better than horizontal IIT. Earlier work on total IIT which found support for the large numbers model ascribed this to the prevalence of horizontal IIT; this finding challenges that presumption.

4.7 IMPLICATIONS AND CONCLUSIONS

There are persuasive reasons for believing that it is worthwhile separating out horizontal and vertical IIT. Theory suggests that their

Table 4.7 Estimated weighted,[1] regression[2] and Tobit analysis for intra-industry trade in horizontally differentiated goods

Independent variables	Expected sign	Dependent variable			
		(1) $HB_j(\pm 15\%)$ (WLS)	(2) $HB_j(\pm 25\%)$ (WLS)	(3) $HB_j(\pm 15\%)$ (Weighted Tobit)	(4) $HB_j(\pm 25\%)$ (Weighted Tobit)
(α_0) Constant		19.048	27.791	1.0817	1.4407
		(4.665)***	(5.941)***	(3.8184)***	(4.9241)***
$(\alpha_1) PD_j$	+	0.0101	−0.0310	0.0014	−0.0016
		(0.3520)	(−0.9477)	(0.7811)	(−0.8756)
$(\alpha_2) SE_j$	−	−0.2045	−0.3578	−0.00128	−0.0198
		(−1.987)**	(−3.3035)**	(−1.9399)**	(−2.9579)***
$(\alpha_3) MS_j$	+	−0.0007	−0.0011	−0.0001	−0.001
		(−2.060)**	(−2.829)***	(−2.9929)***	(−2.5930)***
$(\alpha_4) MNE_j$	+	0.1452	0.4727	0.0092	2.8407
		(1.046)	(2.973)***	(1.0265)	(3.1253)***
N/R^2		77	77	77	77
		0.059	0.220		
Diagnostics Ramsey Reset Specification test	$F(3, 69)$	2.365	2.749		
Jarque Bera Normality test	$(\chi^2, 2df)$	8.542	3.648		
Harvey Heteroscedasticity test	$(\chi^2, 2df)$	0.960	4.696		
Standard error of estimate				17.339	18.173
Log likelihood function				−288.767	−322.125
Squared correlation between observed expected value				0.084	0.277

[1] Weighted using net output in each industry (j) as weights.
[2] Weighted least square regression.
***1% level of significance, **5% and *10%

determinants differ. Moreover, the impact of policy innovations is also likely to differ across markets where the two prevail. Finally, adjustment consequences of trade expansion will differ depending on whether we are dealing with horizontal or vertical IIT.

In this chapter we have used an intuitively plausible and fairly robust criterion to disentangle vertical and horizontal IIT in the bilateral trade of the UK. Our results show that in the UK over two thirds of all multilateral IIT is vertical IIT. This is an important finding and one which some commentators may find surprising. Interestingly however, it is not inconsistent with the findings of Oulton (1990) on the importance of quality factors in UK trade. Our results have obvious implications for modelling the determinants of trade flows. It is also interesting to note that the relative importance of vertical and horizontal IIT differs by country type. This too should help inform and motivate future work on UK trade flows.

Theory suggests that country-specific factors are relevant to the explanation of the pattern of IIT. We therefore estimated a model which incorporates country-specific factors to establish whether they are related to the pattern of horizontal and vertical IIT. Both market size and membership of a customs union are relevant to the explanation of the pattern of the UK's vertical IIT. However, relative factor endowments do not seem to support the neo-factor proportions model – instead this seems to accord with Linder-type trade. This is significant since the neo-factor proportions model is the most well known framework for the explanation of vertical IIT. The obvious question which this poses is whether the finding is a consequence of the measurement of vertical IIT, the measurement of factor endowment differences, or a reflection of a deficiency with the underlying theory? The pattern of horizontal IIT also seems to be fashioned by country-specific factors, though the results are not as strong as with vertical VIIT.

The results of our industry-specific analysis are encouraging in that the explanatory power of at least one of the disaggregated models is comparable to that of the aggregate IIT model. Moreover, the results are also robust to changes in our vertical/horizontal indicator and the levels of significance are high for many of the estimated coefficients in the disaggregated models. Thus measured levels of vertical and horizontal IIT are systematically related to features of production and industrial structure. Indeed the results indicate that HB_j and VB_j are not necessarily related in the same way to these features of industrial structure. By implication the modelling of aggregate IIT will tend to obscure the true underlying relationships.

The empirical evidence presented here supports the view that the industry-specific determinants of vertical and horizontal IIT do differ, but not always in the expected fashion. IIT in vertically differentiated products is not well explained by the small numbers model. Rather we find that vertical IIT is positively related to the number of firms in an industry that is the large numbers model applies. Vertical IIT is also positively linked with vertical product differentiation. By contrast there is no evidence of attribute differentiation being positively related to horizontal IIT and this form of IIT seems to be associated with industries with few firms. Earlier evidence on the determinants of total IIT had been interpreted as supporting the 'large numbers' model, on the presumption that horizontal IIT was the predominant form. But this chapter challenges this presumption for the United Kingdom. The relative importance of vertical IIT may have been persistently understated, but the present work establishes that by 1988 and for the United Kingdom vertical IIT may be the more important type of IIT.

Notes

* The material in this chapter draws heavily on Greenaway, Hine and Milner (1994, 1995).

1. Note that a few analysts equate vertical IIT with the exchange of final goods for intermediates. The usage of vertical to connote different qualities is more common and this is the convention we use throughout.
2. The allocation of categories was based on a concordance between the SITC 5th digit and UK Standard Industrial Classification (SIC) digit 3. Details of the concordance are available from the authors on request.
3. Strictly Grubel-Lloyd indices of the *share* of IIT in the gross trade $(X_j + M_j)$ of an industry rather than absolute levels are reported.
4. Note that the application of the price dispersion criteria to a cif-fob comparison of import and export values means that the *actual* price dispersion range is greater than $\pm$ 15 per cent. The application of this criteria to multilateral trade rather than bilateral trade may also tend to upwardly bias the measurement of horizontal, rather than vertical IIT.
5. Data here were distorted by recording vagaries. For example, IIT in aircraft in trade with Saudi Arabia is suspiciously high. It turns out that this results from the fact that aircraft returned to the UK for repair are treated as an import when they enter the UK and as an export when they return to Saudi Arabia!
6. A potential problem with using unit value indices for international comparisons is the distortions resulting from exchange rate deviations from PPP. If for the sample year in question the exchange rate is significantly under or over-valued, this could distort the unit value indices.

94   *Intra-Industry Trade and Adjustment*

A common way of dealing with this when using aggregate data is to average over a period of years. Since we are dealing with fifth digit data and bilateral transactions, such an option would be intractable. Arguably it is less of a concern with bilateral transactions. Besides which, we have no reason to suppose that 1988 is especially unrepresentative.

7. One could posit a quadratic relationship between the difference in per capita income and the share of IIT. This was investigated, but no statistically significant relationship was evident.

8. The only case of correlation coefficient greater than 0.4 for two RHS variables in any of the results in Tables 4.1, 4.2 and 4.3 is in eq. (2) in Table 4.3. The correlation coefficient between VD_j and MNE_j is 0.57.

References and Further Reading

Abd-el-Rahman, K. (1991) 'Firms' Competitive and National Comparative Advantages as Joint Determinants of Trade Composition', *Weltwirtschaftliches Archiv*, 127, 83–97.

Aw, B.Y. and Roberts, M.J. (1988) 'Price and Quality Comparisons for U.S. Footwear Imports: An application of multilateral index numbers', in Feenstra, R.C. (ed.), *Empirical Methods for International Trade*, Cambridge, MA: MIT Press, pp. 257–75.

Balassa, B. (1967) 'Tariff Reductions and Trade in Manufactures among Industrial Countries', *American Economic Review*, 56, 466–73.

Balassa, B. (1986a) 'Intra-Industry Trade Among Exporters of Manufactured Goods', in Greenaway, D. and Tharakan, P.K.M. (eds), *Imperfect Competition and International Trade*, Brighton: Wheatsheaf Books.

Balassa, B. (1986b) 'The Determinants of Intra-Industry Specialisation in US Trade', *Oxford Economic Papers*, 38, 220–33.

Brenton, P. and Winters, L.A. (1992) 'Estimating the International Trade Effects of "1991": West Germany', *Journal of Common Market Studies*, 30, 143–56.

Cooper, D.N., Greenaway, D. and Rayner, A.J. (1993) 'Intra-Industry Trade and Limited Producer Horizons: An Empirical Investigation', *Weltwirtschaftliches Archiv*, 129, 345–66.

Dixit, A.K. and Stiglitz, J.E. (1977) 'Monopolistic Competition and Optimum Product Diversity', *American Economic Review*, 67, 297–308.

Eaton, J. and Kierzkowski, H. (1984a) 'Oligopolistic Competition, Product Variety, Entry Deterrence and Technology Transfer', *Rand Journal*, 15, 99–107.

Eaton, J. and Kierzkowski, H. (1984b) 'Oligopolistic Competition, Product Variety and International Trade', in Kierzhowski, H. (ed.), *Monopolistic Competition and International Trade*, Oxford: Oxford University Press.

Faini, R. and Heimler, A. (1991) 'The Quality and Production of Textiles and Clothing and the Completion of the Internal Market', in Winters, L.A. and Venables, A.J. (eds), *European Integration: Trade and Industry*, Cambridge: Cambridge University Press.

Falvey, R. (1981) 'Commercial Policy and Intra Industry Trade', *Journal of International Economics*, 11, 495–511.

Falvey, R. and Kierzkowski, H. (1987) 'Product Quality, Intra-Industry Trade and (Im)Perfect Competition', in Kierzkowski, H. (ed.), *Protection and Competition in International Trade*, Oxford: Blackwell.

Feenstra, R. (1984) 'Voluntary Export Restraints in US Autos, 1980–81: Quality Employment and Welfare Effects', in Baldwin, R.E. and Krueger, A.E.O. (eds), *The Structure and Evolution of Recent US Trade Policies*, Chicago: The University of Chicago Press.

Greenaway, D. and Milner, C.R. (1983) 'On the Measurement of Intra Industry Trade', *Economic Journal*, 93, 900–8.

Greenaway, D. and Milner, C.R. (1984). 'A Cross Section Analysis of Intra Industry Trade in the UK', *European Economic Review*, 25, 319–44.

Greenaway, D. and Milner, C.R. (1986) *The Economics of Intra-Industry Trade*, Oxford: Blackwell.

Greenaway, D., Hine, R.C. and Milner, C.R. (1994) 'Country-Specific Factors And the Pattern of Horizontal and Vertical Intra-Industry Trade in the UK', *Weltwirtschaftliches Archiv*, 130, 77–100.

Greenaway, D., Hine, R.C. and Milner, C.R. (1995) 'Vertical and Horizontal Intra-Industry Trade: A Cross Industry Analysis for the United Kingdom', *Economic Journal*, 105, 1505–18.

Grubel, H.G. and Lloyd, P.J. (1975) *Intra-Industry Trade*, London: Macmillan.

Havrylyshyn, O. and Civan, E. (1983) 'Intra-Industry Trade and the Stage of Development', in Tharakan, P.K.M. (ed.), *Intra Industry Trade*, Amsterdam: North Holland.

Helpman, E. (1981) 'International Trade in the Presence of Product Differentiation, Economies of Scale and Monopolistic Competition', *Journal of International Economics*, 11, 305–40.

Helpman, E. (1987) 'Imperfect Competition and International Trade: Evidence from Fourteen Industrial Countries', *Journal of Japanese and International Economics*, 1, 62–81.

Helpman, E. and Krugman, P. (1985) *Market Structure and Foreign Trade*, Brighton: Harvester Wheatsheaf.

Krugman, P. (1979) 'Increasing Returns, Monopolistic Competition and International Trade', *Journal of International Economics*, 9, 469–79.

Lancaster, K. (1979) *Variety, Equity and Efficiency*, Oxford: Blackwell.

Loertscher, R. and Wolter, F. (1980) 'Determinants of Intra-Industry Trade: Among Countries and Across Industries', *Weltwirtschaftliches Archiv*, 116, 281–93.

Oulton, N. (1990) 'Quality and Performance in UK Trade 1978–87', *NIESR Discussion Paper*, 197, London.

Shaked, A. and Sutton, J. (1984) 'National Oligopolies and International Trade', in Kierzkowski, H. (ed.), *Monopolistic Competition and International Trade*, Oxford: Oxford University Press.

Stiglitz, J.E. (1987) 'The Causes and Consequences of the Dependence of Quality of Price', *The Journal of Economic Literature*, 25, 1–48.

Summers, R. and Heston, A. (1988) 'A New Set of International comparisons of Real Product and Price for 130 Countries', 1950–85, *Review of Income and Wealth*, 34, 1–25.

Intra-Industry Trade and Adjustment

Tharakan, P.K.M. (1984) 'Intra-Industry Trade between the Industrial Countries and the Developing World', *European Economic Review*, 26, 213–27.
Torstensson, J. (1991) 'Quality Differentiation and Factor Proportions in International Trade: An Empirical Test of the Swedish Case', *Weltwirtschaftliches Archiv*, 27, 183–94.
Torstensson, J. (1992) *Factor Endowments, Product Differentiation and International Trade*, Lund Economic Studies, No. 47. Lund: University of Lund.
World Bank, (1992) 'Socio-Economic Time Series Access and Retrieval System (STARs)' Version 2.5, April.

APPENDIX 4.1: DATA DEFINITION, SOURCES AND SAMPLE CHARACTERISTICS

Variable Definitions	*Data Source*
a) Dependent Variables	
B_j = Percentage share of total IIT in gross trade $(X_j + M_j)$ of industry j	Trade data (X and M in values and quantities) from OECD data tapes,
HB_j = Percentage share of measured horizontal IIT in gross trade of industry j.	classified according to SITC and recorded at the 5th digit.
VB_j = Percentage share of measured vertical IIT in gross trade of industry j.	
(where j corresponds with 3rd digit of UK SIC – Industry Groups 2–4).	
b) Independent Variables	
PD_j = number of 5 digit SITC categories in each 3 digit SIC (j)	*OECD data tapes*
VPD_j = Percentage share of non-manual employment in total employment of industry j	Business Monitor (1988) 'Report on the Census of Production' (Summary
SE_j = average size of establishment (net output per establishment)	Volume PA 1002), London: Central
$COMP_j$ = number of enterprises in 3 digit SIC group	Statistical Office.
$CONC_j$ = 5 firm (sales) concentration ratio, that is percentage of industry sales of 5 largest enterprises	
MNE_j = Percentage share of total industry sales accounted for by foreign enterprises (in 2 digit group)	

APPENDIX 4.2:   DESCRIPTIVE STATISTICS FOR SAMPLE

Variable	Mean value	Standard deviation	Minimum value	Maximum value
B_j	60.10	17.53	8.40	90.10
VB_j	40.46	16.36	7.10	80.00
HB_j	19.64	17.23	0.00	70.10
PD_j	30.48	38.52	0	297
VPD_j	30.03	10.85	10.00	64.13
SE_j	3.31	12.84	0.09	109.78
$COMP_j$	1586.60	2797.50	24	18688
$CONC_j$	39.18	21.06	9.60	95.60
MNE_j	16.22	12.56	0.01	58.54

5. A Survey of Intra-Industry Trade in the European Union

Marius Brülhart and Robert J.R. Elliott

5.1 INTRODUCTION

During the negotiation and implementation stages of the '1992' Single Market programme, prominent economists anticipated that the pressures for industrial restructuring among EU[1] countries would be considerably stronger than during previous episodes of European integration. Krugman (1987, p. 364) states: 'The question now is whether the further expansion of trade in progress will be equally easy to cope with. The unfortunate answer is, probably not.' Greenaway and Hine (1991, p. 620) suggests that: 'specialisation in Europe may have entered a new phase, and that this could pose greater problems for adjustment'.

These expectations were based on two main developments, both of which were connected to the phenomenon of intra-industry trade (IIT). First, the discovery of high and growing IIT levels in the 1970s had produced a wave of new thinking by trade theorists, which shifted the emphasis of the models away from country-specific trade determinants, generically termed 'comparative advantage', toward industry-specific factors such as increasing returns and external economies. Models of the 'new trade theory', although explaining the existence of IIT, generally predicted that a fall in trade barriers would promote concentration and relocation of industries near their largest markets.[2] Second, most economists agreed on the hypothesis that high levels of IIT were indicative of relatively low trade-induced adjustment costs. Some studies in the late 1980s found evidence of stagnating IIT growth, and therefore concluded that adjustment pressures were becoming more severe. The rapid growth of trade flows among EU countries (Table 5.1) was therefore expected to result in growing

Table 5.1a The post-war boom in intra-EU trade, 1961–77[1]

Country	1961 Imports	Exports	%EU	1967 Imports	Exports	%EU	1972 Imports	Exports	%EU	1977 Imports	Exports	%EU
Belgium-Lux.	20.3	20.1	61.4	23.3	25.3	67.8	31	33.4	74.3	34.3	34	70.1
Denmark	15.5	12.7	55.1	12.3	9.8	47.9	11.1	8.9	46.4	13.9	9.6	47.1
France	3.8	4.7	40.6	5.4	5.2	51.4	8.0	8.0	59.7	9.5	8.9	53.6
Germany	5.5	6.6	41.8	6.7	8.4	47.6	8.7	9.1	51.1	10.0	11.0	49.4
Greece	7.6	1.9	47.9	7.6	2.7	53.1	8.7	3.1	55.6	9.8	4.3	45.9
Ireland	24.5	20.9	72.1	22.8	19.8	72.8	25.6	21.4	73.8	36.2	33.1	72.9
Italy	4.5	4.0	39.7	5.1	5.4	45.4	7.2	7.4	52.8	8.8	9.4	48.0
Netherlands	22.7	20.5	59.8	21.3	20.6	64.7	22.1	26.5	68.7	22.5	27.8	64.3
Portugal	13.8	4.8	50.6	12.3	6.6	49.2	13.3	7.5	50.3	14.7	6.7	50.2
Spain	2.9	3.1	44.4	5.3	2.1	46.8	5.3	3.4	48	5.0	4.1	51.9
UK	3.8	3.6	24.6	4.6	3.7	29.1	5.7	5.0	33.1	10.2	2.9	40.3
EU	6.2	6.2	41.8	7.2	7.1	48.3	9.4	9.4	54.4	11.5	11.6	52.1

[1] *Imports* and *Exports*: all goods, current market prices, in percent of GDP. *%EU*: Proportion of intra-EU trade in total trade
Data source: EU Commission.

Table 5.1b The post-war boom in intra-EU trade, 1985–95[1]

Country	1985 Imports	1985 Exports	1985 %EU	1990 Imports	1990 Exports	1990 %EU	1992 Imports	1992 Exports	1992 %EU	1995 Imports	1995 Exports	1995 %EU
Belgium-Lux.	46.5	44.7	74.4	43.6	44.0	74.4	39.6	39.8	74.4	36.8	41.5	70.5
Denmark	15.1	12.2	46.3	12.5	13.2	50.1	12.5	14.3	51.9	13.0	14.7	51.5
France	11.4	9.9	54.8	11.6	11.0	61.2	10.7	10.9	61.1	10.6	10.6	59.3
Germany	12.9	14.6	50.3	11.8	14.4	53.4	12.3	12.8	55.0	11.6	12.8	54.4
Greece	12.2	6.1	50.0	15.4	6.3	64.2	15.4	6.7	63.6	17.7	6.7	67.0
Ireland	33.9	36.6	67.6	30.7	39.7	71.0	29.2	41.2	70.8	26.8	42.6	61.5
Italy	10.0	8.9	48.2	9.4	9.0	58.0	9.0	8.4	58.7	9.4	10.3	54.1
Netherlands	29.4	39.1	66.3	27.9	33.3	67.6	26.6	31.0	67.5	26.1	30.5	66.1
Portugal	16.9	17.2	52.8	29.2	20.03	70.9	26.6	16.5	74.3	27.0	18.7	73.4
Spain	6.6	7.6	43.5	10.6	7.8	63.2	10.5	7.9	64.7	12.3	11.7	63.8
UK	11.6	10.7	48.9	12.0	10.0	49.8	11.0	10.2	52.7	12.6	11.8	53.2
EU	13.6	13.8	53.8	13.5	13.8	60.1	13	12.8	60.2	13.3	14	58.5

[1] For explanation see notes to Table 5.1a

factor-market friction which in turn could fuel protectionist sentiment and undermine the integration project.

This chapter explores the validity of the second reason for the anticipation of growing adjustment pains in Europe.[3] Greenaway (1987) was first to find that 'IIT may have declined in the EU countries during the late 1970s'. These suspicions were confirmed by Mucchielli (1988), Globerman and Dean (1990) and Greenaway and Hine (1991), who all observed IIT trend reversals for several OECD countries based on relatively small data sets. No comprehensive and recent evidence, however, has as yet been produced to verify these suggestions.

Even if we did find confirmation of a generalized reversal in postwar IIT trends, it might be misleading to draw direct inferences from such a discovery on adjustment costs. The traditional interpretation of IIT has been challenged recently by work on the measurement of *changes* in IIT, now commonly referred to as marginal IIT (MIIT). As shown in Chapter 3, the traditional Grubel-Lloyd (GL) index of IIT is a static measure, in the sense that it describes trade patterns for one time period. Hamilton and Kniest (1991) have shown that the observation of a high proportion of IIT does not justify *a priori* any prediction of the likely pattern of *change* in trade flows. Industrial adjustment, however, is a dynamic concept, relating to the reallocation of resources over time. Even an observed increase in static IIT levels between two periods could 'hide' a very uneven change in trade flows, attendant with *inter-* rather than *intra*-industry adjustment, and with asymmetric rather than symmetric changes. Hence, it might be misleading to infer from rises/falls in IIT that trade expansion entails relatively low/high adjustment costs. We therefore complement the analysis of traditional IIT measures by a comprehensive survey of MIIT patterns in the EU.

Therefore, this chapter presents a comprehensive and statistically disaggregated analysis of IIT and MIIT patterns among the countries of the EU, drawing on the results calculated in the SPES-funded project which underlies most of the research reported in this book. This survey covers the period from 1961 to 1992, the latter being the deadline for the implementation of the Single Market as well as the last year for which customs data on intra-EU trade flows are available. Section 5.2 reports patterns of IIT, Section 5.3 provides the first cross-country analysis of MIIT and Section 5.4 concludes with a summary of the main results.

5.2   A SURVEY OF INTRA-INDUSTRY TRADE IN THE EUROPEAN UNION

Post-war economic integration in the EU contributed to an unprecedented growth of intra-European trade flows. Table 5.1 shows that, between 1961 and 1995, intra-EU trade grew from 12.4 per cent to 27.3 per cent of GDP, and the share of intra-EU flows in total trade rose from 41.8 per cent to 58.5 per cent. The relative expansion of intra-EU trade is particularly pronounced in the 1985–92 period, which coincides with the negotiation and implementation of the Single Market. These general patterns apply with remarkable consistency to the individual EU countries.

It is, therefore, not surprising that economists generally perceive integration-induced trade effects to be one of the main determinants of industrial adjustment in the EU. This is the context within which the IIT-adjustment hypothesis rose to its prominence.

This section provides a descriptive survey of IIT among 12 EU countries. Unadjusted Grubel-Lloyd (GL) indices were calculated from SITC four-digit (1961, 67) and five-digit (1972, 77, 85, 88, 90, 92) trade data supplied by the OECD. We chose such narrow industry definitions in order to minimize the 'categorical aggregation problem' arising from intra-industry product heterogeneity. The combination of these results provides us with the most comprehensive and most disaggregated set of IIT indices compiled for the EU to date.

IIT by country

The twelve panels of Figure 5.2 report IIT patterns separately for the 11 EU trading entities.[4] IIT is calculated in each country for four separate categories of trade: intra-EU trade in all products, intra-EU trade in manufactures, total trade in all products, and total trade in manufactures. This presentation summarizes the IIT results of the country studies in Part Two. We note three salient points:

1.   For the EU average (first panel of Figure 5.2), all four categories of trade flows show broadly increasing IIT trends. Any stagnation of IIT growth is only apparent for intra-EU trade.
2.   IIT is consistently higher for manufactured products than for total trade.
3.   Countries differ considerably in terms of their relative IIT levels for intra-EU and for world-wide trade. Intra-EU IIT has generally

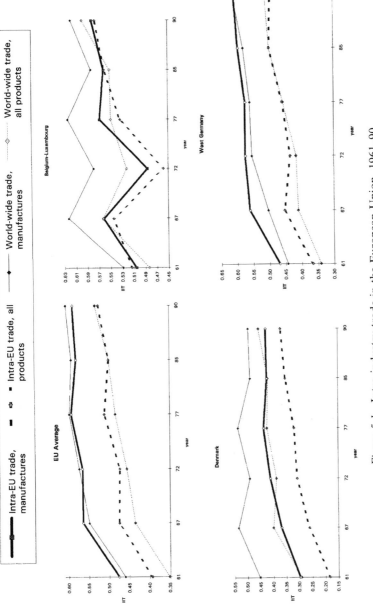

Figure 5.1 Intra-industry trade in the European Union, 1961–90

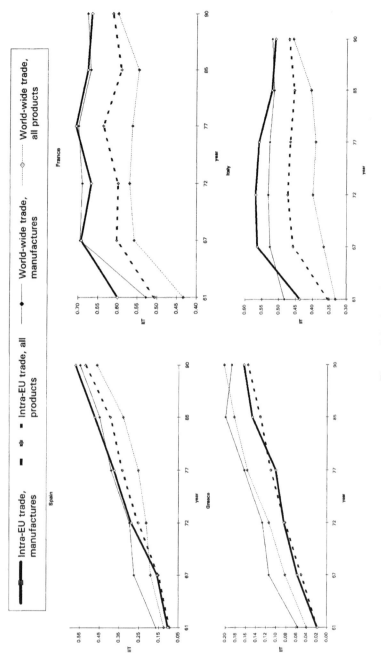

Figure 5.1 (contd.)

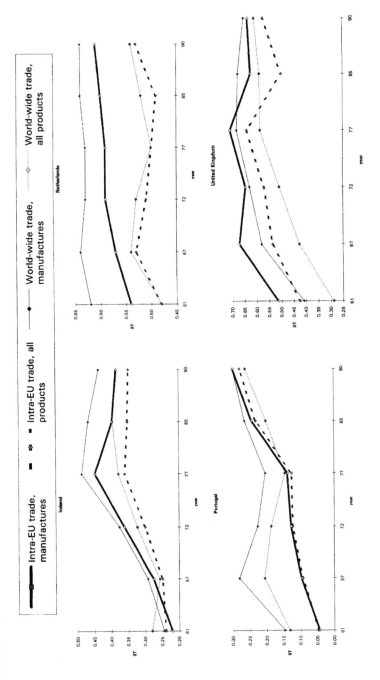

Figure 5.1 (contd.)

been higher than world-wide IIT in Germany, France and Italy. The reverse applies to Belgium-Luxembourg, Denmark, Greece, Ireland and the Netherlands. In Spain and Portugal intra-EU IIT overtook world-wide IIT in the 1970s, while the opposite happened in the United Kingdom.

The comparatively high level of IIT in manufactured products is a well-documented and theoretically established fact. It is more difficult to make inferences from the comparison between intra-EU IIT and world-wide IIT. Our IIT indices are not calculated from bilateral trade flows but from aggregate flows between the base country and either its fellow EU members or the totality of its trading partners. In this framework, world-wide IIT levels are expected *a priori* to be higher than intra-EU IIT, since raising the number of partner countries in the analysis increases the likelihood of net bilateral flows cancelling each other out. Average intra-EU IIT has been roughly at the same level as total IIT of the EU (see the first panel of Figure 5.2). Given the implicit relative upward bias in total IIT levels, this finding suggests that IIT was comparatively higher within the EU than between the EU and the rest of the world.

Of the four trade categories distinguished in Figure 5.1, intra-EU flows show the most interesting IIT patterns. First, this category displays the highest levels of average IIT, and, second, it appears to have witnessed a stagnation of IIT in the later stages of our sample period. Trade in manufactured goods among industrialized nations is also the category most favoured in the theoretical literature of IIT. We therefore scrutinize these trade flows somewhat further, including two additional sample years (1988 and 1992) for a clearer picture of recent developments. Figure 5.2 and Table 5.2 report these results.
We retain three main findings:

1. IIT among EU countries is remarkably high. The number of manufacturing 'industries' identified in the calculations ranges between 365 (1961) and 2169 (1990). In five of our six sample years, over half of all intra-EU trade flows of manufactured goods were matched bilateral exchanges within one of these narrowly defined industries. This finding reinforces the case against those who consider IIT a statistical artefact.
2. IIT levels have *converged* across countries between 1961 and 1990, as countries with lowest initial IIT levels (Greece, Portugal and Spain) witnessed the most pronounced increases. In the latest

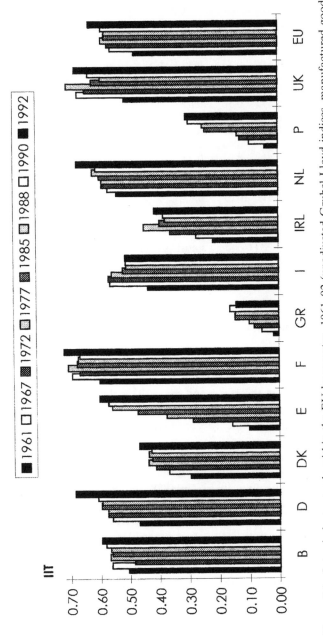

Figure 5.2 Intra-industry trade within the EU by country, 1961–92 (unadjusted Grubel-Lloyd indices, manufactured goods)

108

Table 5.2 Intra-industry trade within the EU by country, 1961–92
(unadjusted Grubel-Lloyd indices[1] underlying Figure 5.2)

Country	1961	1967	1972	1977	1985	1988	1990	1992
Belgium-Lux.	0.51	0.56	0.49	0.57	0.56	0.57	0.58	0.60
Denmark	0.30	0.37	0.41	0.44	0.42	0.44	0.43	0.47
France	0.60	0.69	0.67	0.71	0.68	0.67	0.67	0.72
Germany	0.47	0.56	0.57	0.57	0.60	0.59	0.61	0.68
Greece	0.02	0.06	0.08	0.10	0.15	0.15	0.16	0.15
Ireland	0.22	0.28	0.36	0.45	0.40	0.38	0.38	0.41
Italy	0.44	0.56	0.57	0.56	0.52	0.51	0.51	0.51
Netherlands	0.54	0.57	0.59	0.59	0.60	0.62	0.61	0.67
Portugal	0.04	0.10	0.13	0.14	0.24	0.25	0.30	0.31
Spain	0.10	0.16	0.29	0.38	0.47	0.56	0.57	0.60
U.K.	0.51	0.67	0.65	0.71	0.62	0.59	0.64	0.68
EU[2]	0.48	0.56	0.57	0.59	0.58	0.58	0.59	0.64

[1] Calculated from SITC 5-digit statistics from OECD, for SITC Sections 5–8.
[2] Average of 11 countries, weighted by values of intra-EU manufactured imports and exports

period (1990–92), however, IIT levels appear to have *diverged* again.
3. Looking at average IIT trends across countries, we can distinguish three periods. Intra-EU IIT in manufactures grew with remarkable consistency in the 1960s and early 1970s then it remained roughly stable during the late 1970s and the 1980s, but it resumed its upward trend in the most recent period, 1988–92.

One empirical caveat could qualify the validity of our finding that IIT stagnated in the late 1970s and during 1980s. The SITC classification was revised and refined twice, in 1978 and in 1988. Thus, IIT could have been biased downwards by narrowed-down industry definitions.[5] This issue could only be conclusively resolved either by rearranging all underlying trade data into a consistent classification over time and recalculating IIT indices, or by computing IIT indices for the years immediately before and immediately after the SITC revisions, so as to arrive at an estimate of the impact of reclassification on measured IIT levels. However, IIT rose consistently between 1988 and 1992, when the industry classification remained unaltered. This suggests that the reversal of IIT trend, perceived by various authors in the 1980s, might have been influenced by changes in statistical collation and that, even if the IIT stagnation had been a real phenomenon, it did not extend into the 1988–92 period.

We therefore find that it is premature to diagnose a generalized turnaround in the upward trend of IIT. It also appears that, against early predictions, the implementation of the Single Market did not entail and increase in inter-industry specialization. The broadly increasing tendency and cross-country convergence of intra-EU IIT also runs counter to fears of increased geographical concentration of industries subsequent to economic integration.

IIT by industry

We show in Figure 5.1 that IIT is generally higher in manufacturing industries than in non-manufacturing sectors. This finding is corroborated by the more disaggregated Figure 5.3, where IIT in SITC Sections 5 to 8 is consistently and significantly higher than in Sections 0 to 4. Figure 5.3 also shows that the IIT time trend varies among SITC Sections. The intra-EU trend reversal we have already detected in Figure 5.1 appears to have been driven by developments in SITC

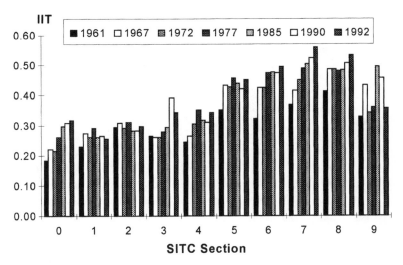

Figure 5.3   Intra-industry trade within the EU by industry, 1961–90 (unadjusted GL indices, weighted across industries, unweighted across countries)

Section 5 (Chemicals) and 6 (Manufactures classified by materials). SITC Section 6 is more important than Section 5 in terms of trade volumes and comprises many traditional, resource-based and relatively declining industries. On the other hand, SITC Section 7 (Machinery and Transport Equipment), which consists mainly of knowledge-based expanding industries, displays continuously rising levels of intra-EU IIT. The results of Figure 5.3, therefore, provide some indication that the observed stagnation of IIT growth in the 1980s was driven by an unevenly-spread relative contraction of resource-based industries, while expanding 'modern' sectors still display growing IIT. The growth of booming sectors thus seems to be more balanced across the countries of the EU than the relative contraction of declining industries.

Although IIT growth in the EU may be slowing down, Figure 5.4 confirms that the proportion of IIT is still considerably higher for intra-EU trade than for trade between the EU and non-EU countries in all SITC sections. The gap between intra-EU and extra-EU IIT is generally larger in sections 0 to 4 than in the manufacturing industries. It can be hypothesized that the EU's Common Agricultural Policy has counterbalanced pressures for inter-sectoral specialization among the Member States and thereby induced a relatively higher proportion of IIT.

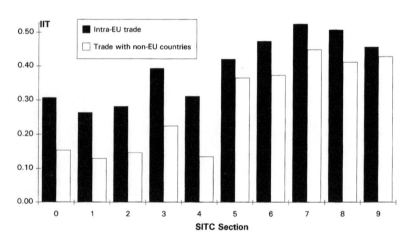

Figure 5.4   Intra-industry trade with EU and non-EU countries by industry, 1990 (unadjusted GL indices, weighted across industries, unweighted across countries)

5.3   A SURVEY OF MARGINAL INTRA-INDUSTRY TRADE

MIIT by country

As shown in Chapter 3, changes over time in GL indices do not convey meaningful information on the symmetry of underlying trade *changes*. We therefore complement the discussion of GL coefficients with Table 5.3, where we report the first comprehensive set of MIIT results computed to date, using the *A* index of Brülhart (1994).[6] Seeking to avoid distortions from industry reclassifications while identifying periods of similar duration, we have chosen the time intervals 1979–83, 1983–87 and 1988–92. End-year data were deflated into base-year prices, so as to retain only real changes in trade flows. The analysis was again conducted at the SITC 5-digit level, but we have concentrated here on intra-EU trade flows.

We note first that average MIIT was highest in the second of our three sub-periods and higher in the last sub-period than in the first one. This finding is in line with the time trend of the average GL index,

Table 5.3   Marginal intra-industry trade in the EU by country, 1979–92
(*A* indices[1])

Country	All product groups (SITC 0–9)			Manufactures (SITC 5–8)		
	1979–83	*1983–87*	*1988–92*	*1979–83*	*1983–87*	*1988–92*
Belgium-Lux.	0.39	0.40	0.35	0.35	0.41	0.36
Denmark	0.24	0.26	0.24	0.23	0.30	0.27
France	0.28	0.39	0.43	0.32	0.44	0.48
Germany	0.41	0.44	0.36	0.43	0.47	0.39
Greece	0.10	0.11	0.08	0.12	0.13	0.08
Ireland	0.17	0.19	0.30	0.21	0.22	0.30
Italy	0.22	0.36	0.24	0.27	0.40	0.27
Netherlands	0.26	0.37	0.36	0.33	0.46	0.40
Portugal	0.20	0.19	0.17	0.20	0.20	0.18
Spain	0.24	0.41	0.34	0.28	0.46	0.38
U.K.	0.20	0.43	0.24	0.28	0.51	0.24
EU[2]	0.29	0.37	0.33	0.32	0.41	0.36

[1] Calculated from SITC 5-digit statistics from OECD (1979, 83, 87) and Eurostat (1988, 92), converted into national currencies using year-average market exchange rates. End-year values deflated using national GDP deflators.
[2] Averages weighted by values of end-year intra-EU manufactured imports and exports

which, after a period of stagnant growth, resumed its upward trend in the early 1990s. While average IIT rose significantly between 1988 and 1992, MIIT in that interval was generally lower than in the mid-1980s. Thus, our data confirm that a rise in IIT levels actually corresponds to a change of trade flows which is necessarily inter-industry in nature. However, it should be noted that average MIIT was still higher in 1988–92 than in 1979–83, and that, in aggregate, we therefore detect no exceptional level of inter-industry trade changes in the run-up to the Single Market deadline.

The cross-country pattern of MIIT resembles that of IIT. Highest MIIT indices were found for Germany, France, Belgium and the Netherlands, whereas Denmark, Ireland, Portugal and Greece appear at the other end of the scale. The UK is an outlier. While, on average, the proportion of IIT since the late 1970s was second highest in British trade (surpassed only by France), the UK only ranks sixth in terms of our MIIT averages. In the most recent subperiod (1988–92), UK manufacturing even exhibited the third-lowest shares of MIIT, with only Greece and Portugal showing lower averages on the *A* index. This indicates that structural inter-industry change was more pronounced

Table 5.4   Marginal intra-industry trade in the EU by industry, 1979–92
(*A* indices[1])

SITC Section	1979–83	1983–87	1988–92
0 (food and live animals)	0.14	0.19	0.21
1 (drink and tobacco)	0.16	0.13	0.18
2 (raw materials, except fuels)	0.15	0.17	0.17
3 (minerals, fuels, lubricants, etc.)	0.20	0.22	0.20
4 (animal and vegetable oils)	0.17	0.25	0.17
5 (chemicals)	0.26	0.30	0.27
6 (manufactures, by material)	0.24	0.31	0.25
7 (machinery and transport)	0.31	0.40	0.33
8 (misc. manufactures)	0.27	0.40	0.34
9 (goods n.e.s.)	0.38	0.36	0.25
0–9 (total trade)[2]	0.25	0.34	0.28
5–8 (manufactures)[2]	0.28	0.37	0.30

[1] Unweighted averages of 11 countries. For data sources and transformations, see Table 5.2.
[2] Weighted across SITC Sections by absolute size of trade changes ($\Delta X + \Delta M$). Note that these figures differ from the bottom row in Table 5.2, since no weighting is applied across countries.

in the UK than in the other 'core' EU economies, and it serves as another remainder that high or growing GL indices can mask considerable inter-industry adjustment.

MIIT by industry

If we look at average A indices across SITC 1-digit sectors, we find that MIIT patterns resemble those of IIT in so far as manufacturing industries exhibit consistently higher average index values than primary sectors (Table 5.4). The highest levels of MIIT are found for all three sub-periods in SITC Sections 7 and 8, which comprise most relatively advanced, R&D intensive industries. This is a further indication that inter-industry trade changes among EU countries were comparatively modest in those sectors which are often considered to be 'strategic'. In other words, it appears that inter-industry adjustment is more pronounced in the relative contraction of traditional industries than in the relative expansion of advanced sectors.[7]

5.4 CONCLUSION

This chapter has provided a comprehensive overview of IIT patterns in the EU for the 1961–92 period. We have paid particular attention to the proposition that industrial adjustment pressures among EU countries have increased in the run-up to the 1992 Single Market deadline, after three decades of what was perceived as smooth adaptation to a continuously more integrated European economy. A protracted post-war rise in intra-industry trade (IIT) had been invoked by numerous economists as the main reason for the relatively frictionless nature of industrial adjustment in Europe.

The incidence of adjustment pressures is examined in a survey of IIT and MIIT patterns in 12 EU countries, calculated from highly disaggregated data. We find some support for earlier results that the continuous rise of average IIT among EU members has come to a halt in the 1980s. However, IIT levels have resumed their upward trend in the 1988–92 period. It must be suspected that at least part of the detected stagnation in IIT growth had been caused by changes in the compilation of trade statistics. It would certainly be premature to diagnose a general reversal of the upward trend in IIT.

The analysis of MIIT does not suggest that trade-induced inter-industry adjustment pressures were particularly strong in the years preceding 1992. On aggregate, therefore, we find no evidence that the pattern of industrial adjustment differed significantly in the run-up to the Single Market deadline compared to earlier stages of European integration.

Averages of IIT and MIIT, however, hide a considerable amount of cross-industry diversity. We find some evidence that growing, advanced industries tend to exhibit higher levels of both IIT and MIIT than more mature, relatively declining sectors. This suggests that inter-industry adjustment is more prevalent in sectors which are in relative decline, whereas the expansion of booming sectors shows comparatively greater cross-country symmetry.

Our explorations have laid bare the need for a further strengthening of the foundation which underpins the IIT-adjustment hypothesis. Our analysis was confined to trade data. The new paradigm that MIIT is of greater relevance to adjustment issues than IIT can only be conclusively examined if trade and production data are merged, particularly if microdata became available to identify both intra- and inter-industry factor movements and wage differentials.[8]

Notes

1. For simplicity, we use the term European Union (EU) throughout this chapter, meaning the pre-1995 Union of 12 Member States.
2. For a comprehensive survey, see Helpman and Krugman (1985). The integration-induced adjustment problem is treated explicitly by Krugman and Venables (1996).
3. The first aspect, namely the relevance of various theoretical approaches for the explanation of intra-EU trade flows and industry location is explored in Brülhart (1996).
4. The figures underlying these charts are reported in Appendix Table 5.1.
5. The two SITC revisions both resulted in an increase in the number of separate 5-digit industries. This inherently lowers the expected GL index, since a narrower industry definition reduces the number of differentiated goods contained within an industry and hence also the potential for IIT flows (see Grubel and Lloyd, 1975, pp. 48f.). Another reason to doubt the economic significance of the perceived levelling-out of IIT lies in the non-linear nature of the GL index, which, given random trade changes, is inherently more likely to fall, the higher its initial level (see Brülhart and Elliott, 1996).
6. See Chapter 3.
7. This finding is supported by the results of a more rigorously categorized analysis of locational shifts in EU industry by Brülhart (1996).
8. The country studies in Part II go some way towards an integrated examination of trade and structural adjustment, but they are constrained by the aggregated nature of industry data.

References

Brülhart, M. (1994) 'Marginal Intra-Industry Trade: Measurement and Relevance for the Pattern of Industrial Adjustment', *Weltwirtschaftliches Archiv*, 130, 600–13.

Brülhart, M. (1996) 'Commerce et spécialisation géographique dans l'Union européenne', *Économie Internationale*, 65, 169–202.

Brülhart, M. and Elliott, R.J.R. (1996) 'A Critical Survey of Trends in Intra-Industry Trade', in Porto, M. (ed.), *Integration and Specialisation*, Coimbra: Curso de Estudos Europeus.

Globerman, S. and Dean, J.W. (1990) 'Recent Trends in Intra-Industry Trade and Their Implications for Future Trade Liberalization', *Weltwirtschaftliches Archiv*, 126, 25–49.

Greenaway, D. (1987) 'Intra Industry Trade, Intra Firm Trade and European Integration', *Journal of Common Market Studies*, 26, 153–72.

Greenaway, D. and Hine, R.C. (1991) 'Intra-Industry Specialization, Trade Expansion and Adjustment in the European Economic Space', *Journal of Common Market Studies*, 29, 603–22.

Grubel, H. and Lloyd, P.J. (1975) *Intra-Industry Trade*, London: Macmillan.

Hamilton, C. and Kniest, P. (1991) 'Trade Liberalisation, Structural Adjustment and Intra-Industry Trade: A Note', *Weltwirtschaftliches Archiv*, 127, 356–67.

Helpman, E. and Krugman, P. (1985) *Market Structure and Foreign Trade*, Cambridge, MA: MIT Press.

Krugman, P. (1987) 'Economic Integration in Europe: Some Conceptual Issues', reprinted in Jacquemin, A. and Sapir, A. (eds) (1989), *The European Internal Market*, Oxford: Oxford University Press.

Krugman, P. and Venables, A.J. (1996) 'Integration, Specialization and Adjustment', *European Economic Review*, 40, 959–67.

Mucchielli, J. (1988) *Principes d'Économie Internationale*, Paris: Economica.

APPENDIX TABLE 5.1: INTRA-INDUSTRY TRADE IN THE EU, 1961–90

	Unadjusted Grubel-Lloyd indices [a]					
	1961	1967	1972	1977	1985	1990
EU Average[b]						
Intra-EU trade, manufactures	0.48	0.56	0.57	0.59	0.58	0.59
Intra-EU trade, all products	0.39	0.48	0.47	0.51	0.50	0.52
World-wide trade, manufactures	0.46	0.55	0.57	0.60	0.59	0.60
World-wide trade, all products	0.35	0.44	0.46	0.48	0.50	0.53
Belgium-Luxembourg						
Intra-EU trade, manufactures	0.51	0.56	0.49	0.57	0.56	0.58
Intra-EU trade, all products	0.51	0.55	0.46	0.53	0.56	0.58
World-wide trade, manufactures	0.53	0.62	0.58	0.62	0.58	0.62
World-wide trade, all products	0.48	0.56	0.52	0.55	0.55	0.60

APPENDIX TABLE 5.1 (*contd.*)

	Unadjusted Grubel-Lloyd indices [a]					
	1961	*1967*	*1972*	*1977*	*1985*	*1990*
West Germany						
Intra-EU trade, manufactures	0.47	0.56	0.57	0.57	0.60	0.61
Intra-EU trade, all products	0.37	0.45	0.44	0.46	0.50	0.50
World-wide trade, manufactures	0.44	0.50	0.55	0.56	0.58	0.61
World-wide trade, all products	0.34	0.41	0.42	0.46	0.50	0.51
Denmark						
Intra-EU trade, manufactures	0.30	0.37	0.41	0.44	0.42	0.43
Intra-EU trade, all products	0.18	0.26	0.31	0.32	0.35	0.37
World-wide trade, manufactures	0.45	0.54	0.49	0.54	0.49	0.49
World-wide trade, all products	0.29	0.40	0.39	0.43	0.42	0.46
Spain						
Intra-EU trade, manufactures	0.10	0.16	0.29	0.38	0.47	0.57
Intra-EU trade, all products	0.09	0.15	0.25	0.33	0.39	0.52
World-wide trade, manufactures	0.16	0.27	0.30	0.39	0.45	0.55
World-wide trade, all products	0.12	0.19	0.21	0.25	0.33	0.46
France						
Intra-EU trade, manufactures	0.60	0.69	0.67	0.71	0.68	0.67
Intra-EU trade, all products	0.51	0.60	0.60	0.64	0.59	0.61
World-wide trade, manufactures	0.53	0.70	0.69	0.70	0.67	0.68
World-wide trade, all products	0.43	0.56	0.57	0.56	0.55	0.60
Greece						
Intra-EU trade, manufactures	0.02	0.06	0.08	0.10	0.15	0.16
Intra-EU trade, all products	0.02	0.05	0.08	0.11	0.13	0.16
World-wide trade, manufactures	0.06	0.11	0.13	0.16	0.20	0.19
World-wide trade, all products	0.04	0.08	0.11	0.16	0.18	0.20
Italy						
Intra-EU trade, manufactures	0.44	0.56	0.57	0.56	0.52	0.51
Intra-EU trade, all products	0.35	0.46	0.47	0.47	0.45	0.47
World-wide trade, manufactures	0.48	0.53	0.53	0.53	0.52	0.52
World-wide trade, all products	0.33	0.37	0.40	0.39	0.41	0.46
Ireland						
Intra-EU trade, manufactures	0.22	0.28	0.36	0.45	0.40	0.38
Intra-EU trade, all products	0.24	0.25	0.30	0.36	0.35	0.35
World-wide trade, manufactures	0.25	0.29	0.38	0.49	0.47	0.44
World-wide trade, all products	0.28	0.26	0.32	0.38	0.40	0.38
The Netherlands						
Intra-EU trade, manufactures	0.54	0.57	0.59	0.59	0.60	0.61
Intra-EU trade, all products	0.48	0.53	0.51	0.50	0.49	0.53
World-wide trade, manufactures	0.62	0.64	0.63	0.63	0.64	0.64
World-wide trade, all products	0.48	0.54	0.53	0.50	0.52	0.54

Portugal

Intra-EU trade, manufactures	0.04	0.10	0.13	0.14	0.24	0.30
Intra-EU trade, all products	0.05	0.09	0.12	0.13	0.23	0.28
World-wide trade, manufactures	0.15	0.28	0.23	0.20	0.27	0.30
World-wide trade, all products	0.13	0.21	0.19	0.15	0.20	0.26

United Kingdom

Intra-EU trade, manufactures	0.51	0.67	0.65	0.71	0.62	0.64
Intra-EU trade, all products	0.42	0.54	0.57	0.64	0.50	0.57
World-wide trade, manufactures	0.41	0.58	0.63	0.68	0.68	0.65
World-wide trade, all products	0.29	0.43	0.51	0.59	0.59	0.61

[a] Calculated from SITC four-digit (1961, 67) and five-digit (1972, 77, 85, 90) data obtained from the OECD, computations by SPES research team; 'all products' = SITC 0–9, 'manufactures' = SITC 5–8.
[b] Trade-weighted averages of 11 EU countries.

Part II
Country Studies

6. Belgium

P.K.M. Tharakan and German Calfat

6.1 INTRODUCTION

The belief that the formation of the European Union (EU) triggered a considerable amount of intra-industry trade (IIT) between the member countries, and that such IIT increases facilitated industrial structural adjustment in the economies concerned, is now part of the conventional wisdom. The rationale behind this idea is relatively straightforward and can be concisely summed up as follows. The factor-intensity factor-endowment concordance criterion which is at the core of the Heckscher-Ohlin inter-industry trade model, presupposes differences in the relative factor endowments of the trading countries. Multilateral trade liberalization in such a world increases the possibility for each country to make use of its comparative advantage and this will lead to increased inter-industry trade. But if the relative factor endowment of the trade-liberalizing countries is similar, the explanatory power of such a model will be diluted. Nevertheless, similarity of income levels will lead to a taste for similar, but differentiated varieties of products. If greater economies of scale can be achieved by concentrating production of particular varieties in particular countries, trade liberalization between such countries will create an increased exchange of different varieties of the same product, that is increased intra-industry trade. And if trade liberalization leads to increased imports of a particular variety of a product matched by an increase in the exports of another variety, the shift of factors of production required will be of an intra-industrial nature. To the extent the skills requirements of the workers and the expertise of the entrepreneurs necessary for such adjustment are less difficult to master than would have been the case in an inter-industry shift, the process would be smoother (see Chapter 3).

The important implications of the above line of reasoning for economic policy in general and commercial policy in particular is evident. Consequently, this proposition deserves rigorous empirical analysis. This chapter explores the patterns of IIT using data for Belgium,[1] which has historically exhibited the highest degree of intra-EU trade orientation as well as above-average levels of IIT (see Chapter 5). We specifically investigate the following questions:

1. What has been the pattern of Belgium's intra-, and extra-EU IIT in recent years?
2. What, if any, are the links between such trade patterns and the adjustment process in Belgium?
3. Does the pattern of intra-EU trade liberalization as revealed by the Single Market Programme (SM) show any link with Belgium's IIT and the adjustment process?

The methodologies used are explained in the relevant sections, and the conclusions emerging from the study are summed up in Section 6.5.

6.2   PATTERNS OF BELGIUM'S INTRA-INDUSTRY TRADE

Recent trends in Belgian IIT

First, a few remarks should be made on the general pattern of the IIT of Belgium. This analysis is based on unadjusted Grubel and Lloyd (GL) indices, which we have calculated at SITC 4 and 5-digit levels for the period 1960–90 and also from the same data averaged to 1 digit level (the main results are reported in Chapter 5).

The GL indices of IIT with a value of 0.75 or more rose from 23 per cent in 1961 to over 27 per cent in 1967. A stable pattern around 24 to 25 per cent set in afterwards and lasted till the end of the period covered here. Note that this is a high percentage compared to most of the other EU countries. The average figures show that Belgium's IIT for all commodities (SITC 0 to 9) rose from 0.48 in 1961 to 0.56 by 1967, but stabilized near that figure till about 1987 and then rose to about 0.60 by 1990. As an average for all commodities, this again is a high figure compared to other EU countries. The average IIT for manufactures (SITC 5 to 8) remained relatively stable during the period 1975–84, but then exhibited some volatility. For total trade and for trade in manufactures, Belgium's intra-EU IIT has systematically shown higher GL indices than its extra-EU IIT.

The analysis of IIT across industries indicates that the average IIT for manufacturing industries is higher than for non-manufacturing industries. Nevertheless, the traditionally held belief that trade in primary products (SITC 0-4) is likely to be determined by traditional comparative advantage is not fully reflected in the statistics. All 5 SITC categories mentioned above showed GL indices between 0.38 and 0.53 in 1990.

Horizontal and vertical IIT of Belgium

In the theoretical IIT literature, a distinction has been made for a long time between vertical and horizontal IIT (VIIT/HIIT). The crucial difference is that the former can explain IIT without vitiating the precepts of the Heckscher-Ohlin (H-O) theorem, while the interaction between economies of scale and (horizontal) product differentiation is an essential ingredient for the theoretical explanation of the latter.

In one class of VIIT models (Falvey and Kierzkowski (1987)), capital intensity or human capital intensity creates 'quality' differences in

Table 6.1 Horizontal and vertical IIT between Belgium and the EU-12

SITC1 Description		IIT	HIIT	Horizontal IIT	Vertical Intra-Industry Trade		
				HIIT % of IIT	VIIT	VIIT % of IIT	HI-Q % of VIIT
	1978						
0	Food, live animal	0.58	0.34	0.60	0.24	0.41	0.56
1	Drink, Tobacco	0.37	0.07	0.18	0.30	0.82	0.44
2	Raw Materials	0.51	0.27	0.52	0.25	0.48	0.78
3	Mineral Fuels	0.45	0.39	0.86	0.06	0.14	0.97
4	Animal/veg. oils	0.60	0.37	0.62	0.23	0.39	0.91
5	Chemicals	0.65	0.30	0.46	0.35	0.54	0.59
6	Manufactures, class by mat.	0.55	0.34	0.61	0.21	0.39	0.50
7	Machinery, Transport Equipment	0.54	0.33	0.61	0.21	0.40	0.70
8	Miscellaneous Manuf.	0.69	0.34	0.49	0.35	0.51	0.44
9	Commodities n.e.s.	0.49	0.00	0.00	0.48	0.99	0.99
	1987						
0	Food, live animal	0.59	0.30	0.52	0.29	0.49	0.65
1	Drink, Tobacco	0.40	0.33	0.82	0.07	0.18	0.75
2	Raw Materials	0.54	0.23	0.43	0.31	0.57	0.77
3	Mineral Fuels	0.62	0.52	0.84	0.10	0.16	0.70
4	Animal/veg. oils	0.70	0.41	0.58	0.29	0.42	0.86
5	Chemicals	0.70	0.40	0.56	0.31	0.44	0.37
6	Manufactures, class by mat.	0.60	0.33	0.55	0.27	0.45	0.42
7	Machinery, Transport Equipment	0.54	0.28	0.53	0.26	0.48	0.64
8	Miscellaneous Manuf.	0.75	0.25	0.34	0.50	0.66	0.13
9	Commodities n.e.s	0.48	0.00	0.00	0.48	1.00	0.98

for calculation methodology, see Chapter 4.

the varieties being produced within an industry. Hence, high-income countries will produce high-quality products, and low-income countries specialize in low-quality products. Yet, the income distribution patterns in the trading countries will lead to the situation in which low income groups in the former will generate demand for low quality varieties which in turn will lead to VIIT. Smeets and Reker (1993) and Greenaway *et al.* (1994) have proposed the methodology which can be used to separate horizontal from vertical product differentiation using import and export unit values (see Chapter 4).[2]

We have made a tentative estimate of Belgium's VIIT using the currently available methodology. In Table 6.1, we report GL indices for the years 1978 and 1987 for intra-, and extra-EU as well as the vertical and horizontal components of the matched flows. Some stylized facts emerge from the analysis of the contents of Table 6.1. Belgium's IIT in manufactures with its EU partners was mainly horizontally differentiated, even though we detect an increase in VIIT between 1978 and 1987. Trade with the rest of the world, however, was mostly of the vertical kind.

Another stylized fact that should be noted is the diminishing share of high-value VIIT in manufacturing VIIT of Belgium with the EU countries. This means that Belgium was specializing into relatively low-price export goods in the vertically differentiated sectors. In contrast, such a tendency is not apparent in Belgian trade with non-EU partners.

To sum up: Belgium has above-average levels of IIT, and such trade has been generally increasing over the 30-year period covered in the study. The intra-EU IIT of Belgium is higher than its extra-EU IIT. Belgium's IIT with its EU-partners is mainly of a horizontal type and with the rest of the world, of a vertical type. But the level of Belgium's horizontal IIT with the EU partners is declining together with the share of high quality component of the VIIT.

6.3   INTRA-INDUSTRY TRADE AND STRUCTURAL ADJUSTMENT

Adjustment and trade

Structural adjustment, defined as a process by which factors of production shift from sectors which are stagnant or declining to sectors with sustainable prospects, is a persistent process, but can be disruptive and counterbalance the discounted gains from specialization. Factors contributing to this process consist of a number of elements such as the speed of technological change, changes in consumption patterns and increasing exposure to international trade. The disentangling of the effects of the changes in trade specialization on the structure of the economy is not straightforward since most of the effects occur simultaneously with other related developments.

In this section, we investigate the link between trade patterns and the structural change in Belgium. The main thrust of the investigation is to test the validity of the generally held assumption that high levels of IIT and specialization (triggered by economic integration) cause less adjustment costs than inter-industry trade. We proceed in three steps:

1. an accounting approach is used to decompose the different sources of change in the most sensitive of the adjustment variables, employment;
2. correlations are calculated between trade-related variables and variables related to adjustment; and
3. the relationship between the indices of marginal IIT and certain adjustment related variables is analysed.

Trade and industrial employment: an accounting approach

Following Kol and Mennes (1983), we can decompose the change in employment into changes in domestic demand, trade surplus and changes in productivity using the following identity:

$$\Delta L = \lambda_1 [u_0 \Delta TDD - TDD_1 \Delta mp + \Delta E] + Q_0 \Delta \lambda \qquad \ldots (6.1)$$

where ΔL stands for changes in employment, Q is output, λ is a coefficient for labour intensity, which is equal to the inverse of p (labour productivity $= Q/L$), TDD represents total domestic demand, ΔE represents the change in exports, Δmp stands for the change in import penetration, and the subscripts 0 and 1 indicate the initial and end years of the period analysed for changes in employment.

Table 6.2 shows the sources of employment change in Belgium during 1986–91. These figures are aggregated from a detailed sectoral breakdown (which is available from the authors on request). The most important point that emerges from the table is that the principal cause of employment loss is the productivity increase. The increase in production ('Output effect'), particularly through the contribution of

Table 6.2   Sources of employment change in Belgium 1986–91

Total Change	−27618
Productivity Effect	−114312
Output Effect	+86694
Domestic Consumption	+50025
Trade	+36669
Import Penetration	−11481
Export Expansion	+48150

* based on 90 NACE 3-digit industrial sectors

domestic consumption and export expansion has helped to cushion the employment losses.

The combined effect of domestic consumption and trade shows a positive impact on employment. This result seems to indicate that for the Belgian economy, the detrimental import penetration effect on employment has not been substantial. Analysis of the sectoral break-down showed that there were only a few industries in which the import effect exceeded the positive contribution of domestic consumption. These industries include knitting, ready-made clothes and accessories, cotton, bodies for vehicles and electronic machinery. In most in-dustries, however, the negative effect of import penetration is out-weighed by the positive employment effect of exports. The positive contribution to changes in employment derived from export increases is specially important in the following sectors: assembly of motors, cocoa and chocolates, carpets and plastics. Some of these sectors have already been identified as high performers in a study of the compara-tive advantage of Belgian industry (Tharakan and Waelbroeck (1988)).

Correlation analysis of trade and changes in production and employment

To complement the insights from the use of the accounting meth-odology, we have further explored the relationship between various adjustment indicators and trade patterns of Belgium. Using cross-section regression analysis, we examined the relationship between the proportional employment change during the period 1980–90 and a series of performance and trade variables. The results, presented in Table 6.3, show that the most important variable explaining employ-ment changes in this period has been output changes. This is in accordance with the results obtained in the accounting analysis. The regression results also capture the importance of trade (either in the

Table 6.3 Regression analysis of Belgian manufacturing employment changes 1980–90

Independent variable	Equation number					
	(1)		(2)		(3)	
		t-ratio		t-ratio		t-ratio
Constant	-0.407	-5.08***	-0.345	-8.14***	-0.349	-7.87***
Change in Output	0.458	4.98***	0.474	5.23***	0.472	5.11***
Change in Import Penetration	-4.57E-05	-1.70*	-3.98E-05	-1.51*	-4.09E-05	-1.54*
Change in Export Expansion	0.0013	1.88*	0.0013	1.76*	0.0014	2.04**
A Index	0.092	0.821				
B Index			0.013	0.863		
GHME Index					-1.50E-10	-0.155
F	7.76		7.78		7.53	
R²	0.272		0.272		0.266	

Notes:
- calculations based on 78 NACE 3-digit industrial sectors
- An asterisk denotes significance at 10 per cent, two asterisks denote significance at 5 per cent and three asterisks denote significance at 1 per cent.
- Dependent variable = DEMPL = change in sectoral employment = $[(EMPL_t - EMPL_{t-n})/(0.5*(EMPL_t + EMPL_{t-n})]$. D Output is weighted in the same manner like DEMPL. Import penetration = $M_i/(P_i + M_i - X_i)$. Export Expansion = X_i/P_i.

form of import penetration or export expansion). Both trade variables have the expected sign. But their level of significance is weak, especially when compared to that of the output changes. None of the measures of marginal IIT seem to be related to net employment changes. Note, however, that this analysis is of a preliminary nature, given the lack of consensus on appropriate specification. In particular, absolute employment changes are but a crude measure of adjustment.

Patterns of specialization and trade performance

The changes in the trade specialization can be captured through indices of marginal IIT (MIIT). One of the useful MIIT indices is the Brülhart (1994) *B* index which can indicate a sector's revealed specialization 'into' or 'out' of specific industries (see Chapter 3). The index varies between -1 and 1. When the index is negative, it indicates that imports have increased more than exports. And at -1 only imports have increased, with the exports remaining unchanged. An index of 1 indicates the opposite case. Finally, the *B* index with a value close to zero denotes high MIIT.

6.4   INTRA-INDUSTRY TRADE ADJUSTMENT AND THE SINGLE MARKET PROGRAMME

Background

The impressive research effort that has been already invested in investigating the welfare implications of the completion of the Single Market (SM) still leaves room for the analysis of other policy relevant issues such as the likely nature of the trade patterns that have emerged and will continue to take shape as a result of the SM and the adjustment costs of these trade changes.[3]

In Section 6.2, we analysed the IIT patterns of Belgium, and in Section 6.3, we investigated the link between IIT and adjustment. The SM programme provides us with the possibility of examining the above two points within the context of the dismantling of non-tariff barriers within the EU. The conventional measure of IIT (GL index) will show high values if exports match imports even if such exports and imports account for only a fraction of the turnover of the industry. Therefore, we have chosen to apply also Jacobsson's (1988) index of intra-industry specialization (IIS), because this measure contains an explicit link between domestic production and trade.[4]

We have used the B coefficient to regroup the Belgian industrial sectors into: low-MIIT $(B < -0.5)$ and high-MIIT $(-0.5 \leq B < 0)$ 'out' specialization, and high-MIIT $(0 \leq B \leq 0.5)$ and low-MIIT $(B > 0.5)$ 'in' specialization. We found that 62 per cent of the industries included in the sample yielded negative values ('out specialization') of the B index. However, this specialization 'out' reflecting a deteriorating trade balance does not seem to have been accompanied by a proportionate decrease in employment and production. It could well be that, as indicated by the analysis in the preceding sub-section, increasing domestic consumption outweighed the negative impact of deteriorating trade balance at the sectoral level. The period 1985–90 was characterized by intensive adjustment of the intra-industry type in 78 per cent of the industrial sectors $(-0.5 \leq B \leq 0.5)$. It is in fact these categories that have shown employment losses.

The most striking fact that emerges from the empirical analysis contained in section 6.3 is that inter-industry specialization does not show a clear relationship with net employment losses, while such losses – somewhat counterintuitively – seem to be concentrated in sectors showing significant intra-industry adjustment.

We attempt to answer the following two questions:

1. Have IIT and intra-industry specialization (IIS) increased more in the sectors which are relatively open to intra EU trade?
2. Are there indications that the adjustment process has been less difficult in sectors where IIT and IIS is high, and, if so, to what extent is this linked to the degree of intra-EU liberalization?

The completion of the Single Market and trade patterns

Although no tariff barriers remain within the EU, a number of non-tariff barriers continued to affect the intra-EU trade until the full implementation of the SM. The identification of the sectors most likely to be affected by the Single Market (SM) was carried out by the Commission (CEC, 1988a, b, 1990), on the basis of the following indicators: the level of non-tariff barriers (norms, security regulations, government procurement policies, border formalities, and so on); the degree of market penetration by intra-Community imports; the fragmentation of the Community Market, measured through the price dispersion for identical products; and the potential economies of scale.

The classification of industries according to internal EU non-tariff barriers was first presented by Buigues and Ilzkovitz (1990). Using this list, we have regrouped a sample of 106 Belgian industries (NACE 3-digit) into three categories.

1. *Highly Protected Sectors (H)*: this group includes high-tech public procurement and traditional public procurement and regulated sectors.
2. *Moderately Protected Sectors (M)*: under this category we find mass consumer products, and certain capital and intermediate goods that are still subject to technical, administered and fiscal barriers.
3. *Low or Unaffected Sectors (L)*: this category includes the remaining sectors, assuming the existence of no major intra-EU trade impediments.

It should be noted that the inventory of NTBs was based on the firms' perceptions of the likely effects of completion of the SM, as recorded in 1985. In other words, we still do not have data for what could be called 'the day after the completion of the SM'. There are strong indications that liberalization in certain important areas such as government procurement policies has not made the expected progress.

The results reported in Table 6.4 can be used to analyse the proposition that trade liberalization fosters IIT and IIS. The first im-

Table 6.4   IIT and IIS 1986 and 1991, classified by pre-SM non-tariff barriers

Degree of Single Market Barrier	High		Moderate		Low	
number of industries	12		26		82	
year	1986	1991	1986	1991	1986	1991
average GL	82.87	79.21	75.64	72.32	73.91	73.93
average IIS	0.36	0.35	0.453	0.454	0.36	0.37
Value Share of Total X + M Intra EC Trade	7.10	7.58	37.74	33.80	54.42	57.56
Change in						
IIT	−1.14		−3.04		3.21	
'A' Index	0.320		0.712		0.470	
IIS	−0.04		9.48		11.12	
EC import penetration	35.26	40.90	55.05	54.08	40.77	44.52
NON EC import penetration	15.00	9.82	17.42	19.17	10.17	11.76

portant point that emerges from the table is that only a relatively small percentage (7.1 per cent) of Belgian intra-EU trade was subject to high NTBs. The corresponding percentage is higher for the 'moderate' (37.7 per cent) and 'low' (54.4 per cent) categories.

Average IIT remained constant in the category with low internal barriers and decreased in the two other categories. However, the differences in average IIT changes across categories are not statistically significant. The intra-industry specialization index (IIS) shows a small increase in the category with 'low' NTBs and a small decrease in the category with 'high' NTBs, but here again the differences are not statistically significant.[5] The differences in the EU import penetration variable, however, are significant at 5 per cent level. This suggests that Belgian industry was indeed faced with stronger import competition in the sectors which had been most affected by NTBs. This result is mirrored in the results obtained for marginal IIT (MIIT), using the Brülhart (1994) *A* index. MIIT is substantially lower than the average in those industries which had been subject to high NTBs, which again points to relatively strong inter-industry trade adjustment triggered by the implementation of the Single Market.

The Single Market and structural adjustment

Table 6.5 provides indicators which provide further clues relating to the question about the relationship between the Single Market and adjustment.

From the 'political economy of protection' theory we know that pressure groups tend to react against trade liberalization if it leads a

Table 6.5 Structural changes in industry 1986–91, classified by pre-SM non-tariff barriers

Variable	High		Moderate		Low	
Number of industries	12		26		60.	
Change in employment (%)						
Weighted average	−15.57		−10.95		1.87	
Change in value added (%)						
Weighted average	−0.79		16.67		29.81	
Change in turnover (%)						
Weighted average	15.95		26.09		13.79	
	1986	1991	1986	1991	1986	1991
Share of Employment	12.65	11.14	28.31	26.53	59.04	62.33

decline in employment. In the context of our analysis the crucial question is whether IIS has increased substantially in the liberalized sectors, and what effect it has had on employment. As can be seen from Table 6.5, the share of employment of industries belonging to the category of less affected sectors has consistently increased, while the share of the more affected sectors shows signs of decline. When we consider the average changes in employment in each group (all changes in the structural variables have been weighted by the share of each variable in the total), the comparison indicates substantial employment losses during the period 1986–91 in the sectors subjected to internal EU barriers. The differences between the groups are significant at the 5 per cent level of confidence.

The results on value added and turnover are less clear. Although the changes in value added seem to confirm a tendency towards higher positive changes when we move from the highly protected group to the less protected, the differences are not statistically significant. A similar picture holds for the changes in turnover.

Taking into account all the results reported in this section, it appears that the Single Market did affect Belgian industry even in the early implementation period 1986–91. Industries which were particularly sensitive to the dismantling of NTBs exhibit relatively high marginal *inter*-industry trade, increased import penetration and weak employment and output performance.

6.5 CONCLUSIONS

In a comprehensive and disaggregated analysis, we found that Belgium has comparatively high levels of IIT, and that such trade has been generally increasing over the 30 year period covered by the study. In addition it is shown that the intra-EU IIT of Belgium is higher than its extra-EU IIT and the former has been growing faster than the latter.

The effort to answer the question whether there is a link between the detected pattern of IIT and structural change in Belgian industry yielded some counterintuitive results. Arguably the most interesting fact that emerged from that part of the analysis was that inter-industry specialization does not show any clear relationship with net employment losses and that such losses seem to be concentrated in sectors having significant intra-industry adjustment.

However, the attempt to verify the possible relationship between adjustment on the one hand and the early implementation of the Single

Market yielded some noteworthy results. The much repeated claim of intra-EU liberalization leading to frictionless structural change was contradicted by our results for Belgium, which indicate that the most affected industries were subject to painful *inter*-industry adjustment.

Notes

1. The data used for the analysis pertain to Belgium-Luxembourg, although we consistently refer only to Belgium.
2. At the theoretical and methodological level we have some reservations about VIIT analysis in its present state. We have stated them in some detail elsewhere (Tharakan and Kerstens, 1995). At the theoretical level, our critique of the current version of the Flam-Helpman-Falvey-Kierz-kowski model consists mainly of the fact that low-cost and probably less formally trained workers do not necessarily produce 'low quality' products in all industries any more than high capital intensity leads to across-the-board increase in 'quality' in all varieties. At the methodological level, one may question whether the ratio of export to import unit prices always reflect what the VIIT models seek to quantify.
3. See CEC (1988a, b, 1990), Winters and Venables (1991) and Winters (1992).
4. Jacobsson's intra-industry specialization index for industry i is defined as:

$$IIS_i = \frac{2(\min M_i, X_i)}{P_i + AC_i},$$

where P_i = Value of the domestic production in industry i, AC_i = Apparent Consumption = $(P_i + M_i) - X_i$, and M_i and X_i have the same meaning as in the definition of the GL index.
5. An interesting point to note is the high IIS index found in the category with 'moderate' NTBs, although the index has remained stationary during the period studied. If we decompose this category into 'consumer', 'capital' and 'intermediate' goods, one finds the highest figures (0.53 in 1986 and 0.57 in 1991) for intermediate goods, and the lowest (0.38 in 1986 and 0.49 in 1991) for consumer goods. The higher degree of intra-EU import penetration (55.05 per cent in 1986) indicates a great amount of competition in this category.

References

Commission of the European Communities (CEC) (1988a) 'The Economics of 1992', *The European Economy*, 35, March.
CEC (1988b) *Research on the Cost of Non-Europe: Basic Findings*, 16 vols., Brussels: European Commission.

134 *Intra-Industry Trade and Adjustment*

CEC (1990) 'The Impact of the Internal Market by Industrial Sector: The Challenge for the Member States', *The European Economy – Social Europe, Special Edition.*

Brülhart, M. (1994) 'Marginal Intra-Industry Trade: Measurement and Relevance for the Pattern of Industrial Adjustment', *Weltwirtschaftliches Archiv*, 130, 600–13.

Buigues P. and Ilzkovitz F. (1990) 'Belgium National Report', in 'The Impact of the Internal Market by Industrial Sector: The Challenge for the Member States', *The European Economy.*

Falvey, R.E. and Kierzkowski, H. (1987) 'Product Quality, Intra-Industry Trade and (Im)Perfect Competition', in Kierzkowski, H. (ed.), *Protection and Competition in International Trade*, Oxford: Blackwell.

Greenaway, D., Hine R., Milner C. and Elliott R. (1994) 'Adjustment and the Measurement of Marginal Intra Industry Trade', *Weltwirtschaftliches Archiv*, 130, 356–67.

Greenaway, D., Hine R.C. and Milner, C. (1994b) 'Country-Specific Factors and the Pattern of Horizontal and Vertical Intra-Industry Trade in the UK', *Weltwirtschaftliches Archiv*, 130, 77–100.

Hamilton, C. and Kniest, P. (1991) 'Trade Liberalisation, Structural Adjustment and Intra-Industry Trade: A Note', *Weltwirtschaftliches Archiv*, 127, 356–67.

Jacobsson, S. (1988) 'Intra-Industry Specialisation and Development Models for the Capital Goods Sector', *Weltwirtschaftliches Archiv*, 127, 356–367.

Kol, J. and Mennes L.B.M. (1983) 'Trade and Industrial Employment: An Accounting for Growth Approach with and Application for the Netherlands'. *EADI Proceedings.*

Smeets, D. and Reker C. (1993) 'Intra-Industry Trade and European Integration: The German Experience', Paper prepared for the fourth SPES Workshop at the University of Antwerp, October 1993.

Tharakan, P.K.M. and Kerstens, B. (1995), 'Does North-South Horizontal Intra-Industry Trade Really Exist? An Analysis of the Toy Industry', *Weltwirtschaftliches Archiv*, 131, 86–105.

Tharakan, P.K.M. and Waelbroeck, J. (1988) 'A study on the Comparative Advantage of the Belgian Manufacturing Industries'. mimeo, University of Antwerp.

Winters, L.A. and Venables A.J. (1991) *European Integration: Trade and Industry*, Cambridge: Cambridge University Press.

Winters, L.A. (1992) *Trade Flows and Trade Policy after '1992'*, Cambridge: Cambridge University Press.

7. France

Mohamed Harfi and Christian Montet

7.1 INTRODUCTION

Like its trading partners in the EU, France has become progressively more trade-oriented since World War II. The degree of openness, measured by the ratio of exports and imports to GDP, amounted to more than 30 per cent at the end of the 1980s, compared to about 11 per cent immediately after the war. The relative importance of foreign trade more than doubled over the 1970s and 1980s. Now, France is simultaneously confronted with the completion of the Single Market and the growing participation in trade of low-wage countries, mainly located in south-east Asia.

All these changes may have a significant influence on French welfare. However, the resulting effects are neither well understood nor well documented, and fears remain of possible negative effects from a further opening to trade. Worries concerning trade issues commonly relate to the evolution of manufacturing employment, the level of low-skilled wages, or the survival of 'the rural life'. Many commentators complain about the unfair influence in trade negotiations of big countries like the USA and Japan. GATT negotiations on agriculture were largely perceived in France as a typical case of the negative influence of the USA. This argument tends to strengthen the case of those arguing in favour of a stronger European Union. Other arguments are more oriented towards putting a halt to French trade liberalization altogether. The development of trade with the newly industrialized and developing countries is widely perceived as a threat for French industries and thus for French jobs. Low wages and so-called 'social dumping' are seen as unfair sources of advantage on international markets, calling for all kinds of protection: antidumping tariffs, countervailing duties, quotas, and so on.

Even the completion of the Single Market is suspected of threatening some French traditional industries. There are fears that France could lose market share after a market-driven regional reallocation of activities in the EU. This popular concern finds support in scholarly theorizing about the likely effects of the completion of European

135

integration. Will it change specialization structures in a way similar to that experienced in the USA? Will regional specialization lead to an increase in inter-industry trade while until now the bulk of new intra-European trade has been of the intra-industry trade (IIT) type?

The purpose of this chapter is to document the evolution and effects of French trade patterns in order to glean a better understanding of the adjustment issues. Section 7.2 will discuss the main features of French trade over the period 1961–90 with a particular emphasis on various aspects of IIT. Section 7.3 analyses the link between changes in trade and changes in structural variables for the manufacturing sectors. This section includes an accounting analysis of the effects of trade on jobs, the estimation of simple statistical relationships between trade and employment, a grouped analysis of the effects in different industries and finally an attempt to link these changes with specialization. The main conclusions are summarized in Section 7.4.

7.2   THE EVOLUTION OF FRENCH TRADE, 1961–90

After a general overview of French exports and imports, this section will report the evolution of intra and inter-industry trade, with an implicit focus on adjustment issues. Particular emphasis will be put on the vertical or horizontal nature of IIT, as it might be hypothesized that vertical IIT creates a mainly Heckscher-Ohlin type of adjustment, in contrast to horizontal IIT.

Aggregate trade flows

While generally positive during the 1960s, the French trade balance has been in deficit since the first oil shock in 1973 (except for small surpluses in 1975 and 1978). Following the second oil shock (1979), a large deficit appeared, and the situation worsened further after the expansionary policy pursued in 1981–82 by the socialist government. Several devaluations of the French franc together with other factors, such as expansions of the US and other economies, helped to improve the situation in the second part of the 1980s, although the deficit remained large until 1991. It is worth noting that trade with other EU countries is mainly responsible for the structural deficit, since the trade balance with extra-EU countries improved with the devaluations at the beginning of the 1980s and was in surplus from 1983 to 1990. Globally, the balance improved significantly in 1992 and surpluses have been recorded since then. This was partly due to the policy of 'competitive deflation' of the second part of the 1980s, and also to a relative decline in imports resulting from the economic downturn in the early 1990s. The visible trade deficit is generally counterbalanced by surpluses on trade in services.

Beyond the global balance of trade it is interesting to look at the sectoral balances, in order to assess the relative performance of different industries. Table 7.1 shows sectoral balances at the SITC 1-digit level. France has relatively large deficits in Sections 2 to 4: raw materials; mineral fuels and mineral/vegetable oil. France has traditional surpluses in Sections 0 and 1 (food and drink), which reflects the relative advantage of France in agricultural products, and is influenced by the Common Agricultural Policy. A relative advantage in wine and related products is typically reflected in the surplus of Section 1.

For manufactured goods the picture is mixed. Over the period considered, only Section 7 maintained a surplus, mainly driven by car and aircraft industries. Trade in chemicals (Section 5) was in deficit in 1980, but swung into surplus by 1992. The balances of Sections 6 and 8 ('traditional' manufactures) changed from surplus in 1970 to deficit in 1992. In the long run, however, French trade has been relatively balanced in every major industrial section. Many commentators have contrasted this situation with the existence of dominant poles of exports in countries such as Japan (automobile, consumer electronics), Germany (cars, engineering products), and the United States (aerospace, computers, chemicals). The lack of such dominant poles in France is often interpreted as a weakness of the French economy. However, the link between strong performance in a few sectors and economic welfare is not entirely clear.

The separate analysis of intra-EU and extra-EU trade, reveals that France has a strong surplus in agricultural products with the EU but a persistent deficit in manufactures. Table 7.2 shows the breakdown of trade flows for France's main trading partners: the EU, the rest of world and, among the latter, the United States and Japan. The striking feature is the relative importance of trade within the EU. Exports to EU were never less than 53 per cent of total exports between 1970 and 1992 and peaked in our last sample year at 63 per cent. The percentages for imports were similar: never below 52 per cent, and over 65 per cent in 1992.

The share of trade with the US fluctuated between 4 and 9 per cent for exports, and 6 to 10 per cent for imports between 1970 and 1992. One can probably trace these fluctuations to changes in the franc/dollar

Table 7.1 France's trade balance by SITC section

SITC (1) sections	World			Intra-EU			Extra-EU		
	1970	1980	1992	1970	1980	1992	1970	1980	1992
Food (1)	44	1,931	4,100	713	1,583	4,240	-669	350	-146
Drink, tobacco (2)	214	1,380	3,865	154	492	1,362	60	891	2,502
Raw materials (3)	-1,061	-2,813	-1,627	407	932	1,115	-1,468	-3,725	-2,740
Minerals, fuels (4)	-1,915	-22,517	-11,731	-160	-2,152	-1,045	-1,756	-20,561	-10,690
Oils, fats (5)	-128	-308	-165	-39	-164	-143	-90	-142	-21
Chemicals (5)	106	-612	3,687	-240	-1,737	-744	345	1,136	4,434
Manufactures, by materials (6)	236	280	-1,377	-447	-2,344	-3,452	683	2,677	2,092
Machinery, transport (7)	1,090	5,797	4,580	-426	-1,704	-5,546	1,516	7,579	10,577
Misc. manuf. (8)	51	-1,539	-8,479	-362	-2,050	-5,648	413	543	-2,774
0-9	-1,183	-16,951	-6,483	-299	-6,077	-9,601	-885	-10,811	3,118

Data from EUROSTAT, External Trade and Balance Payments, Statistical yearbook.

Table 7.2 Geographical breakdown of French trade, 1970–92

	World		Intra-EU		Extra-EU		United States		Japan	
	Exports Million ECU	Imports	Exports %	Imports %	Exports %	Imports %	Exports %	Imports %	Exports %	Imports %
1970	17,739	18,922	58	56	42	44	5	10	1	1
1975	41,981	43,682	53	52	47	48	4	8	1	2
1980	80,151	97,102	55	52	44	48	4	6	1	2
1985	128,180	141,642	54	59	46	40	9	6	1	2
1990	174,499	191,777	63	65	37	35	6	7	2	3
1992	192,361	199,361	63	66	37	34	6	7	2	3

Data from EUROSTAT, External Trade and Balance of Payments, Statistical yearbook exchange rate, as well as to the progression of European integration, which tends to diminish the relative importance of trade with the USA. Japan's share in French trade increased steadily, reflecting the gradual removal of barriers and the industrial growth of that country.

Trends of French intra-industry trade: 1961–90

Table 7.3 shows the evolution of Grubel-Lloyd (GL) indices for trade of France with all its trading partners (the world) over our eight sample years, calculated at the SITC 4- and 5-digit levels and aggregated to the SITC 1-digit level. A sharp rise in average IIT can be observed at the beginning of the period: from 1961 to 1967. The GL index rose from 0.43 to 0.56 for all commodities and from 0.53 to 0.70 for manufactures. Between 1967 and 1977, the GL index stabilized around 0.57 for all commodities and around 0.69 for manufactures. After 1977, a slight decline in French IIT can be observed, followed by a rise in the period 1985–90, which confirms that GL indices fluctuated within a relatively narrow range between 1967 and 1990.

Table 7.3 also shows the relative importance of IIT for manufactures compared to primary products. On average, the value of the GL index is below 0.45 in Sections 0–4, while the average for manufactures is constantly above 0.65. It is well known that the scope for product differentiation is greater in manufactures giving rise to higher IIT than in the more homogeneous primary industries. What is striking in the long-term results is the stability of this situation.

We have also distinguished between trade within the EU and trade outside the EU (detailed results are available from the authors on request). Our results illustrate that France's trade with its European partners is predominantly IIT, while trade with the rest of the world is more of the inter-industry type. Throughout our sample period, the GL indices with the EU are high, above 0.6 for manufactures and above 0.5 for all commodities. By contrast, for trade with non-EU countries the GL indices averaged 0.35 for all commodities. We observed, however, an increase in IIT for French trade with non-EU countries since the end of the 1970s. The index rose from 0.30 in 1977 to 0.42 in 1990. Trade with countries such as Japan and the USA has become increasingly intra-industry in nature, and trade with the NICs and developing countries appears to display a similar transformation (see Muchielli and Mazerolle, 1989).

Table 7.3 French IIT 1961–90: total trade, by SITC sections

SITC section	Description	Intra-industry trade (Grubel-Lloyd indices)[1]							
		1961	1967	1972	1977	1978	1985	1987	1990
0	Food, live animals	0.36	0.31	0.29	0.34	0.35	0.35	0.40	0.38
1	Drink, tobacco	0.52	0.50	0.39	0.35	0.30	0.20	0.18	0.20
2	Raw materials	0.31	0.38	0.40	0.41	0.41	0.38	0.40	0.39
3	Mineral fuels	0.16	0.17	0.18	0.14	0.13	0.21	0.20	0.25
4	Mineral/vegetable oils	0.26	0.31	0.38	0.38	0.41	0.43	0.51	0.44
5	Chemicals	0.61	0.68	0.65	0.74	0.61	0.57	0.56	0.58
6	Manufactures, classified by materials	0.43	0.64	0.66	0.67	0.66	0.66	0.69	0.66
7	Machinery, transport equipment	0.61	0.74	0.72	0.70	0.67	0.69	0.72	0.73
8	Miscellaneous manufactures	0.53	0.72	0.69	0.73	0.73	0.74	0.70	0.65
9	Commodities n.e.s	0.01	0.01	0.29	0.46	0.28	0.27	0.31	0.91
0–9	All commodities	0.43	0.56	0.57	0.56	0.54	0.55	0.60	0.60
5–8	Manufactures	0.53	0.70	0.69	0.70	0.66	0.67	0.68	0.68

[1] Calculated from 4-digit (1961, 1967) and from 5-digit (1972, 1977, 1985, 1990) OECD data, weighted by current trade values in each year

Horizontal and vertical intra-industry trade, 1978–87

In this section we examine the quality of French exports relative to the quality of imports, within IIT. In order to separate a horizontal components and a vertical component in total IIT, we used the simple method suggested by Abd-El-Rahman (1991) and adapted by Greenaway *et al.* (1994), using the standard 0.85–1.15 interval of unit value ratios for the delineation of horizontal IIT (HIIT). Table 7.4 reports the horizontal–vertical decomposition.

The primary sectors (SITC 0–4) have a lower level of IIT than manufactures, but they do not display a distinctive pattern of vertical

Table 7.4 Horizontal and vertical intra-industry trade, 1978 and 1987

	1978		Intra-EU			Extra-EU	
SITC	Description	IIT	% of IIT		IIT	% of IIT	
			HIIT	VIIT		HIIT	VIIT
0	Food, live animals	0.38	47	53	0.16	44	56
1	Drink, tobacco	0.37	7	93	0.10	0	100
2	Raw materials	0.43	53	47	0.14	37	63
3	Mineral fuels	0.42	89	11	0.05	76	25
4	Mineral/vegetable oils	0.46	78	22	0.16	77	23
5	Chemicals	0.55	52	49	0.51	23	77
6	Manufactures, classified by materials	0.67	64	36	0.34	32	68
7	Machinery, transport equipement	0.71	72	28	0.43	56	44
8	Miscellaneous manufactures	0.64	24	76	0.59	10	90
	1987		Intra-EU			Extra-EU	
SITC	Description	IIT	% of IIT		IIT	% of IIT	
			HIIT	VIIT		HIIT	VIIT
0	Food, live animals	0.43	60	40	0.21	32	68
1	Drink, tobacco	0.19	82	19	0.08	59	41
2	Raw materials	0.38	50	50	0.19	39	61
3	Mineral fuels	0.37	83	18	0.08	18	82
4	Mineral/vegetable oils	0.55	39	61	0.17	58	42
5	Chemicals	0.53	59	41	0.49	28	72
6	Manufactures, classified by materials	0.68	60	41	0.47	32	68
7	Machinery, transport equipement	0.72	56	44	0.50	44	56
8	Miscellaneous manufactures	0.64	35	65	0.63	24	76

or horizontal IIT both in terms of time trends and of cross-country differences.

Manufactures display a more consistent picture, as the importance of vertical differentiation generally increased between 1978 and 1987. In addition, we find a significant difference in vertical IIT (VIIT) shares for intra- and extra-EU trade. With its EU partners, France has a majority of HIIT in manufactures, both in 1978 and in 1987. In contrast, IIT with non-members of the EU is largely vertical. These results are consistent with a Heckscher-Ohlin (or Falvey-Kierzkowski) explanation of trade, and they are confirmed by an econometric analysis performed at a more detailed geographical level by Harfi and Oulmane (1995). French IIT with its EU partners therefore appears to reflect determinants of specialization which generally differ from the neo-classical forces, while much of what is measured as IIT between France and non-EU countries constitutes matched trade of different qualities and is thus determined mainly by traditional factors shaping comparative advantage.

7.3 TRADE AND STRUCTURAL ADJUSTMENT IN THE 1980s

Few economists would hold trade liberalization responsible for unemployment in the long run. But adjustments to changes in trade patterns may create temporary unemployment, due to the fact that job losses in some industries are not immediately compensated by job creation in other industries. Furthermore, the skills required in shrinking and expanding industries are generally not identical. It is, therefore, important to examine the link between changes in trade flows and changes in employment.

The issue has given rise to a series of theoretical and empirical controversies among academics. In France, most of the studies have used input–output techniques to evaluate the labour content of imports and exports (Vimont, 1993; Mathieu and Sterdyniak, 1994; Bonnaz *et al.*, 1994; Messerlin, 1995). This study takes a new approach to evaluate the link between trade patterns and employment change.

Grouped analysis of employment and trade changes

The pattern of structural adjustment is related to the direction of change in imports and exports. It is intuitively clear that industries where both imports and exports have increased may have a change in employment different from those where exports increased and imports decreased. Industries were thus grouped into four categories according to the direction of exports and imports, and for each group we computed the changes in gross output, employment and gross output per worker between 1979 and 1990 (Table 7.5). The bulk of industries (80 per cent) experienced a simultaneous increase in both exports and imports during the period. A smaller group experienced an increase in imports and a decrease in exports (14.3 per cent). Only 4.3 per cent had a decrease in both exports and imports and the remaining 1.4 per cent had an increase in exports coupled with a decrease in imports.

Table 7.5   Grouped analysis of French industry performance

	Import increased Export increased	Import decreased Export increased	Import increased Export decreased	Import decreased Export decreased
Number of industries	167	3	30	9
Gross output per worker 1990	0.503	1.28	0.905	0.997
Gross output per worker 1979	0.34	0.782	0.697	0.757
Change in Gross output (%) 1979–90	23.70	76.20	−20	−2.40
Change in employment (%) 1979–90	−16.30	7.60	−38.40	−25.90
Change in Gross output/worker 1979–90 (%)	47.90	63.80	29.80	31.80
Employment 1979	3,778,816	17,206	465,299	65,539
Employment 1990	3,161,724	18,509	286,721	48,520

Strikingly, the three industries in the latter group experienced an increase in employment (+7.6 per cent), when employment was falling in all the other groups. Strong export performance appears to be related to job as well as productivity gains. As could be expected, the more pronounced loss in employment (in percentage terms) occurred in the group where exports fell and imports increased (−38.4 per cent). This simple analysis is useful in showing that the pattern of structural adjustment is related to the direction of changes in trade flows. However, we need a more comprehensive analysis to isolate the respective effects of trade and other determinants of industrial performance.

Trade and jobs: an accounting analysis

In order to assess the link between the evolution of trade and changes in industrial employment, we first apply a simple accounting procedure to isolate the effects of trade and other variables on employment in each industrial sector. We made our calculations on data for the years 1979 and 1990 as base and end periods. We used compatible production and trade data, given by INSEE (National Accounts) for output and trade data and SESSI (Statistics division of the Ministry of Industry) for employment and related data (number of firms and so on). The classification is NAP 600 and NAP 100 used by both institutions, which have been related to the SITC when required. All values were deflated into 1980 prices.

The 1980s have been characterized in France by an important decline in manufacturing employment and large changes in labour productivity. Table 7.6 shows the main results of the accounting procedure across all industrial sectors. Between 1979 and 1990, total employment has declined by 811,386. On its own, growth in domestic demand, with unchanged productivity would have implied an increase of 940,813 in employment. Hence, the decline is due to the trade effect and the productivity effect. It is clear from Table 7.6 that the productivity effect is mainly responsible for the job losses. Combined productivity changes and trade changes implied a decrease of 1,752,200 units but trade counts for only 18 per cent of this total.

Table 7.6   Trade effects on employment in French manufacturing:
an accounting approach

Sources of employment change 1979–90	
Employment change	−811,386
Productivity effect	−1,437,134
Output effect	625,748
Domestic demand	940,813
Imports	−740,637
Exports	425,571
Trade	−315,066

During the 1979–90 period, early devaluations of the FF in the EMS restored some French competitiveness. However, most of the period was characterized by the 'franc fort' policy, and thus some degree of overvaluation of the currency. Since industrial trade is quite sensitive to exchange rate changes, a more accommodating exchange-rate policy might have led to a less severe accounting effect of trade on employment.

Correlations between trade and employment change

We now explore some simple bivariate relationships between trade changes and employment adjustment. For the 1979–90 period, we found a correlation coefficient between percentage changes in employment and percentage changes in exports of 0.184, which is not statistically significant. Similarly, we find no significant relationship between changes in employment and changes in imports ($r = 0.132$). These results again indicate the importance of non-trade and productivity changes in determining employment changes.

What about the relationships between net job changes and the structure of trade changes? We have analysed the correlations between various indices of IIT and marginal IIT (MIIT) and sectoral employment change. The hypothesis of smoother adjustment in the presence of (M)IIT means that the changes in employment, whether positive or negative, should be more important in industries where the share of (M)IIT is low (see Figure 7.1).

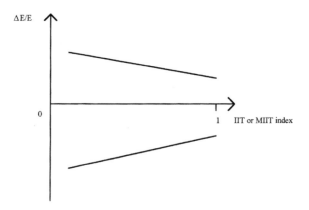

Figure 7.1   IIT and change in employment

Thus, we split our industry sample into two groups, according to the sign of the employment change. The correlations between changes of employment and various indices of IIT are presented in Table 7.7. As

Table 7.7 Employment Change and (M)IIT, 1979–90

correlation coefficients (205 industries)	change in employment negative	positive
	161 industries	*44 industries*
A index	0.316*	−0.157
GL (1990)	0.244*	−0.224
GL (1979)	0.198**	−0.211
ΔGL	0.040	−0.022

T test, statistically significant at the 1% (*), 10% (**) levels

expected, the correlation coefficient between *A* indices and employment changes in the group which has experienced a decrease in employment is positive and significant, while the correlation coefficient for the other group is negative, but not significant. For the GL, the relation has also the expected signs, but the coefficients are lower than the previous one and they are not significant for the industries which have experienced an increase in employment. For ΔGL, the coefficients are very low and not significant, which confirms that the change in the value of the GL indices during a period of time cannot be taken as a good indicator of MIIT.

Although all correlation coefficients are relatively low, it is interesting to note that the most significant one is obtained for the group of industries which represents more that 75 per cent of French manufacturing. We therefore conclude that there is some relation between the level of (M)IIT and industrial adjustment.

Intra-industry specialization and adjustment

For the study of adjustment issues indices of intra-industry specialisation (IIS) are often better suited than indices of IIT. High IIT indices may in fact have little significance in industries where trade flows are small relative to domestic production and apparent consumption. We thus calculated an index of IIS for the French industrial sectors (at the NAP 100 level), using the formula suggested by Jacobsson (1988):

$$IIS = \frac{2Min(X, M)}{P + AC} \qquad \ldots (7.1)$$

where P = value of domestic production in the particular industry and AC = apparent consumption (AC = P − X + M).

We rewrote the index as the product of three components according to the following equation:

$$IIS = \frac{2Min(X,M)}{X+M} \cdot \frac{X+M}{P} \cdot \frac{1}{2 - \frac{(X-M)}{P}} \qquad \ldots (7.2)$$

The first term on the right hand side of equation (7.2) is the GL index. The second term will be called degree of openness (OD), since it reflects the relative importance of trade with respect to domestic output. The last term will be called trade performance index (TPI). Its value is equal to 0.5 if trade is exactly balanced; it is lower than 0.5 if the sectoral trade balance is negative, and it is higher than 0.5 otherwise. In order to assess first the relations between IIS indices and their three components according to equation (7.2), a series of correlations have been computed for NAP 600 industries. Table 7.8 shows that IIT is associated with relatively high levels of IIS. One can also find a positive relation between IIS and the degree of openness. Since, the degree of openness could reasonably be taken as a proxy for the extent of trade liberalization in a given industry, one can infer that the level of intra-industry specialization tends to be higher in industries which are subject to low trade impediments. This result confirms earlier studies which found a negative relationship between IIT and the level of protection across industries (see, for example, Ray, 1987).

Table 7.8   French intra-industry specialization

	IIS (1990)		Change in IIS (1979–90)
(X + M)/P (OD)	0.607	Change in (X + M)/P	0.385
TPI	0.074	Change in TPI	0.160
GL 1990	0.356	Change in GL (1979–90)	0.231

All coefficients are statistically significant at the 5% level (*t* test).

We have linked IIS measures and structural change variables in order to test the hypothesis that IIS entails smooth adjustment. We correlated IIS measures with employment changes, splitting the industry sample into two according to the sign of employment change. The coefficients (obtainable from the authors on request) have the expected signs. We can therefore conclude that the French data lend some support to the hypothesized link between IIT/IIS and structural adjustment.

7.4 CONCLUSIONS

This chapter documents the evolution of French trade over the period 1960–90. We have concentrated on the distinction between intra and inter-industry changes in trade. These changes were related to structural adjustment, especially employment changes. According to the accounting approach, about 300,000 of the net 800,000 manufacturing jobs lost during the 1980s were lost due to the effect of changes in trade. The study provides some support for the presumed link between IIT and smooth adjustment. However, the relatively crude nature of our data and methodology calls for further research on the issue.

Can one infer predictions about the likely effects of further European integration from the observations made for the 1960–90 period? The relative decline of IIT with the EU partners will probably continue alongside a relative increase of IIT with the rest of the world. The movement of 'Europeanization' of firms, through foreign direct investment, mergers and alliances, will tend to reduce horizontally differentiated IIT, but also to stimulate another type of IIT (intra-firm trade). The exploitation of scale economies in industries where the products are relatively homogeneous will tend to generate more inter-industry trade. France might, therefore, face increased pressures of structural adjustment through delayed responses to (and further progression of) European integration.

References and Further Readings

Abd-el-Rahman, K. (1991) 'Firms' Competitive and National Comparative Advantages as Joint Determinants of Trade Composition', *Weltwirtschaftliches Archiv*, 127, 83–97.
Bonnaz, H., Courtot, N. and Nivat, D. (1994) 'Le contenu en emplois des échanges industriels de la France avec les pays en developpement', *Economie et Statistique*, 279–280, 13–33.
Globerman, S. and Dean, J.W. (1990) 'Recent Trends in Intra-Industry Trade and their Implications for Future Trade Liberalisation', *Weltwirtschaftliches Archiv*, 126, 25–49.
Greenaway, D. and Milner, C.R. (1986) *The Economics of Intra-Industry Trade*, Oxford, Blackwell.
Greenaway, D., Hine, R. and Milner, C. (1994) 'Country-Specific Factors and the Pattern of Horizontal and Vertical Intra-Industry Trade', *Weltwirtschaftliches Archiv*, 130, 77–100.
Grubel, H.G. and Lloyd, P.J. (1971) *Intra-Industry Trade*, London, Macmillan.

Harfi, M. and Oulmane, N. (1995) 'Vertical Differentiation and Factor Proportions in French Manufacturing Trade', Paper presented at the University of Coimbra, November.

Harfi, M. and Montet, C. (1994) 'Intra-Industry Trade, Specialization and Adjustment in France (1960–1990)', SPES Workshop No. 6 at the University of Nottingham, September.

Jacobsson, S. (1988) 'Intra-Industry Specialisation and Development Models for the Capital Goods Sector', *Weltwirtschaftliches Archiv*, 124, 14–37.

Krugman, P. (1993) 'What do Undergrads Need To Know About Trade', *The American Economic Review, Papers and Proceedings*, 83(2), 23–6.

Lancaster, K. (1982) 'Comments on Krugman', in Bhagwati, J. (ed.), *Import Competition and Response*, Chicago: The University of Chicago Press.

Lawrence, R. (1987) 'Trade Performance as a Constraint on European Growth', in Lawrence, R. and Schultze, G.L. (eds), *Barriers to European Growth, A Transatlantic View*, Washington: Brookings Institution.

Mathieu, C. and Sterdyniak, H. (1994) 'L'émergence de l'Asie en développement menace-t-elle l'emploi en France?, *Observations et diagnostics économiques*, 48, January.

Messerlin, P.A. (1995) 'The Impact of Trade and Foreign Investment on Labour Markets: The French Case', The OECD Jobs Study Working Paper Series, No. 9, Paris, OECD.

Muchielli, J.L. and Mazerolle, F. (1989) 'Commerce intrabranche et intégration européenne', in Laussel, D. and Montet, C. (eds), *Commerce international en concurrence imparfaite*, Economica, Paris.

Oulmane, N. (1994) 'Echange intra-branche et différenciation verticale des produits', *Mémoire de DEA*, Université de Montpellier I.

Ray, E.J. (1987) 'Evidence on the Political Economy of Protection: A Survey', *Mimeo*, Ohio State University.

Tortensson, J. (1991), 'Quality differentiation and factor proportions in international trade: an empirical test of the Swedish case', *Weltwirtschaftliches Archiv*, 127, 183–94.

Vimont, C. (1993) *Le commerce extérieur français créateur ou déstructeur d'emplois?*, Paris, Economica.

Wood, A. (1994) *North-South Trade, Employment and Inequality*, Oxford, Clarendon Press.

8. Germany

Heinz-Dieter Smeets

8.1 GERMANY'S FOREIGN TRADE PATTERNS

In the past 30 years the development of foreign trade in the Federal
Republic of Germany[1] has been marked by a steep rise in nominal
exports and imports of goods and services. Only recently has this
progression slowed down. For almost the whole of this period the
trade balance showed a surplus, which reached its peak level in 1989.
Subsequently the surplus decreased considerably due to German reunification, but it gradually recovered in the following years. The impressive and continuous increase of German foreign trade over time
can be seen in Figure 8.1, which shows real exports and imports of
goods. In 1960 the relation of foreign trade (export and import of
goods) to GDP amounted to about 24 per cent. By 1990 this ratio rose
to about 57 per cent reflecting Germany's growing dependence on
foreign trade. Since 1991, the ratio has fallen back to about 50 per
cent. This reflects the effects of German unification since intra German
trade has replaced trade with foreign countries.

European integration has significantly contributed to the increased
trade orientation of the German economy. This is manifested in the

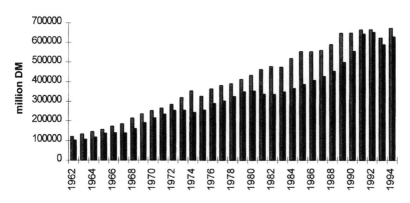

Figure 8.1   Real exports and real imports of goods (1991 prices)
Source: Council of Economic Experts, Report 1995–6.

151

growth of intra-European trade, whose percentage of GDP increased from 10 per cent in 1960 to about 25 per cent in 1985. Consequently, the percentage of intra-European goods trade in aggregate goods trade rose from approximately 40 per cent in 1960 to more than 60 per cent in 1992 (Figure 8.2). The largest increases occurred during the 1960s and 1980s. We find an apparent decline of the intra-EU trade share after 1992, but it must be suspected that this is influenced by the change in customs data collection after implementation of the Single Market.

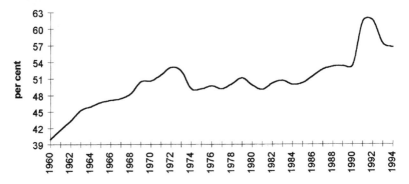

Figure 8.2   Intra-European share of German merchandise trade
Source: Council of Economic Experts, Report 1995–6.

Since 1960, the percentage of manufactured products in total merchandise exports increased only slightly. Imports, however, followed a different trend. In 1960 the manufacturing industries accounted for approximately 55 per cent of aggregate goods imported, whereas in the early 1990s the proportion had increased to over 70 per cent. This development indicated growing import penetration, which might be expected, *a priori*, to have led to considerable structural adjustment.

The extent of the adjustment pressures generated by rising trade volumes and the necessary reallocation of resources may also depend upon the type of foreign trade. For an assessment of such reallocation, it seems appropriate to differentiate between inter- and intra-industry trade. Structural adjustment refers to the transition from one equilibrium to another, and adjustment 'problems' occur if the transition is protracted by the existence of market imperfections. One of these market imperfections which is often focused on is the segmentation of labour markets through occupational and geographical immobility. If factor intensities between firms are similar, then we should expect labour to transfer from one firm to another with comparative ease. It is this situation that most commentators have in mind when discussing adjustment in the intra-industry trade setting. For inter-industry trade they expect very different factor intensities between firms that allow transferability of labour only after more or less complete retraining (see Chapter 3).

Given the potential importance of intra-industry trade for the adjustment problem, this chapter will first examine the development of intra-industry trade in the Federal Republic of Germany from 1960 until 1990. The role of European integration in this development will also be considered. Furthermore, attention will be given to the adjustment effects that were associated with trade changes. The discussion of structural adjustment is based mainly on results for manufacturing industries.

8.2 THE EVOLUTION OF GERMAN INTRA-INDUSTRY TRADE

The level of intra-industry trade over time

All calculations presented in this chapter for German IIT are based on SITC 4 and 5-digit OECD trade data for the period from 1961 to 1990. Therefore, this study provides the most comprehensive set of disaggregated IIT indicators for Germany to date. This is true for the time coverage as well as for the level of statistical disaggregation. Previously published studies on German IIT (for example Schuhmacher, 1983) came to the general conclusion that the level of IIT increased significantly during the 1960s and 1970s, especially vis-à-vis the European neighbours. It could also be shown that even trade with developing countries was to a certain extent of the intra-industry type. All these studies end, however, in the second half of the 1970s at the latest.

The IIT indices, as reported in the following, are Grubel-Lloyd (GL) indices unadjusted for trade imbalances. For 1961 and 1967 indices were calculated from SITC 4-digit level data while for all other years SITC 5-digit data could be employed. As a result, the number of product groups considered here increased from almost 600 in 1961 to more than 3000 in 1990. This may bias the measure of IIT upwards in the 1960s. Furthermore even the GL indices for the 1970s and 1980s

are not perfectly comparable because of changes in the SITC-classi-
fications in 1978 and 1988.

In order to investigate the relationship between European integration and German IIT, we grouped Germany's trading partners into
five country aggregates:[2] EU6, EU12 and 'All Countries', as well as
the 'Rest of Europe' (EU12 minus EU6 = 'ROE' or 'EU-Newcomers')
and the Rest of the Word ('All Countries' minus EU12 = 'ROW').

The results show consistently that Germany has shared in the general rise in IIT in industrial countries since 1960. During this period
the most pronounced rise in the share of IIT was to be observed during
the 1960s while we detect a lower rate of increase over the last two
decades. Moreover, this general trend holds for each of the country
aggregates looked at. As far as the level of IIT is concerned, a systematic difference appears between the predominantly manufacturing
sections 5–8, showing high IIT levels, and the remaining, mainly primary, sectors, which display considerably lower IIT. The patterns of
German IIT with the EU12 (Table 8.2) is similar to IIT with all
countries (Table 8.1).

Table 8.1   Intra-industry trade 1961–90: all countries

SITC Section	1961	1967	1972	1977	1985	1990
0	0.22	0.29	0.32	0.37	0.45	0.49
1	0.32	0.33	0.33	0.39	0.40	0.45
2	0.24	0.32	0.29	0.35	0.34	0.35
3	0.21	0.31	0.18	0.28	0.40	0.37
4	0.31	0.43	0.36	0.47	0.59	0.44
5	0.43	0.48	0.52	0.53	0.57	0.62
6	0.48	0.53	0.62	0.63	0.61	0.65
7	0.35	0.39	0.45	0.45	0.51	0.59
8	0.53	0.61	0.63	0.63	0.63	0.60
9	0.35	0.41	0.48	0.48	0.52	0.57
5–8	0.44	0.50	0.55	0.56	0.58	0.61
0–9	0.34	0.41	0.42	0.46	0.50	0.51

To highlight the influence of European integration on IIT, we
looked at the country aggregates EU6, ROE and ROW in a second
step. Figures 8.3 and 8.4 show that the level of IIT for the aggregated
sections 5–8 and 0–9 is consistently highest within EU6. More strikingly, however, the development of German IIT against ROE and
ROW shows roughly the same level and trend, at least as far as
aggregated SITC 1-digit sections are concerned. Therefore, the

Table 8.2 Intra-industry trade 1961–90: EU12

SITC Section	1961	1967	1972	1977	1985	1990
0	0.18	0.35	0.32	0.47	0.48	0.52
1	0.31	0.28	0.29	0.25	0.41	0.49
2	0.35	0.42	0.45	0.44	0.41	0.40
3	0.20	0.14	0.09	0.20	0.34	0.29
4	0.37	0.57	0.39	0.43	0.57	0.44
5	0.42	0.52	0.54	0.54	0.58	0.62
6	0.44	0.58	0.64	0.67	0.63	0.62
7	0.48	0.52	0.55	0.55	0.55	0.62
8	0.54	0.62	0.57	0.63	0.63	0.58
9	0.38	0.53	0.51	0.42	0.41	0.37
5–8	0.47	0.56	0.57	0.60	0.60	0.61
0–9	0.37	0.45	0.43	0.46	0.50	0.50

subsequent joining of the EU by those countries which are included in ROE does not seem to have affected the development of IIT vis-à-vis Germany significantly.

A more detailed analysis of the sector-specific development of German IIT shows that only for agricultural goods did the GL index with the ROE increase noticeably between 1972 and 1990 without, however, reaching the level of EU6. In all other sections GL indices for ROE remained close to the GL indices for non-European countries.

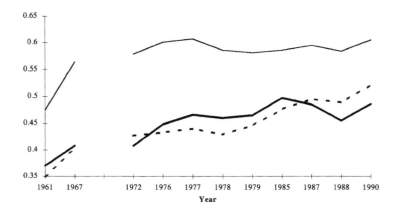

— EU6, ▬ ROE ---- ROW.

Figure 8.3 Grubel-Lloyd indices, Sections 5–8

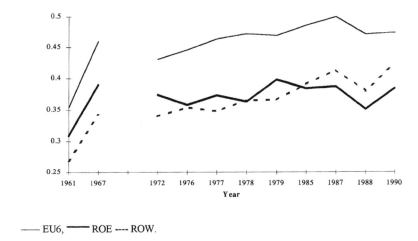

Figure 8.4   Grubel-Lloyd indices, Sections 0–9

This could be interpreted as a first indication that the level of IIT does not seem to be determined primarily by formal integration but by other factors such as regional proximity. Otherwise, it would have been expected that IIT with ROE would have increased compared to ROW during the 1970s and 1980s, because the ROE contains countries which joined the EU over the last two decades. These results may support demand-side explanations of IIT being based on consumer preferences, which may be more similar for close European neighbours as represented by EU6 (four of these countries share a common border with Germany) compared with ROE (only one of these countries shares a common border with Germany) and, even more plausibly, with ROW.

Horizontal versus vertical intra-industry trade

The results reached so far indicate that Germany has a high level of IIT which may have caused comparatively low costs of structural adjustment. In addition to the overall level of IIT it is, however, of special interest for structural adjustment whether the traded goods are horizontally differentiated (alternative combinations of attributes) or vertically differentiated (alternative qualities). For, if IIT is vertically differentiated, this trade can be explained by a revised version of the well-known Heckscher-Ohlin-Samuelson theorem. That, in turn,

Table 8.3 The share of horizontal intra-industry trade

Section	1972 Europe 6	1972 Europe 12	1972 All countries	1978 Europe 6	1978 Europe 12	1978 All countries	1987 Europe 6	1987 Europe 12	1987 All countries	1990 Europe 6	1990 Europe 12	1990 All countries
0	32.1	33.5	27.9	33.2	37.8	29.1	38.3	32.7	33.4	36.2	35.1	34.2
1	0.0	0.0	7.6	12.9	23.5	11.7	21.1	20.6	31.3	31.6	29.1	36.8
2	22.6	23.2	28.4	33.3	41.5	35.5	28.0	33.2	30.1	31.8	31.4	25.7
3	41.5	39.7	35.6	38.5	34.6	42.1	31.0	28.0	37.8	51.9	50.4	40.7
4	50.9	47.7	29.5	73.2	56.4	44.4	38.0	48.1	42.1	64.0	56.5	41.3
5	27.6	28.4	30.4	35.2	35.5	31.2	32.5	34.2	36.6	32.2	33.1	34.0
6	33.0	34.5	26.9	36.8	36.5	33.7	33.4	37.6	32.8	36.4	35.7	36.5
7	24.2	23.9	31.5	26.2	23.0	23.6	22.1	27.8	27.1	24.4	25.4	28.9
8	16.3	18.5	20.6	26.6	20.3	17.7	24.6	20.5	12.4	26.0	25.1	20.0
9	15.7	3.5	0.0	0.0	29.8	18.9	0.0	0.0	10.4	64.1	70.8	0.0

makes quite clear that adjustment problems under these circumstances will coincide with those known from the (unfavourable) inter-industry-trade case. Therefore, Table 8.3 gives an overview of the qualitative structure of German IIT for the 1-digit SITC sections and against the three country aggregates EU6, EU12 and All Countries. Following Abd-el-Rahman (1991) and Greenaway *et al.* (1994a), quality is measured with reference to the unit values of exports and imports. Horizontal IIT (HIIT) is defined as that part of total IIT in a (5-digit) product group where the ratio (r) between the unit value of exports (UVEX) and the unit value of imports (UVIM) is greater than 0.85 and less than 1.15. For $r < 0.85$ and $r > 1.15$, IIT is defined as vertical (VIIT).

The level of German HIIT vis-à-vis European countries (EU6, EU12) increased in all sections between 1972 and 1990. Nevertheless, the average share of HIIT in manufactured goods between Germany and its European neighbours increased only slightly from about 25 per cent in 1972 to about 30 per cent in 1990. This reveals that only one-quarter to one-third of German IIT is in horizontally differentiated goods, while the bulk of IIT consists of vertically differentiated goods representing different qualities. We define matched trade in industries where the ratio of export to import unit values exceeds 1.15 as high-quality-export VIIT, while a ratio of below 0.85 represents low-quality-export VIIT. Defined in this way, Germany's trade in the manufacturing industry is characterized mainly by high quality exports, which comprise between about 45 to 65 per cent of total IIT.

Marginal intra-industry trade and international specialization

The analysis so far has been based on indices which measure the extent of IIT as a proportion of total trade at a point in time. But, as discussed in Chapter 3, changes in the GL index may not capture potential adjustment costs, and measures of marginal IIT (MIIT) can, therefore, be useful to complement traditional IIT analysis. MIIT was quantified in this study according to Brülhart's (1994) *A* and *B* indices.

We have calculated *A* indices from SITC 5-digit trade figures, deflated into base-year values by the consumer price index, over the periods 1961–67, 1972–77 and 1978–87, and we report the results in Figures 8.5a to 8.5c. It can be seen that indices rarely exceed 0.50, with some exceptions in the manufacturing sectors (SITC 5–8). The generally low level of *A* indices indicates that trade-induced specialization occurred mainly at the inter-industry level.

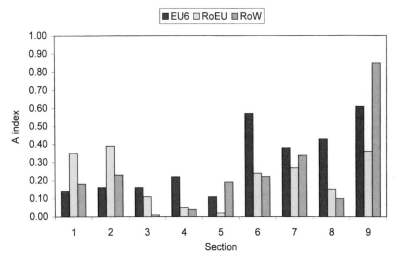

Figure 8.5a   German MIIT, 1961–67 (*A* indices by SITC Section)

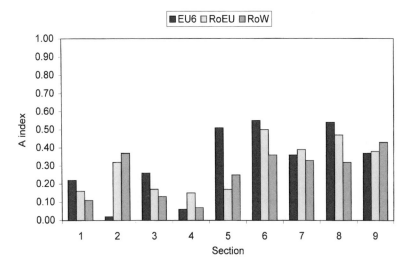

Figure 8.5b   German MIIT, 1972–77 (*A* indices by SITC Section)

During the 1960s, Germany's MIIT within EU6 showed the highest level compared to the other country aggregates for the manufacturing industry (sections 5–8). Over time, however, the indices for all country aggregates have converged in sections 5 to 8. This development is

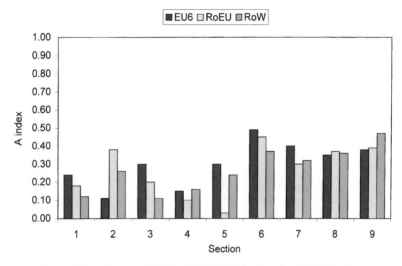

Figure 8.5c   German MIIT, 1978–87 (*A* indices by SITC Section)

mainly caused by a decrease of German MIIT within EU6 and by a
strong increase with the other country groups. This is especially obvious for ROE during the 1970s and may be caused by the first enlargement of the EU in 1973. The second (southern) enlargement,

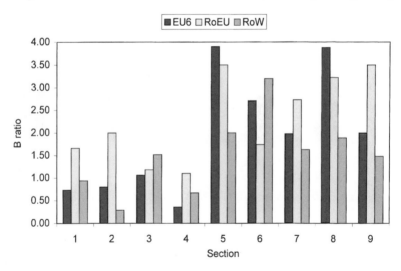

Figure 8.6a   German 'trade performance', 1961–67 (ratios of positive to
negative *B* indices)

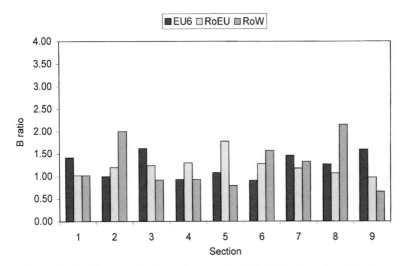

Figure 8.6b German 'trade performance', 1972–77 (ratios of positive to negative *B* indices)

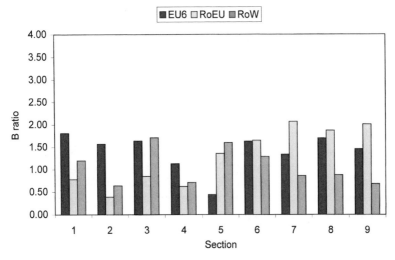

Figure 8.6c German 'trade performance', 1978–87 (ratios of positive to negative *B* indices)

however, is not (positively) reflected in the data. Rather, *A* indices for the 1980s decreased slightly.

Whether this inter-industry change of trade flows worked to Germany's advantage or disadvantage in terms of sectoral trade performance is indicated by the values of the *B* index. This measure is positive where exports grew more than imports and negative in the reverse case. Since, by definition, any average of Bs over several product groups will yield invalid results, Figures 8.6a to 8.6c report the ratio of industries with positive Bs relative to the industries with negative *B*s.

International 'competitiveness' was especially strong for the German manufacturing industries during the 1960s vis-à-vis Germany's European neighbours. In the manufacturing sectors, all *B* ratios exceed the value of one, and some even exceed three. These *B* ratios decreased sharply against all country groups to about 1 to 1.5 in the 1970s. During the third sub-period (1978–87) they increased again, especially for ROE while they decreased even further for ROW. Thus, Germany's manufacturing industries continued to improve their trade performance throughout our sample period, but at a decelerating rate.

The sharp fall in the *B* ratios between 1961–67 and 1972–77 was presumably driven by the break-down of the Bretton-Woods system. This ended a long period of undervaluation of the Deutsche Mark which had favoured German exporters. At the same time, the international 'competitiveness' of the agricultural sector against the ROE steadily decreased after the enlargement of the EU to the south. This can be seen from the *B* ratios for SITCO (food products) in Figures 8.6a to 8.6c, which fell from more than 1.6 in the first period (1961–67) to 0.8 in the third period (1978–87).

Another possible way to look at sectoral trade performance is to calculate the ratio of the number of industries with positive Bs relative to those with negative Bs, as done before, but weighting them with different factors. This was done on the basis of NACE 3-digit data for 95 manufacturing industries (NACE 221 to 495) by weighting *B* indices for the country aggregates EU6, EU12 and ROW according to the level of production, employment and trade respectively. The results are summarized in Table 8.4.

Independent of the country aggregate, all *B* indices are larger than 1. This result indicates that changes in German trade have on average worked towards the economy's advantage. Weighting according to 1980 levels of production and trade gives *B* ratios of about 5 for Europe and 2 for ROW. A comparison with the unweighted ratios shows in both cases that sectors which improve their trade performance were the ones which were already highly trade-oriented and especially productive at the outset. Quite a different picture, however, results from weighting Bs according to 1980 levels of employment. For EU6 the

Table 8.4 Marginal intra-industry trade and structural adjustment 1980–87

	EU 6		EU 12		ROW	
	A Index	B Index	A Index	B Index	A Index	B Index
Unweighted		2.89		4.00		1.63
Production-weighted		5.26		5.61		1.94
Employment-weighted		4.80		3.51		1.11
Trade-weighted	0.54	5.32	0.52	5.68	0.49	1.97

B ratio again increases from about 3 in the unweighted case to about 5 after weighting. Weighted *B* ratios for EU12 and ROW, however, exhibit a less favourable evolution of trade flows than the unweighted ratios. This indicates that the trade performance of sectors with above-average employment levels was generally below the average for trade with EU newcomers and the ROW. Vis-à-vis these country aggregates, Germany seems to be specializing out of low-productivity, labour-intensive industries and into highly productive and less labour-intensive industries. For the EU6, on the other hand, German trade flows worked to the economy's advantage in terms of employment. This evolution may be explained by assuming that against the original EU members Germany specialized into (high-tech) sectors which intensively use skilled labour. Measured against the trade-weighted *A* index, changes in trade were of a predominantly intra-industry nature as far as Europe is concerned and of an inter-industry nature for ROW. However, the differences among A indices are comparatively small.

8.3 STRUCTURAL CHANGE AND ADJUSTMENT

We now consider the relationship between trade patterns and the structure of German production in the manufacturing industries. As Greenaway and Milner (1986, p. 80) have pointed out, 'the exchange of differentiated products (IIT) by a country with the rest of the world can change without any change in its production structure and therefore without affecting specialization'. In this sub-section, we therefore examine whether and how the pattern of German trade has affected the structure of German manufacturing industries.

By looking at German manufacturing in general it can be seen that that the share of this sector's value added in total value added increased slightly during the 1960s and reached its peak in 1970–71 at about 37 per cent. During the 1970s and 1980s, however, this share fell continuously to about 32 per cent in 1990. After German reunification there was a further significant decrease in the relative importance of manufacturing, due to rationalization of unproductive enterprises in East Germany and a boom in service industries. The share of manufacturing employment in total employment has been decreasing continuously over time. It stood at 45 per cent in 1960 to reach 33 per cent in 1990 and 27 per cent in 1994, after German reunification. Given this pronounced relative contraction of manufacturing as a whole, it is important to assess how the sectoral pattern of change has affected structural adjustment.

To investigate the relationship between trade and industrial performance, simple correlation coefficients were first calculated between trade performance (measured by the growth rates of German exports to, and imports from various country aggregates) and industrial performance (measured by changes in output, establishment numbers and employment). These results, reported in Table 8.5, are based on a data set comprising 95 NACE 3-digit manufacturing industries (NACE groups 221 to 495) in 1980 and 1987.

First, the correlation coefficients are in general relatively small. This indicates that changes in the pattern of trade flows have at best a partial influence on German industrial performance, in spite of Ger-

Table 8.5   Trade and industrial performance: correlation coefficients 1980–87

	Production	*Value Added*	*Changes in:* Establishments	*Employment*
Total trade				
Exports	0.19*	0.15	0.12	0.07
Imports	0.08	0.01	0.41**	−0.22*
EU12 trade				
Exports	0.06	0.04	0.02	0.12
Imports	0.26**	0.19*	0.36**	−0.17*
IIT 80	0.08	0.10	0.08	0.09
IIT 87	0.09	0.11	−0.02	−0.02
ΔGL	0.01	0.02	−0.16	−0.16
A index	0.11	0.07	0.07	0.01
B index	−0.02	−0.01	−0.06	−0.13
GHME	0.04	0.04	0.44**	−0.09

Statistical significance (t tests): 0.01: **, 0.1: * (95 observations).

many's high trade orientation. Second, exports for all country aggregates are positively correlated with employment. Third, imports are negatively correlated with employment but positively correlated with production.

Although correlation coefficients are in most cases not statistically significant, these results may suggest that growing imports from Europe put competitive pressure on German industries which squeeze employment and increase productivity. Changes in imports from ROW, however, have no simple association with changes in production and employment. This may be caused by the predominantly inter-industry nature of trade with regard to this country group going along with a lower elasticity of substitution between imported and domestically produced goods. The same substitution effect may, on the other hand, also cause the positive association between exports to ROW and German production, as well as employment, since under inter-industry trade the employment increasing effect of rising exports is not offset by any increase in imports in the same industry.

Since the relationship between trade and industrial performance was found to be rather weak, the association between trade structure measured with IIT and MIIT indices, and industry performance was tested in a second step. Although the highest correlation coefficient reached 0.44, the relationship is generally still rather weak.

The results of these calculations can be summarized as follows. First, there is nearly no association between the level of the GL index and the growth rate of employment. This result holds true independently of the country aggregate under consideration. Second, looking at MIIT, the picture is less clear cut. Within Europe there is a negative relationship between MIIT and employment growth, while a positive relationship is found against the ROW. This is consistent with our results on trade performance. While German MIIT within Europe seems to be dominated by the negative import effect on employment, MIIT against ROW seems to be dominated by the positive export effect on employment. It should be stressed, however, that few of the correlation coefficients are statistically significant. Third, the higher MIIT, the higher is generally the growth rate of production. Fourth, when export growth exceeds import growth, as reflected in a positive B index, this is accompanied by an above-average rate of job losses. It is to be expected that the causation here runs from employment to the trade balance: decreasing employment means increasing productivity which makes German trade more competitive.

8.4 SUMMARY AND CONCLUSIONS

In general, the level of German IIT measured in terms of the GL-index is rather high. After a sharp rise in German IIT during the 1960s, the remainder of our sample period was characterized by only small further increases. A generalized decrease in the level of IIT, as recently experienced by some other countries, did not emerge in Germany.[3]

The level of German IIT with regard to the original EU countries is significantly higher than with new EU member countries and the ROW. This result holds consistently across industries. We detect, however, a somewhat surprising absence of a catching-up effect by the new EU members during the 1970s and 1980s. This result may indicate that the formal process of European integration did not significantly affect the level of IIT. It was mainly the ROW countries against which a relative increase of the level of German IIT could be observed during the 1980s. This might reflect in part the increased internationalization of production exploiting low labour costs in developing countries.

Only about one third of German IIT has been characterized by horizontally differentiated goods of roughly equal quality. However, in the bulk of industries Germany exports high-quality goods and at the same time imports low quality goods.

By looking at MIIT measured in terms of A indices, it can be seen that new trade in the 1980s was often of a predominantly inter-industry character. The level of German MIIT was generally the highest for manufacturing sectors. According to B indices, Germany became more competitive between 1978 and 1987, especially against the new EU member countries. Weighted B ratios indicate that Germany is moving out of low-productivity labour-intensive industries and into highly productive and less labour-intensive industries. Towards the original EU countries, however, German trade flows worked to the economy's advantage in terms of employment. The explanation for this finding is probably that Germany specialized in skilled labour-intensive industries vis-à-vis the original EU members.

In conclusion, we found little evidence that for Germany IIT leads to less adjustment frictions than inter-industry trade. Moreover, European integration does not seem to have generated increased IIT for Germany. Thus, policy makers' often revealed preference for regional rather than global trade liberalization, as a means of minimizing adjustment problems, seems to be largely unfounded – at least as far as the German experience is concerned. General growth of the German economy was presumably the main cause for the smoothness of adjustment during most of the post-war period. This suggests that although the creation of the European Single Market may do little to ease adjustment problems because of an expansion of IIT, it may help because of the faster growth prospects it generates.

Notes

1. Since 1991 data refer to unified Germany.
2. EU6=Belgium, France, Germany, Italy, Luxembourg, The Netherlands; EU12 = EU6 + United Kingdom, Ireland, Denmark (all since 1973), Greece (since 1981), Spain and Portugal (both since 1986).
3. A general but temporary decrease in the German level of IIT was observed between 1987 and 1988, which probably resulted from the second revision of the SITC classification in 1988.

References and Further Reading

Abd-el-Rahman, K. (1991) 'Firms' Competitive and National Comparative Advantages as Joint Determinants of Trade Composition', *Weltwirtschaftliches Archiv*, 127, 83–97.

Brülhart, M. (1994) 'Marginal Intra-Industry Trade: Measurement and Relevance for the Pattern of Industrial Specialization', *Weltwirtschaftliches Archiv*, 130, 600–13.

Buigues, P., Ilzkovitz, F. and Lebrun, J.-F. (1991) 'Industrieller Strukturwandel im europäischen Binnenmarkt: Anpassungsbedarf in den Mitgliedstaaten', in Kommission der Europäischen Gemeinschaften, *Europäische Wirtschaft*, Brussels: Soziales Europa.

Greenaway, D. and Milner, C. (1986) *The Economics of Intra-Industry Trade*, Oxford: Blackwell.

Greenaway, D., Hine, R. and Milner, C. (1994a) 'Country-Specific Factors and the Pattern of Horizontal and Vertical Intra-Industry Trade', *Weltwirtschaftliches Archiv*, 130, 77–100.

Greenaway, D., Hine, R.C., Milner, C. and Elliott, R. (1994) 'Adjustment and the Measurement of Marginal Intra Industry Trade', *Weltwirtschaftliches Archiv*, 130, 418–27.

Hamilton, C. and Kniest, P. (1991) 'Trade Liberalisation, Structural Adjustment and Intra-Industry Trade: A Note', *Weltwirtschaftliches Archiv*, 127, 356–67.

Schuhmacher, D. (1983) 'Intra-Industry Trade between the Federal Republic of Germany and Developing Countries: Extent and Some Characteristics', in Tharakan, P.K.M. (ed.), *Intra-Industry Trade*, Amsterdam: North-Holland.

Vona, S. (1991) 'On the Measurement of Intra-Industry Trade: Some Further Thoughts', in *Weltwirtschaftliches Archiv*, 127, 678–700.

9. Greece

Alexander H. Sarris, Pyrros Papadimitriou and Athanassios Mavrogiannis

9.1 INTRODUCTION

Greece formally joined the European Union (EU) in January 1981, and as one would expect, given the small size of Greece relative to that of the EU, this development has had a major influence on both Greece's structure of production and of international trade. The purpose of this chapter is to study the structure of international trade of Greece, with special emphasis on intra-industry trade (IIT), and to analyse industrial adjustment, especially as it relates to trade performance, in the post accession period.

There are three phases that one can distinguish in the process of Greek integration with the EU (Katseli, 1990). The first covers the period of the association agreement until accession (1962–80). This period was characterized by rapid economic growth and gradual elimination of tariff barriers coupled with active use of domestic policy instruments for the selective protection of industrial activity. The second phase covers the immediate post-entry period (1981–86), and is characterized by slow economic growth, faster dismantling of existing trade barriers, and a series of measures aimed at restructuring industrial activity but also prolonging protection afforded to selected sectors. The third phase started in 1987 and is characterized by repeated macro stabilization programmes and slow growth, in view of large internal imbalances, elimination of all remaining protection and export subsidy measures, and liberalization of the domestic financial system, international capital flows, international transactions in services, and public procurement. Many of these liberalization measures were taken in accordance with the completion of the Single Market by the EU.

There have been very few studies of Greek industrial and overall trade in general and IIT in particular. Sarris (1988) analysed the developments of trade and protection in Greece from 1960 to 1980, and showed that while tariff protection had significantly declined, non-tariff protection in the form of other border and internal taxes had not. He also showed that export propensity for several industries had significantly increased, aided by export subsidy policies that were in force before EU accession. Import penetration, however, had also increased, particularly in the products traditionally exported by Greece. Katseli (1990) showed that protection had declined after accession for the traditional import competing sectors, while it had not for the modern ones. Giannitsis (1988) showed that trade competitiveness had declined in almost all traditional industrial sectors after accession, but had increased slightly in modern sectors, and in sectors where protection had increased. Other relevant studies of Greek industrial trade include those of Katsos and Spanakis (1983), Alexakis and Xanthakis (1992), and Mardas (1992). The latter reported some figures on Greek IIT, but at a rather aggregated level.

From a theoretical viewpoint, Greece was and still is a country rather dissimilar to the core EU countries, in the sense that it is characterized by low income per capita (on a purchasing power basis the per capita GDP of Greece is 63 per cent of the EU12 average), a low degree of industrialization (industry, including mining, electricity and construction, makes up 22.2 per cent of GDP compared to 33.1 per cent for the rest of EU12), and geographical peripherality. Trade theory suggests that under such conditions trade with the more developed countries will be more of the inter-than of the intra-industry type. Trade liberalization which followed integration with the EU might then lead to inter- rather than intra-industry specialization, and adjustment pressures might be quite large. It is the purpose of the chapter to disentangle some of these effects empirically.

In Section 9.2, the trends in Greece's IIT are discussed. Greek IIT is subdivided into its horizontal and vertical components in Section 9.3. Section 9.4 analyses industrial adjustment between 1978, one of the latest pre-accession years, and 1987. In Section 9.5 post-EU accession changes in industrial employment are analysed and related to changes in trade performance. Section 9.6 provides a conclusion.

9.2 GREEK INTRA-INDUSTRY TRADE 1961–90

The evolution of Greek trade flows

The period 1960–90 witnessed a substantial opening of the Greek economy. The share of merchandise exports in GDP increased continuously from 5.8 per cent in 1960 to 14.2 per cent in 1990, while the share of merchandise imports in GDP increased from 14.6 per cent to a peak of 35.7 per cent in 1985, and retreated in 1990 to 27.4 per cent. This decrease is to a large extent due to the stabilization programmes that in one way or another have been in effect since 1986. Growing import penetration meant that the deficit in merchandise trade grew from about 9 to 12 per cent of GDP in the pre-accession period to 13 to 20 per cent in the period after 1980. The merchandise deficit in Greece is counterbalanced by surpluses in the services and capital accounts.

There have been substantial and rapid structural changes in both Greek exports and imports over the period 1960–90. In the early 1960s, more than 90 per cent of Greek exports consisted of products in SITC categories 0, 1, and 2 (Food and live animals, Beverages and tobacco, and Inedible crude materials except fuels). Only 8.2 per cent of exports were in manufacturing (SITC categories 5 to 8). On the eve of EU accession this picture had changed considerably. The share of manufactures in total exports was about 55 per cent, while the share of SITC 0 to 2 products had dropped to 40 per cent. By 1990, ten years after accession, the share of manufactures in total exports had remained at 55 per cent, while the share of SITC 0 to 2 products had declined further to about 27 per cent.

Within manufactures, however, certain 'low technology' sectors occupy large shares. For instance, clothing (SITC 84) accounted in 1990 for 89 per cent of total exports of SITC section 8, or 20.8 per cent of total merchandise exports. Textiles, non-metallic mineral manufactures, iron and steel manufactures, and non-ferrous metal manufactures (SITC 65 to 68) accounted for 85 per cent of trade in SITC section 6, or 20 per cent of all merchandise exports. These five sectors accounted for 74 per cent of all manufactured exports.

In 1961, 74 per cent of Greek imports consisted of manufactures. This share slightly dropped to 69 per cent by 1977, but increased again after accession to reach 72 per cent in 1990. The fact that the manufacturing share of exports and imports has stayed roughly unchanged in the first ten years of accession is consistent with the fact that the share of manufacturing in Greek GDP has stagnated in the same period (from 18 per cent in 1980 to 16 per cent in 1988).

The observed changes over time in Greek trade with the other 11 member countries of the pre-1995 EU are much less dramatic than the changes in the overall pattern of Greek trade. The EU12 had been the destination of 40 to 54 per cent of Greek exports, and the source of 45 to 56 per cent of Greek imports before accession, with no marked change between 1960 and 1980. After accession, the share of Greek exports destined for the EU12 rose considerably (reaching 64 per cent by 1990), as did the share of Greek imports coming from EU12 (reaching 64 per cent in 1990). The developments for manufacturing trade are similar.

Intra-industry trade

Previous cross-country analyses of IIT including Greece (for example Greenaway and Hine, 1991), showed a generally rising pattern of IIT for Greece until the early 1980s, and a stagnation thereafter. The unadjusted Grubel-Lloyd (GL) index computed for Greece on the basis of 3-digit SITC trade data, suggested that, by 1985, 46 per cent of Greek manufacturing trade was intra-industry. Similarly, Mardas (1992), using 3-digit SITC data showed that IIT in many 3-digit product groups was quite high. In this section the values of GL indices for Greece over the period 1961 to 1990 are reported, computed from disaggregated trade data at the SITC 4- and 5-digit level, and aggregated to 1-digit SITC Sections.

Table 9.1 lists the GL indices for all 1-digit sections, as well as total (SITC 0–9), non-manufacturing (SITC 0–4), and manufacturing (SITC 5–8) trade of Greece with the EU12, the non-EU12 countries,

Table 9.1   Grubel-Lloyd indices over time for trade with the world, EU12 and non-EU12 countries

A. Trade with EU12 countries

SITC	1961	1967	1972	1977	1985	1990
0	0.018	0.034	0.073	0.061	0.059	0.096
1	0.003	0.014	0.090	0.298	0.141	0.186
2	0.035	0.053	0.061	0.116	0.121	0.070
3	0	0.155	0.116	0.416	0.192	0.598
4	0.020	0.004	0.010	0.143	0.140	0.066
5	0.009	0.077	0.071	0.129	0.102	0.079
6	0.027	0.109	0.156	0.205	0.233	0.212
7	0.015	0.012	0.033	0.026	0.056	0.062
8	0.023	0.116	0.174	0.110	0.168	0.264
9	0	0	0	0.086	0.686	0.090
SITC 0–9	0.018	0.050	0.082	0.110	0.131	0.156
SITC 0–4	0.017	0.035	0.076	0.143	0.093	0.138
SITC 5–8	0.018	0.058	0.084	0.100	0.147	0.164
Trade imbalance						
SITC 0–9	0.461	0.360	0.470	0.393	0.330	0.374

Table 9.1   (contd.)

B. *Trade with non-EU12 countries*

SITC	1961	1967	1972	1977	1985	1990
0	0.036	0.058	0.075	0.084	0.066	0.141
1	0.001	0.001	0.025	0.032	0.044	0.229
2	0.051	0.125	0.120	0.164	0.260	0.200
3	0	0.021	0.023	0.040	0.055	0.348
4	0.078	0.014	0.015	0.044	0.008	0.087
5	0.059	0.192	0.205	0.414	0.235	0.215
6	0.186	0.229	0.259	0.230	0.225	0.195
7	0.028	0.060	0.053	0.109	0.084	0.079
8	0.280	0.302	0.170	0.195	0.212	0.200
9	0	0	0	0.620	0.298	0.409
SITC 0–9	0.046	0.083	0.107	0.128	0.117	0.197
SITC 0–4	0.019	0.050	0.069	0.079	0.083	0.249
SITC 5–8	0.086	0.164	0.147	0.170	0.172	0.166
Trade imbalance						
SITC 0–9	0.243	0.252	0.444	0.455	0.433	0.234

C. *Trade with the world*

SITC	1961	1967	1972	1977	1985	1990
0	0.030	0.059	0.085	0.098	0.109	0.151
1	0.004	0.007	0.055	0.124	0.135	0.281
2	0.052	0.123	0.138	0.187	0.241	0.178
3	0	0.041	0.071	0.173	0.181	0.446
4	0.060	0.013	0.011	0.169	0.100	0.143
5	0.029	0.166	0.119	0.249	0.197	0.166
6	0.118	0.187	0.242	0.284	0.304	0.260
7	0.022	0.026	0.041	0.072	0.080	0.078
8	0.185	0.240	0.232	0.204	0.202	0.273
9	0	0	0	0.250	0.556	0.210
SITC 0–9	0.040	0.082	0.114	0.157	0.183	0.203
SITC 0–4	0.022	0.054	0.092	0.145	0.164	0.236
SITC 5–8	0.057	0.114	0.127	0.163	0.200	0.188
Trade imbalance						
SITC 0–9	0.350	0.306	0.459	0.427	0.382	0.316

Source: Computed from OECD 4-digit (1961, 1967) and 5-digit (1972, 1977, 1985, and 1990) data.

and the world, over time. The indices have been computed using the OECD trade data as available (that is 4-digit data for 1961 and 1967 and 5-digit data for the later years). The first observation is that the share of IIT in total trade of Greece is much lower than previously computed with aggregated 3-digit data. In 1990, after a period of continuous increase in IIT, only 20 per cent of the total trade of Greece with the world, and 19 per cent of manufacturing trade was of the intra-industry type. This contrasts with figures of the order of 45 per cent computed earlier with three digit data (Greenaway and Hine, 1991). It also contrasts with much higher levels of IIT for the other EU countries calculated with the same type of detailed data.

Turning to trends, it is quite obvious that the share of IIT has increased substantially over the three decades 1960–90. The increase appears to be strong in the post-accession period, and particularly so in the non-manufacturing sections (SITC 0–4) for the most recent period. This is due largely to liberalization of imports from the EU in these products. Table 9.1 shows that IIT in manufacturing (SITC sections 5–8) is generally higher than IIT in primary product industries (SITC sections 0–4), as one would expect. However, the difference is not large, and in 1990 average IIT was higher in the primary sectors (SITC 0–4) than in the manufacturing sectors (SITC 5–8). This is due to the large increase of IIT in Greek trade with non-EU12 countries after 1985.

An interesting finding is that Greek IIT in manufactures is lower with the EU than with non-EU countries for all periods. This means that, despite the overall increase in IIT, Greece's exports to and imports from the EU12 were and remain more dissimilar compared to trade with non-EU12. Thus, integration with the EU does not (yet) seem to have created a production structure that tends towards the average EU composition of industries.

One of the reasons for the low degree of IIT in Greece is the significant imbalance of aggregate Greek trade. In Table 9.1 the relative trade imbalance, measured by the ratio of the difference between total imports and total exports to the sum of total imports and exports, is shown at the bottom of every set of GL indices for trade with a given country group, and it is clear that Greece has been characterized by significant trade deficits all throughout the period. Even if, however, the GL indices are adjusted for overall trade imbalance Greek IIT still remains quite low (less then 30 per cent).

Marginal intra-industry trade

To assess the change over time in the structure of Greek trade, the concept of marginal IIT (MIIT) is employed (see Chapter 3). The following measures are used. First, we employ the simple change in the value of the GL index. Second, the absolute measure of MIIT proposed by Greenaway *et al.*, (1994b) (GHME measure) is used, which is simply the change in the absolute value of IIT. Finally the *A* index proposed by Brülhart (1994) is utilized. Our analysis draws on data for the years 1978 and 1987 (both expressed in 1978 values). These two years are chosen for two reasons. First, 1978 is one of the last years before Greek accession to the EU, while 1987 is a year well past the initial adjustment. Second, 1978 is the first year where Greek trade data are compiled according to the SITC revision 2, while 1987 is the last such year. Hence the period spans both the period of interest to Greece and one where the analysis would not be complicated by changes in international trade data classification.

Table 9.2 presents aggregated results concerning MIIT for Greek trade with EU12 and non-EU12 between 1978 and 1987. The first thing to notice is that Greek trade with the EU12 expanded considerably in the early post-accession period, and in almost all sectors, while trade with non-EU12 largely contracted. IIT with EU12 (as measured by GHME) generally increased in all sectors, while IIT with non-EU12 countries increased by much smaller amounts.

The *A* index generally takes values closer to zero than 1. This implies that the changes in trade of Greece with EU12 between 1978 and 1987 were mostly of the inter-industry type. The same was the case for trade with non-EU12 countries.

The GHME index, which gives absolute changes in IIT, suggests that the bulk of the change in Greek IIT with EU12 has been in SITC sections 0 (food), 6 (raw material based manufactures) and 8 (miscellaneous manufactures). These three sections account for 86.1 per cent of all the change in IIT between the two periods, as measured by the GHME index, and they accounted for the bulk of Greek exports in most years (about 67 to 68 per cent of all exports in the 1977–90 period), albeit for only 38 per cent of total Greek trade in 1978. Thus, it appears that the bulk of change in Greek IIT has occurred in the traditional export sectors. By contrast the sector with the highest base year trade (SITC 7, Machinery and transport) has exhibited a very small change in IIT. The changes in Greek IIT with the non-EU12 countries are similar to the above. It thus appears that Greek IIT has expanded in the more traditional Greek export industries, implying that the liberalization that has accompanied Greek accession has opened up many of the traditionally protected Greek sectors to international competition and imports.

Table 9.2 Marginal IIT of Greece with EU12 and non-EU12, 1978–87
(All trade and IIT numbers are in constant 1978 million US dollars[1])

A. Trade with EU12

SITC Section	Trade in 1978 (X + M)	Change in trade 1978–87	Change in GL 1978–87	A index	Change in IIT (GHME)
0	557	1487	0.077	0.160	252
1	120	123	−0.066	0.118	4
2	258	70	0.032	0.106	17
3	290	−26	−0.062	0.263	−25
4	66	116	0.304	0.499	57
5	536	360	−0.018	0.087	22
6	1179	1093	0.069	0.184	407
7	1816	−292	0.046	0.053	63
8	434	887	−0.006	0.117	121
9	2	−1	0.564	0.000	1
SITC 0–9	5259	3818	0.053	0.142	919
SITC 0–4	1292	1770	0.021	0.180	306
SITC 5–8	3965	2049	0.065	0.123	613

B. Trade with Non-EU12

SITC Section	Trade in 1978 (X + M)	Change in trade 1978–87	Change in GL 1978–87	A index	Change in IIT (GHME)
0	828	−291	0.073	0.040	27
1	159	−26	0.067	0.140	9
2	509	56	0.008	0.044	15
3	1458	−72	−0.035	0.619	−46
4	18	12	−0.012	0.039	0
5	216	94	−0.094	0.200	1
6	866	108	0.115	0.149	133
7	1511	−555	0.025	0.037	−3
8	176	226	0.031	0.123	53
9	5	36	0.645	0.613	28
SITC 0–9	5745	−411	0.049	0.092	217
SITC 0–4	2972	−320	0.013	0.068	5
SITC 5–8	2768	−127	0.076	0.096	185

Source: Computed from OECD data
[1] The deflation is done by first translating 1987 dollar trade values into Greek drachmas using the 1987 exchange rate, then deflating by the wholesale price deflator to 1978 and finally transforming to dollars with the 1978 exchange rate

9.3   QUALITY DIFFERENTIATION IN GREEK INTRA INDUSTRY TRADE

Vertical IIT (VIIT) involves the simultaneous export and import of products in the same industry, where imports are systematically of lower or higher quality than exports (see Chapter 4). Conversely, horizontal IIT (HIIT) involves simultaneous exports and imports of similar quality products of the same industry. The phenomenon is potentially important for policy analysis, as quality may be important for commercial success in an increasingly competitive market, and VIIT is likely to involve greater adjustment costs than HIIT. Trends in the volume of Greek IIT with the EU in products that are vertically differentiated can provide information concerning the gradual evolution of the division of labour within the enlarged EU. For instance, if domestic production is moving towards higher quality exports within an industry, it might imply that potentially more skilled and fewer unskilled workers are needed. Similarly, if the volume of HIIT is increasing it might imply lower adjustment pressures.

The methodology applied is as follows (see also Chapter 4). Given an industry (defined at the 3-digit or higher level), the volume of IIT as well as the ratio of the unit value of exports to that of imports is computed for each 5-digit sub-industry of that industry. Subsequently, the IIT of this sub-industry is assigned to one of three groups. Group A consists of sub-industries which exhibit a relative export unit value ratio larger than 1.15. Group B consists of sub-industries which exhibit a relative export unit value ratio smaller than 0.85, and group C consists of those sub-industries with relative export unit value ratio between 0.85 and 1.15. IIT in group A is considered high-quality VIIT (HQVIIT), while that falling in group B is considered low quality VIIT (LQVIIT).

Table 9.3 exhibits the breakdown of manufacturing IIT of Greece with the EU12 and non-EU12 from 1972 to 1990 into vertically and horizontally differentiated groups. The most marked pattern seems to be the rising share of low quality VIIT in Greece's IIT with EU12. While not more than 43 per cent of Greek IIT with the EU12 was LQVIIT in the pre-accession period, it then rose to as high as 63 per cent, and has not fallen below 55 per cent. This can be contrasted with the slight decline in the same share in IIT with non-EU12, which has declined from 44 per cent in the pre-accession period to 38 per cent in 1990. Coupled with the fact that the overall proportion of manufactured IIT in total manufactured trade of Greece is still much lower

Table 9.3 Vertical and horizontal intra-industry Trade of Greece in manufacturing industries (million 1978 $, except where indicated)

A. Trade with EU12

	1972	1977	1978	1985	1987	1990
Total IIT (TIIT)	113.0	344.3	435.0	727.0	1412.2	1981.6
HQ Vert. IIT (HQVIIT)	61.0	193.2	160.3	126.3	295.3	481.1
LQ Vert. IIT (LQVIIT)	44.8	125.5	186.4	454.3	887.7	1103.4
Horiz. IIT (HIIT)	7.1	25.6	88.3	146.4	229.2	397.1
HIIT/TIIT (Per cent)	6.3	7.4	20.3	20.1	16.2	20.0
HQVIIT/TIIT (Per cent)	54.0	56.1	36.9	17.4	20.9	24.3
LQVIIT/TIIT (Per cent)	39.7	36.5	42.9	62.5	62.9	55.7

B. Trade with non-EU12

	1972	1977	1978	1985	1987	1990
Total IIT (TIIT)	102.2	470.3	344.2	469.9	712.8	907.6
HQ Vert. IIT (HQVIIT)	39.4	158.3	121.7	126.0	280.8	323.6
LQ Vert. IIT (LQVIIT)	33.1	210.9	139.4	190.7	248.6	342.8
Horiz. IIT (HIIT)	29.7	101.0	83.1	153.3	183.3	241.2
HIIT/TIIT (Per cent)	29.1	21.5	24.1	32.6	25.7	26.6
HQVIIT/TIIT (Per cent)	38.6	33.7	35.4	26.8	39.4	35.7
LQVIIT/TIIT (Per cent)	32.4	44.9	40.5	40.6	34.9	37.8

Source: Computed from OECD data

than comparable figures from other EU12 member countries, it appears that only a negligible share of total manufactured trade of Greece is of the HQVIIT variety (only about 4.6 per cent of total manufacturing trade, 4.0 per cent of total trade with EU12 and 5.9 per cent of total trade with non-EU12 countries).

A high share of HQVIIT in manufactures implies that the country is specializing in high-quality products and could imply something about the demand for skilled labour. From Table 9.3 it can be seen that trade falling into this has grown more slowly than total manufacturing IIT. The growth of the volume of HQVIIT between 1978 and 1990 has been 185 per cent compared to a growth in total manufacturing IIT of 271 per cent. HQVIIT with the EU12 has grown over the same period by 200 per cent compared with IIT growth of 356 per cent. Finally HQVIIT with non-EU12 countries has grown by 166 per cent in line with the 164 per cent growth in overall manufacturing IIT with non-EU12. For reference the growth in total trade (exports plus imports) of Greece over the same period has been 60 per cent It thus appears that IIT of the EU with Greece has developed into the exchange of lower-quality products from Greece against higher quality products from the EU.

9.4   MANUFACTURING PRODUCTION AND TRADE 1978–87

The analysis of the previous sections utilized only trade data. Since the ultimate objective of our study is to assess the implications of trade performance for industrial adjustment, one needs to analyse production along with trade data. In order to do this, we need to have matching data for trade and other economic variables. As no official concordance between domestic production and trade data exists for Greece, the classification had to be done by the authors. A concordance was compiled between the Greek industrial classification and NACE, as well as the between NACE and the SITC, Rev. 2. This yielded a set of 64 manufacturing 'industries' aggregated at about the 3-digit level (the complete list of industries and correspondence with the NACE classification is presented in Sarris *et al.* (1994)). Some industries had to be omitted, as it was impossible to allocate them satisfactorily to a NACE category (these amounted to about 10 per cent of production). Production and employment data came from the census of industry in Greece (various years), which covers all establishments with 10 or more employees, while the trade data came from the OECD 5-digit statistics.

The calculations reported in Tables 9.1 to 9.3 were repeated for the new sample of industries, to see if the trends and results identified earlier were robust to a change in product classification. Table 9.4 shows various measures of adjustment and trade for all of the included industries for the years 1978, 1985, and 1987. Examining the trends in IIT, it can be noticed that the GL index is in the same range as found earlier. Comparing the GHME index between 1978 and 1987 for EU12

Table 9.4 Production and trade developments of Greek industry 1978–87
(All monetary values in 1978 million $)

	1978	1985	Change 1978–85 (%)	1987	Change 1985–87 (%)	Change 1978–87 (%)
Value of Production	9411	14119	50.0	13217	−6.4	40.5
Number of Workers ('000)	270	320	18.5	319	−0.2	18.3
Number of Establishments	3176	7576	138.5	7576	0.0	138.5
Value of Exports	2554	3198	25.2	3223	0.8	26.2
Value of Imports	5675	5698	0.4	6940	21.8	22.3
Exports to EU12	1285	1402	9.1	1985	41.6	54.5
Imports from EU12	3132	3822	22.0	4335	13.4	38.4
Av. Export Propensity[1]	0.169	0.161		0.160		
Av. Import Penetration[2]	0.453	0.343		0.410		
IIS Index	0.070	0.055		0.059		
A Index (rel. to 1978)		0.120		0.105		
Trade with the whole world						
GL	0.186	0.190		0.174		
GHME (relative to 1978)		162		285		
VIIT	686	1195	74.2	1236	3.4	80.2
HQVIIT	207	325	57.6	313	−3.8	51.6
LQVIIT	479	869	81.3	923	6.2	92.5
HIIT	799	495	−38.0	500	1.0	−37.4
Trade with EU12						
GL	0.117	0.122		0.139		
GHME (relative to 1978)		121		362		
VIIT	229	447	95.0	791	77.2	245.5
HQVIIT	88	133	51.2	195	47.0	122.2
LQVIIT	141	314	122.2	596	89.9	322.0
HIIT	267	134	−49.8	104	−22.3	−61.0
Trade with non-EU12						
GL	0.163	0.155		0.169		
GHME (relative to 1978)		−54.1		26.1		
VIIT	241	320	32.9	489	52.6	102.8
HQVIIT	95	148	54.7	210	42.4	120.3
LQVIIT	146	173	18.5	279	61.4	91.3
HIIT	353	246	−30.3	121	−50.9	−65.8

Source: Computed by authors from Greek census of industry and OECD data
[1] Export propensity is defined as the ratio of exports to total domestic supply, namely the sum of production and imports.
[2] Import penetration is defined as the ratio of imports to total apparent consumption, namely the sum of domestic production plus imports minus exports.

and non-EU12 trade, the same conclusion is reached, namely that IIT has grown much more in Greek trade with EU12 than with non-EU12 countries.

Between 1978 and 1985 production of all manufacturing industries increased by 50 per cent, the number of manufacturing establishments increased by 138.5 per cent, but manufacturing employment increased by only 18.5 per cent. It appears that the average size of manufacturing establishments decreased considerably both in terms of production and employment. This might, however, be due to the fact that small establishments, formerly not represented in the census, increased their employment above the threshold level of 10, and were hence included in the statistics for 1985.

Total manufacturing exports and imports appear to have grown at much slower rates than domestic production, with imports virtually unchanged between 1978 and 1985. This is due to a large extent to large declines in imports of the ship repair industry, an industry that is heavily dominated by the public sector. If this industry is excluded, imports would have grown by about 17 per cent which is still below the growth rate of production. Exports to EU12 grew much less than total exports, while imports from EU12 grew much more than total imports. This could very well be the consequence of the liberalization of Greek trade vis-à-vis the EU that took place after accession, as Greek exports to the EU were already largely liberalized before 1980 but EU exports to Greece were less so.

Turning to changes between 1985 and 1987, it should be noted that this period was characterized by a stabilization programme in Greece, implying a substantial decline in aggregate demand. One would, therefore, expect declines in production and imports. It can be seen from Table 9.4 that aggregate manufacturing production indeed declined between 1985 and 1987. However, employment and the number of establishments remained unchanged, which is due largely to the rigidities of the Greek labour market (Katseli, 1990). Exports remained stable between 1985 and 1987, but contrary to what one would expect, total imports increased substantially.

For the whole period 1978–87, total exports and imports have grown less than domestic production, but exports to and imports from the EU12 grew by as much as or more than production. These trends might be due to the product composition of Greek trade, which on the export side is concentrated on labour intensive and hence internationally very competitive sectors (for example textiles, shoes) while on the import side it is concentrated in technology and capital intensive goods. Labour intensive goods are relatively protected within the EU, and hence one would expect some trade reorientation of Greek exports toward the EU markets. Non-competing imports, however, were never subject to significant barriers, and hence imports from the EU would not be expected to increase by much, given that the EU has always been Greece's largest trade partner.

When the figures for HQVIIT and LQVIIT are examined the trends obtained are in line with the earlier discussion, namely that the amount of LQVIIT has grown much more than that of HQVIIT, and that the growth of LQVIIT seems to be much larger in trade with the EU12 than in trade with non-EU12 countries.

The overall conclusion of the above analysis is that the Greek industrial sector seems to be concentrating into a range of relatively low quality products within the EU. Furthermore, the low degree of HIIT, implies that Greek industry is bound to face a major adjustment and competitiveness problem in the course of further EU integration and internal market completion.

9.5 INDUSTRIAL ADJUSTMENT AND TRADE PERFORMANCE

Grouped analysis

The objective of this section is to examine the relation between trends in industrial employment and trade performance. To this end an accounting decomposition of post-accession employment changes in our 64 Greek manufacturing industries is first presented. Employment change between two periods can be broken into a part that is due to changes in domestic output, and a part due to changes in productivity. The output effect, in turn, can be subdivided into a part due to a change in domestic demand, and one due to a change in net exports. Finally the trade component can be broken into changes in exports and changes in imports.

Table 9.5 presents the accounting analysis of employment changes for all Greek manufacturing for the periods 1978–85, 1985–87, and the total interval 1978–87. Between 1978 and 1987 total manufacturing employment (in the 64 industries considered) increased by 49,500, or 18.3 per cent. Almost all of this increase was accomplished in the period 1978–85. However, there appear to be opposing influences on employment from the output and productivity developments. If

Table 9.5 Accounting analysis of manufacturing employment in Greece
1978–87 (all figures in '000 employees)

	1978–85		1985–87		1978–87	
Total Empl. Change	49.9	(50.5)	−0.4	(0.6)	49.5	(51.1)
Productivity Effect	−68.9	(−54.2)	−16.7	(−17.1)	−82.2	(−68.4)
Output Effect	118.7	(104.7)	16.3	(17.7)	131.6	(119.5)
Domestic Demand	31.8	(102.3)	29.6	(39.5)	54.4	(143.2)
Trade	86.9	(2.3)	−13.4	(−21.8)	77.2	(−23.7)
Exports	28.2	(28.4)	25.3	(25.6)	52.0	(52.5)
Imports	58.7	(−26.0)	−38.7	(−47.4)	25.2	(−76.2)

Note: Figures in parentheses exclude the industry involved in ship repairs.
Source: Computed by authors.

productivity had stayed the same over the period, manufacturing employment would have grown by much more, by 131,600 or 2.7 times
more than the actual total employment growth of 49,500. Productivity
changes by themselves appear to have led to a substantial downward
pressure on the number of manufacturing jobs, as they would have
entailed a loss of 82,200 jobs by 1987, *ceteris paribus*.

The output-induced manufacturing job expansion of 131,600 jobs
appears at first sight to be due to a larger extent to trade developments
than to domestic demand expansion. This, however, is the result of
changes in the ship repair industry. In 1987, this industry accounted
for a mere 1.1 per cent of total manufacturing sales and 4.5 per cent
of total industrial employment. However, it experienced substantial
import reduction over the period (this was the result of deliberate
government policy aimed at protecting the Greek shipyards), which
translates into a very large positive contribution to domestic employment, and swamps the effects of all other industries. If this industry is
excluded from the accounting analysis, as indicated by the figures inside parentheses, then trade appears to have contributed negatively to
changes in manufacturing employment (largely through increases in
imports), and it is mainly domestic demand that has maintained industrial employment.

Regression analysis

The accounting method does not allow for inferences concerning
causality or even correlation between employment changes and trade
performance. In particular, it assumes that productivity developments

are independent of trade developments. To avoid these problems regression analysis is employed. The question investigated is whether post EU-accession industrial employment changes in Greece are related to trade performance and trade structure. The underlying hypotheses are the following. First, it is hypothesized that sectors with strong export orientation should fare well within the EU, as far as employment is concerned, given that the liberalization of EU trade for Greek exports should increase exports to the EU. Second, the employment in sectors characterized by large initial import penetration should not be affected much after EU accession, as traditionally such sectors were already not very protected in Greece, and as the share of EU in Greek imports was already quite high. Third, sectors that exhibit significant MIIT, should display relatively stable employment levels, the reason being that increases in IIT are related to intra-sectoral labour adjustment and hence small labour flows across sectors. Fourth, sectors with good trade performance, namely exhibiting net export growth should be those with increasing employment. Fifth, increases in domestic demand should be positively associated with employment growth, and finally improvements in labour productivity should be negatively associated with employment growth.

The model employed relates changes in employment to several variables aimed at testing the hypotheses stated above. The first hypothesis is tested by including the average export propensity (EP) in the beginning and ending years as a proxy for export orientation (expected sign positive). The second hypothesis is tested by including the average import penetration (IP) in the beginning and ending years (expected sign negative or insignificant). The third hypothesis is tested by including the A index of MIIT (expected sign positive), while the fourth hypothesis is tested by including the B index of Brülhart (1994) (expected sign positive). It was found that these latter two indices were uncorrelated with each other and with the GHME index. The final class of variables involves those tracking domestic developments. The change in domestic apparent consumption (ΔD) is utilized to test the fifth hypothesis (expected sign positive), while the change in labour productivity (ΔPROD) is used for the final test (expected sign negative). Since it is not clear whether there is an influence of trade and domestic demand on productivity, equations both with and without the productivity variable were estimated.

In preliminary investigations it was found that the export propensity and import penetration variables were strongly correlated with the changes in domestic consumption, albeit uncorrelated between them.

It was also found that all the other regressors were uncorrelated. Hence the estimated regressions included either the change in domestic demand, or the export penetration and import propensity variables.

Table 9.6 illustrates the results of regressions of employment changes between 1978 and 1985, as well as between 1978 and 1987. All variables have the expected signs. The results suggest a significant influence of trade-related variables on employment changes, irrespective of whether productivity is included or not. They also suggest more robust relations in the regressions for 1978–85 changes than in those for 1978–87. This was expected for the reasons discussed earlier. From the regression for 1978–85, it appears that the coefficients of domestic demand, productivity, marginal IIT, and trade performance are all of

Table 9.6   OLS regression results for determinants of post-EU accession sectoral changes in Greek industrial employment

	Employment changes between 1978–1985			
Constant	0.057	0.028	0.060	0.048
A	0.340**	0.372**	0.458**	0.460***
B	0.128***	0.099**	0.010	0.010
ΔD	0.417***	0.305***		
ΔPROD	−0.296***		−0.082	
EP			0.350***	0.348***
IP			−0.057	−0.064
Corr. R^2	0.493	0.343	0.341	0.327
	Employment changes between 1978–87			
Constant	0.046	−0.034	−0.038	−0.041
A	0.246	0.359*	0.315	0.319
B	0.126*	0.070	−0.074	−0.075
ΔD	0.397***	0.340***		
ΔPROD	−0.264**			−0.009
EP			0.775***	0.774***
IP			−0.023	−0.023
Corr. R^2	0.446	0.397	0.222	0.222

Note: Dependent variables $\Delta L = 2(L_t - L_{to})/(L_t + L_{to})$. The ΔD and ΔPROD variables are defined as the absolute changes in consumption or productivity, divided by the average (beginning and end periods) consumption and productivity respectively. The EP and IP variables are defined as the simple averages of beginning and ending year EP and IP values.
* – significance at 10% level
** – significance at 5% level
*** – significance at 1% level

the expected sign and significant. When the change in domestic demand is excluded, it turns out that export propensity emerges as a very significant determinant, while productivity is insignificant. While in the accounting method it was seen that the exclusion of the shipbuilding industry affected the results considerably, there was no such difference found in the regression results. For the 1978–87 period the variables still exhibit the expected signs, but with lower statistical significance, and this is to be expected for the reasons discussed earlier (influence of the stabilization programme). The major pattern that emerges from both sets of regressions is that trade performance and structure are strongly correlated with employment growth. This implies that trade developments, which are expected to be significantly influenced by further EU integration, are bound to remain important for industrial employment in Greece.

9.6 SUMMARY AND CONCLUSIONS

It has been shown in this chapter that the bulk of Greek external trade is of the inter-industry type, despite significant increases in IIT over the last three decades. It was found furthermore that most of Greek IIT is vertically differentiated, and that, in the manufacturing sector, Greece tends to increasingly specialize toward inferior quality goods within the EU. This implies that adjustment pressures in the context of EU integration are likely to be significant for Greece, as trade seems to be governed mostly by 'traditional' factor proportion type of comparative advantage.

The accounting analysis of employment changes in the post EU accession period suggested that domestic demand changes and productivity effects had the most significant influence, with trade factors (especially increases in imports) making negative contributions. The regression analysis verified this initial finding with respect to demand and productivity influences, but revealed that trade performance both in terms of changes in IIT as well as in terms of net export performance are significant determinants of Greek industrial employment changes.

The analysis was based largely on data for the period before the onset of the EU internal market programme. The years 1988 to 1992 in Greece can be characterized as adjustment years, since considerable liberalization vis-à-vis the EU12 has taken place in view of Single Market programme. From some preliminary analysis (Sarris *et al.*, 1994) it appears that aggregate manufacturing production stagnated during the period, but with markedly different behaviour across groups of sectors. The sectors that were characterized by high intra-EU non-trade barriers, and are hence sensitive to the liberalization of the internal market programme, experienced increases in their output, while the sectors exhibiting low intra-EU12 non-trade barriers, and are hence less sensitive to the Single Market programme, experienced a large decline in the period 1988–90 and a sharp recovery afterwards, for an overall loss of production for the whole period. It thus appears that the low sensitivity sectors are much more volatile than the sensitive sectors, and that EU trade liberalization in the context of the Single Market programme has not hurt the sensitive sectors.

The results of this chapter raise some policy issues. On the one hand positive trade performance and positive changes in IIT appear to contribute to increasing employment in the manufacturing sectors. This implies that trade liberalization in the context of a more open EU, if it leads to export expansion and increasing intra-industry specialization, is likely to have a positive overall impact on employment. On the other hand, EU liberalization seems to be associated with the Greek manufacturing sector moving toward a lower quality product mix, something with obvious disadvantages, albeit indeterminate impact on growth. The detected specialization pattern is driven by market forces shaping the new economic geography of Europe, and it is not clear how and to what extent this trend can be influenced by policy. Further research is clearly required for a full understanding of these processes.

References and Further Reading

Abd-el-Rahman, K. (1991) 'Firms' Competitive and National Comparative Advantages as Joint Determinants of Trade Composition', *Weltwirtschaftliches Archiv*, 127(1).
Alexakis, P. and Xanthakis, M. (1992) 'Export Performance of Greek Manufacturing Companies. Export Subsidies and Other Factors', *Economia Internationale*, 45(2), May.
Brülhart, M. (1994) 'Marginal Intra-Industry Trade: Measurement and Relevance for the Pattern of Industrial Adjustment', *Weltwirtschaftliches Archiv*, 130, 600–13.
Giannitsis, A. (1988) 'Entry into the European Community and Effects on Industry and International Trade', *mimeo*, Athens: Centre for Mediterranean Studies.

Greenaway, D. and Hine, R.C. (1991) 'Intra-Industry Specialization, Trade Expansion and Adjustment in the European Economic Space', *Journal of Common Market Studies*, 24(6), December.

Greenaway, D., Hine, R.C. and Milner, C. (1994a) 'Country-Specific Factors and the Pattern of Horizontal and Vertical Intra-Industry Trade in the UK', *Weltwirtschaftliches Archiv*, 130, 78–100.

Greenaway, D., Hine, R.C., Milner, C. and Elliott, R. (1994b) 'Adjustment and the Measurement of Marginal Intra Industry Trade', *Weltwirtschaftliches Archiv*, 130, 418–27.

Grubel, H.G. and Lloyd, P. (1975) *Intra Industry Trade*, London, Macmillan.

Hine, R.C., Greenaway, D. and Milner, C. (1994), 'Changes in Trade and Changes in Employment: An Examination of the Evidence from UK Manufacturing Industry 1979–87', *mimeographed*, University of Nottingham.

Katseli, L.T. (1990) 'Economic Integration in the Enlarged European Community: Structural Adjustment of the Greek Economy', in Bliss, C. and de Macedo, J.B. (eds), *Unity with Diversity in the European Economy: The Community's Southern Frontier*, Cambridge: Cambridge University Press for the Centre for Economic Policy Research.

Katsos, G. and Spanakis, N.I. (1983) *Industrial Protection and Integration*, (monograph), Athens: Centre for Planning and Economic Research.

Mardas, D. (1992) 'The consequences of the Unified Market on Greek Export Trade. An Intra-Industry Analysis', Athens: Greek Centre for European Studies (EKEM), [in Greek].

Sarris, A.H. (1988) 'Greek Accession and EC Commercial Policy Toward the South', in Mennes, L.B.M. and Kol, J. (eds), *European Trade Policies and the Developing World*, London: Croom Helm.

Sarris, A.H., Papadimitriou, P. and Mavrogiannis, A. (1994), 'Manufacturing Trade, Specialisation and Adjustment of Greece in the Course of European Integration', *mimeographed*, Department of Economics, University of Athens.

10. Ireland

Marius Brülhart, Dermot McAleese and Mary O'Donnell

10.1 INTRODUCTION

A small open economy such as Ireland can serve as a useful case study for the assessment of trade effects. Over the last three decades, the combined value of Ireland's imports and exports has risen from around 60 per cent to over 105 per cent of GDP, a level now surpassed in the European Union (EU) only by Belgium-Luxembourg (Figure 10.1). This rapid expansion of trade took place against a background of an increasingly open trade regime. The milestones in Irish trade liberalization were the Anglo-Irish Free Trade Agreement of 1965, accession to GATT in 1967, membership of the EEC in 1973 and the ongoing implementation of the EU's '1992' Single Market programme.

Ireland also presents a particularly well suited case for the analysis of foreign direct investment (FDI). During the 1980's foreign direct investment increased sharply throughout the OECD rising over fivefold

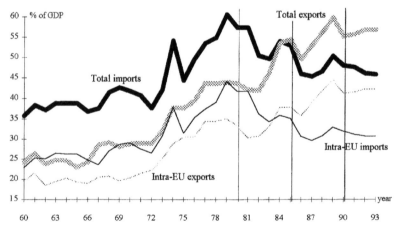

Figure 10.1   Irish merchandise trade 1960–93
Source: Commission of the European Communities (1993)

between 1982 and 1990. Ireland has benefited to an unusually high degree from this trend, which has continued in the 1990s (Thomsen and Woolcock, 1993). The importance of FDI to Ireland is evident from the large proportion of total gross output and employment in the manufacturing sector accounted for by foreign firms. In 1983, foreign firms accounted for 46 per cent of gross output and 38 per cent of employment. By 1990 this had risen to almost 55 per cent of output and 45 per cent of employment. While the economic effects of FDI in Ireland have been well documented, until now, there has been no full analysis of the contrasting trade patterns of foreign and domestic firms.

Much research has been devoted to exploring the pattern of industrial adjustment associated with Ireland's increasingly liberal trade environment. Until recently, measurement of intra-industry trade indices suggested that trade-induced adjustment in the Irish manufacturing sector had taken the form of restructuring *within* industries rather than *between* them. NESC (1989), however, found that the share of *intra*-industry trade (IIT) had ceased to rise in the late 1970s and that trade flows of an *inter*-industry nature were again becoming more important. This change in trade patterns was seen as significant for the Irish economy, because adjustment pressures associated with inter-industry trade are generally believed to be stronger than those associated with IIT. It was argued that Ireland could suffer stronger adverse effects from industrial relocation pressures following both the EU Single Market programme and the process leading towards Economic and Monetary Union, than it had experienced at the earlier stages of trade liberalization. Our objective is to provide a deeper examination of the validity of these arguments, through three main questions; first, how has IIT behaved over time? second, does IIT have higher adjustment costs than inter-industry trade? and third, does IIT differ for foreign and domestically owned firms?

This chapter is arranged as follows. First, there will be a brief assessment of Irish IIT trends over the period 1977–91 using standard Grubel-Lloyd measures. Patterns of marginal IIT (MIIT) during this time will also be reviewed. Second, moving beyond the analysis of pure trade flows, we study the link between trade patterns and changes in the structure of Irish industry. The common assumption that the higher the proportion of IIT, the less severe are the costs arising from trade-induced industrial restructuring, is examined. We also investigate the importance of trade patterns relative to other determinants of structural change. This was made possible by the availability of a data set combining Irish trade and production figures under the same classification (NACE), albeit at a relatively high level of aggregation (70 product groups).

Third, we examine the importance of foreign-owned industries. We recalculate MIIT and IIT indices separately for foreign-owned and domestic-owned sectors. Significant differences are found between the two sectors in terms of IIT activity over time. These findings are interesting and highly relevant to an analysis of the effect of FDI. Finally, Section 10.5 summarizes our findings and draws some general conclusions.

10.2   IRISH IIT 1977–91: GENERAL TRENDS

Figure 10.2 suggests that Irish IIT has tended to level out since 1977. We detect pronounced drops in IIT after 1977 and 1987. Thus, the steady growth of Irish IIT which has been observed since the 1950's (see McAleese 1976, 1979 and Chapter 5), appears to have come to a halt.

There is the possibility that the decline of Irish IIT growth in the manufacturing sectors could be attributed to rising trade balance surpluses (see Figure 10.1), biasing the GL indices downward. Our calculations of Aquino-adjusted GL indices,[1] however, suggest that aggregate trade imbalances do not explain the fluctuations of the un-adjusted GL measures. Figure 10.2 shows that the Aquino adjustment leaves the broad level and trend of observed IIT unchanged. The increasing trade surplus therefore does not explain the apparent levelling-off of Irish IIT.

Another possible reason for the calculated decline in IIT stems from the possibility that the increased number of product groups distinguished at the fifth digit of Irish trade statistics gave rise to this observation. Indeed, Figure 10.2 shows that the drops in Irish IIT after 1977 and 1987, coincided with the introduction of revised and more disaggregate SITC classifications. Irish IIT appears to have increased in the aftermath of both revisions, between 1978 and 1987, as well as between 1990 and 1991. However, these IIT increases were somewhat less steep after 1978 than during the 1960s and 1970s.[2] Furthermore, due to increasing product diversity and statistical precision, the number of product groups had also been growing fast prior to the 1980s, when GL indices had been *rising* rapidly.[3] Increasing statistical disaggregation did not halt the rise of Irish IIT in the 1960s and 1970s. While it may explain the IIT drops after 1977 and 1987, it thus might

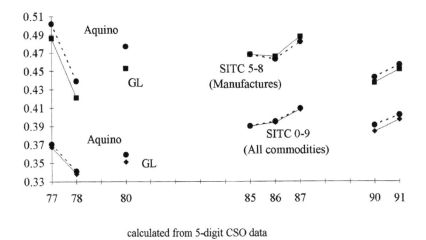

calculated from 5-digit CSO data

Figure 10.2 GL unadjusted and Aquino-adjusted indices for total trade

not be the only cause of the stagnation in IIT growth observed in the 1980s. It has been shown that widening the definition of an 'industry' from five-digit to three-digit product groups results in the same trend in IIT over time (Brülhart and McAleese, 1995).

One way of estimating the importance of inter-industry adjustment is through the calculation of MIIT indices. The first four columns of Table 10.1 report *A* indices of MIIT. We find that Irish MIIT was higher in the 1980s than in the 1960s. This pattern holds for both intra-EU and non-EU trade, and for manufactured as well as for other products. While the comparison of static IIT measures points to a recent slowdown in IIT growth (Figure 10.2), MIIT indices tell a seemingly different story, namely that trade changes were more intra-industry in nature in the 1980s than in the 1960s.

This finding is particularly striking if we consider that our MIIT data set for the 1960s distinguished only 400 product groups (238 of which are in SITC 5 to 8), while the data for the 1980s are disaggregated into 1755 sectors (1339 of which are in SITC 5 to 8). In order to compare like with like, we have also calculated 1978–87 MIIT SITC 5 to 8 from less disaggregated figures, namely at the four and three-digit levels. These results are shown in Table 10.2. It appears even more clearly through these results that MIIT was considerably higher in the 1980s than in the 1960s.

The intuitive explanation of the seemingly conflicting MIIT and IIT results is relatively straightforward. The low initial levels of Irish IIT in

Table 10.1 Vertical and marginal IIT 1978-87, by SITC sections[a]

| SITC section | Description | MIIT[b] | | | | Horizontal and Vertical IIT[c] | | | | | |
| | | 1961–67 | | 1978–87 | | 1978 | | | 1978 | | |
		EU	non-EU	EU	non-EU	IIT	VIIT	HI-Q (%)	IIT	VIIT	HI-Q (%)
0	Food, live animals	0.14	0.05	0.23	0.03	0.19	0.16	36.1	0.22	0.18	41.1
1	Drink, tobacco	0.02	0.03	0.27	0.01	0.31	0.27	78.6	0.35	0.31	82.2
2	Raw materials	0.09	0.22	0.08	0.05	0.15	0.12	70.0	0.16	0.14	58.0
3	Mineral fuels	0.11	0.00	0.02	0.02	0.03	0.03	29.6	0.15	0.15	20.9
4	Animal/veg. oils	0.00	0.04	0.14	0.01	0.25	0.21	60.3	0.14	0.12	26.6
5	Chemicals	0.29	0.26	0.33	0.18	0.42	0.24	61.3	0.43	0.36	33.6
6	Manufactures, class. by materials	0.26	0.13	0.21	0.14	0.43	0.35	72.1	0.41	0.36	66.7
7	Machinery, transport equipment	0.11	0.22	0.24	0.38	0.35	0.29	74.0	0.53	0.25	67.8
8	Miscellaneous manufactures	0.55	0.40	0.29	0.33	0.55	0.45	40.0	0.50	0.44	47.7
9	Commodit. n.e.s.	0.17	0.69	0.44	0.08	0.57	0.57	100.0	0.49	0.49	99.8
0–9	All products	0.19	0.20	0.24	0.23	0.34	0.27	62.6	0.41	0.29	56.6
5–8	Manufactures	0.24	0.23	0.25	0.25	0.42	0.29	63.7	0.46	0.32	56.0

[a] calculated fom 5-digit OECD data.

[b] A-indices weighted by sectoral trade changes (Brülhart (1994)).

[c] IIT = unadjusted GL indices; VIIT $= (\sum_i \{2^* \min X_i, M_i\})/(\sum_{i,j}\{X_{i,j} + M_{i,j}\})$, where $UV_i < 0.85$ or $UV_i > 1.15$, and $0.85 \leq UV_j \leq 1.15$; HI-Q $= 100^* (\sum_k \{2^* \min X_k, Y_k\})/(\sum_i \{2^* \min X_i, Y_i\})$, where $UV_k > 1.15$, and $0.85 > UV_i > 1.15$; for total Irish trade.

Table 10.2 MIIT and statistical aggregation

Time Period	Level of aggregation	No. of industries	EU	Non-EU
1978–87	3-digit	151	0.31	0.50
1978–87	4-digit	528	0.27	0.36
1978–87	5-digit	1339	0.25	0.25
1961–67	4-digit	238	0.24	0.23

the 1960s facilitated a rise in IIT even though the expansion of trade was very imbalanced at a sectoral level. In the 1978–87 period, initial IIT was considerably higher, so that trade expansion brought about a relatively smaller rise in IIT, even though the trade change was less sectorally imbalanced than in the 1960s.

These findings emphasize the need for careful interpretation of the detected IIT stagnation for industrial adjustment in Ireland. Further evidence can be drawn from our NACE data set, which underlies the calculations reported in the next section. The average A index calculated for the 70 industries in the sample is 0.48 for the 1980–90 period. Interestingly, it was lower in the first half of the decade, at 0.31 for 1980–85, than in the second half, at 0.41 for 1985–90. This further cautions us against interpreting the stagnation of IIT as a sign of re-emerging pressures for inter-industry adjustment.

Table 10.1 also reports some patterns of Irish VIIT. Looking at the average proportion of VIIT relative to IIT, we find that more than two thirds of total Irish IIT was vertical, both in 1978 and 1987. The proportion of VIIT relative to IIT is relatively stable across SITC sections and over the two sample years. The columns 'HI-Q' show that more than half of Irish VIIT in our sample years took the form of high-valued Irish exports. This share of high-value VIIT in total VIIT diminished slightly between 1978 and 1987. VIIT may be influenced heavily by the well-documented phenomenon of transfer pricing by MNEs (Ruane and McGibney, 1991). Thus, the VIIT evidence may be taken as another pointer to the importance of the foreign sector in Irish industry and trade.

10.3 INDUSTRIAL ADJUSTMENT AND TRADE PATTERNS 1980–90

Changing trade patterns are of interest mainly because of their effects on a country's production structure. In 1990, the combined value of

world-wide industrial imports and exports amounted to 125.4 per cent
of Irish manufacturing output. Intra-EU exchanges dominate Irish
trade. Of total Irish manufactures trade in 1990, 72.9 per cent flowed
to and from fellow EU Member States. Between 1980 and 1990, Irish
intra-EU trade in manufactures has grown by 66.4 per cent in real
terms and domestic production increased by 54.4 per cent. Yet, in the
same period, industrial employment fell by 13.6 per cent. Without
further examination, these figures indicate a high and growing trade
dependency of Irish industry, strongly geared towards the European
Union. At a first glance, they also suggest a trade-induced rationalization process, yielding considerable productivity gains at the expense
of employment growth. These suppositions are investigated in this
section.

The importance of trade for employment change: accounting method

A widely used empirical technique to assess the impact of changes in
trade flows on changes in employment is the accounting method.[4] The
basis for this method is the identity

$$E_{it} \equiv \frac{O_{it}}{P_{it}} \equiv \frac{1}{P_{it}}(C_{it} + X_{it} - M_{it}), \qquad \ldots (10.1)$$

where E_{it} is employment in the ith industry in year t, O is output, P is
labour productivity, C is domestic consumption, X represents exports
and M stands for imports. From this static identity, the following relationship between *changes* in employment and production variables
can be derived, applying the weights suggested by Hine *et al.* (1994).

$$\Delta E_i \equiv \underbrace{\frac{2}{(P_{it} + P_{i(t+n)})}}_{a}(\underbrace{\Delta C_i}_{b} + \underbrace{\Delta X_i}_{c} - \underbrace{\Delta M_i}_{d}) - \underbrace{\frac{\Delta P_i(E_{it} + E_{i(t+n)})}{(P_{it} + P_{i(t+n)})}}_{e},$$

$$\ldots (10.2)$$

where terms *a* to *d* determine the effect of output changes on employment, and *e* defines the productivity component in the explanation
of employment change. The output effect is decomposed into the
contribution of three parameters: changes in domestic consumption
(*b*), changes in exports (*c*) and changes in imports (*d*).

   Table 10.3 reports the results of the accounting analysis conducted
on our NACE data set for the 1980s. Over the whole decade, Irish
manufacturing employment shrank by 31,000, which represents a

Table 10.3 Sources of change in industrial employment, 1980–90
(thousand persons)

Sources of employment change	Time periods		
	1980–90	*1980–85*	*1985–90*
Total change	−31	−37	6
Productivity effect	−94	−55	−39
Output effect	63	18	45
Dom. consumption	41	−4	45
Trade	22	22	0
Imports	−32	4	−36
Exports	54	18	36

decline of 13.6 per cent from the initial level. Our analysis suggests that this decline was caused by increases in productivity which far surpassed the increases in demand. Had productivity remained unchanged and demand increased as it did between 1980 and 1990, then employment would have grown by 67,000.[5]

We have conducted this analysis mainly to isolate the employment effect of external trade flows. The demand pull created by the improved trade performance of the 1980s obviously contributed positively to employment growth. One third of the output effect was created by the improvement in the trade balance. Figure 10.1 shows that most of the relative export growth occurred in the first half of the decade. This is reflected in Table 10.3, which shows that, between 1980 and 1985, the improved trade balance was the only positive determinant of employment growth. Trade gains were outweighed, however, by a slump in domestic consumption and considerable productivity increases, so that a huge net loss of manufacturing jobs occurred despite the successful external performance. A reversal of fortunes occurred in the second half of the decade: the external trading position had stabilized, thus not contributing to net employment creation, while domestic demand increased markedly and productivity growth slowed down. These factors led to a small net increase in industrial employment between 1985 and 1990.

Judging by these results, the net employment effect can be easily offset by changes in domestic factors. While trade was buoyant, domestic factors still led to a considerable net loss of manufacturing jobs, and when a gain in net employment did occur, trade did not account for any of it.

Not too much, however, should be read into results obtained by the accounting method. This technique is of limited usefulness, since the productivity effect is assumed to be independent from the other variables.[6] It does not seem realistic to assume away any causal connection between trade performance and productivity gains. Table 10.2 shows that the productivity effect was the most important source of change in net employment. Interestingly, the greatest gains in productivity appear to have coincided with the most marked improvement in Ireland's external trading position. Thus, it cannot be ruled out that improved trade performance was intricately linked with productivity gains and produced only a small positive or even a negative net effect on the level of industrial employment in Ireland.

Structure of trade and industrial adjustment: correlation analysis

Correlation analysis provides another method of investigating the relationship between trade patterns and industrial performance. The impact of two aspects of trading patterns are investigated. First we look at the indicators of trade *performance*, namely percentage changes in exports and imports and the Brülhart (1994) *B* index, which captures the net change in sectoral trade balances.

Then, we study the relevance for industrial adjustment of various indicators of trade *structure*. We test whether the IIT index, both in its static form and in first differences, is negatively related to adjustment pressures (defined as net changes in output or employment), as is often assumed. This same exercise is then carried out with measures of MIIT (see Chapter 3).

We have calculated correlation coefficients between, on one hand, these various indicators of trading patterns (trade-related variables) and, on the other hand, two measures of change in industrial structure, namely output and employment changes (production-related variables). These results are reported in Table 10.4.

The first row of results in Table 10.4 shows that, as expected, increases in exports tended to be accompanied by increases in employment and output. Somewhat more surprising are the coefficients in the second row. Changes in imports also relate positively to employment and output changes, though to a somewhat lesser extent. This result might reflect the high proportion of intermediate goods in Irish imports, destined to a major part for the many subsidiaries of multinational firms located in Ireland.

Table 10.4 Changes in intra-EU manufactures trade and industrial
performance, 1980–90
Correlation Coefficients, all Sectors

Trade-related variables	Production-related variables					
	Employment change[a]			Output change[a]		
	1980–90	1980–85	1985–90	1980–90	1980–85	1985–90
Trade performance						
Δ Exports	0.32***	0.25**	0.25**	0.50***	0.47***	0.23*
Δ Imports	0.17	0.24**	0.14	0.43***	0.46***	0.29**
B index	0.31***	0.11	−0.03	0.30***	0.00	−0.08
Trade structure						
GL (base year)	0.13	0.07	0.28**	0.12	0.07	0.28**
GL (end year)	0.12	0.10	0.39***	0.08	0.04	0.36***
Δ GL	−0.03	0.04	0.09	−0.05	−0.04	0.05
A index	0.19	0.06	0.38***	0.25**	0.21*	0.36***
C measure	0.33***	0.23*	0.28**	0.58***	0.46***	0.29***
GHME measure	0.38***	0.36***	0.28**	0.58***	0.53***	0.31***

[a] Employment change = $\Delta E = (\{E_{1990} - E_{(1990-n)}\}/\{[E_{1990} + E_{(1990-n)}]*0.5\})*$ 100, likewise for production change.
Statistical significance (*t* tests): 0.01:***, 0.2: **, 0.1:* (70 observations).

Looking at trade performance measured by *B* indices, we find that the coefficients for the whole 1980–90 period are positive and significant, in line with *a priori* expectations. However, no significant correlation appears for the sub-periods 1980–85 and 1985–90 which is surprising. Interestingly, the reverse pattern emerges for the indices of trade structure. Over the whole period, GL and *A* indices display a relatively weak association with employment and output growth, but for 1985–90, this relationship is positive and significant throughout.[7] It thus appears that, taken over the whole decade, employment and output changes were more closely related to trade *performance*, while for the sub-period 1985–90, it was trade *structure* which showed a closer link with changes in the underlying production activities. We tentatively interpret this result as an indication that employment and output growth are more closely related to trade *performance* in the long term than in the short term, due to considerable year-to-year volatility in sectoral trade balances. Close inspection of the data suggests that the high correlations between industrial growth and (M)IIT in the 1985–90 period are a result of the exceptional rise in that era of 'hi-tech' industry grown largely out of an unprecedented influx of direct foreign investment.

The strongest correlations of all appear in the last two rows of Table 10.4. MIIT measured in values rather than percentages appears to be very closely associated with industry performance. This result, however, is difficult to interpret. Value measures of MIIT contain two dimensions. On one hand, they report matched trade, and on the other hand, they are strongly related to total sectoral trade expansion or contraction. Therefore, they are determined both by changes which affect countries asymmetrically (the forces underlying international specialization) and by changes that affect industries symmetrically in all countries (global demand or technology changes).[8]

While this correlation analysis shows that trade performance and MIIT are related to the performance of Irish industry, the calculated coefficients all lie well below unity. Obviously, such a univariate exercise cannot determine the importance of changing trade patterns for the structure of Irish industry relative to other determinants. Indeed, our analysis has confirmed the finding of our accounting exercise that trade flows are by no means the only determinant of Irish industrial structure, in spite of Ireland's high trade orientation. Other factors such as changes in demand, technology and industrial policy are also important shaping forces of adjustment.

Sectoral trade performance and industrial specialization: grouped analysis

Correlation analysis suggests that both the sectoral trade *performance* and sectoral trade *structure* were related to industrial growth in the 1980s. It appears that, at least in the long term, trade performance is positively related to employment and output growth. There was also some evidence of a positive link between MIIT and industrial performance, mainly for the 1985–90 period. We now investigate these links further, conducting a grouped analysis based on the values of the *B* index. We have allocated our 70 industries to four categories, as defined in Table 10.5. Average changes in employment, output and aggregate trade values were calculated for each category. The results of these calculations, reported in Table 10.5, allow a separate analysis of sectors with high and with low MIIT.

First, however, we ignore the level of MIIT and concentrate on trade performance. Thus, we distinguish between specialization *into* a sector (Categories III and IV) and *out of* a sector (Categories I and II).

We have calculated the ratio of the number of industries with positive
Bs relative to the number of industries with negative Bs using various
different weights.[9] The unweighted ratio of industries with positive Bs
to industries with negative Bs is 1.19 (38 positive and 32 negative
NACE Groups). Weighting NACE Groups according to 1980 *trade
volumes*, we obtain a ratio of 1.50; weighting according to 1980 levels
of *production*, the ratio is 1.31; but weighting according to 1980 levels
of *employment*, it stands at 0.99. This result indicates that the change
in Irish trading patterns mostly worked to the economy's advantage in
terms of pure trade performance and production, but not in terms of
employment. The sectors which improved their trade performance
were the ones which were already highly trade-oriented and productive
in 1985, whereas the trade performance of sectors with above-average
employment levels generally worsened. Ireland seems to be specializing
out of low-productivity labour-intensive industries and *into* highly
productive and less labour-intensive sectors.

This development is mirrored by the average changes in industry
variables for each category, reported in columns [E] to [G] of Table
10.6. As expected, increases in employment and production are greater
in the sectors which Ireland specialized *into* (Categories III and IV)
than in the industries which Ireland was specialized *out of*.[10] This result
is in line with the positive correlation between the B index and industrial performance, found in Table 10.4. However, the distinction
between high and low MIIT also seems to be significant. In terms of
net job creation, industries of Category II, whose sectoral trade balances deteriorated while displaying a high level of MIIT, performed
better than the sectors contained in Category IV, which had experienced pronounced improvements in their sectoral balances. These results confirm our inferences from the correlation analysis, namely that
both the distinction between sectors with improved or deteriorated
trade *performance* and the distinction between (marginal) intra- and
inter-industry trade are relevant for industrial adjustment and specialization in Ireland.[11]

Table 10.5 Industry categories according to MIIT patterns

Categories	Definition	MIIT	Specialization
I	$B < -0.5$	low	out
II	$-0.5 \leq B < 0$	high	out
III	$0 \leq B \leq 0.5$	high	in
IV	$B > 0.5$	low	in

Table 10.6   Industrial specialization in Ireland 1980–90, by MIIT categories

Category [A] No. of Industries	[B] Empl. 1980	[C] Output 1980 (IR£ bn)	[D] Intra-EU Trade 80 (IR£ bn)	[E] Average Δ Empl.[a] (%)	[F] Average Δ Outp.[a] (%)	[G] Average Δ Trade[a] (%)
I	21	61,100	2.37	1.81	−35.8	3.6	6.4
II	11	53,405	1.00	0.83	3.6	12.5	70.2
III	15	50,574	1.47	1.01	7.8	116.2	126.3
IV	23	63,191	2.96	2.96	−11.7	66.9	81.8
Total	70	228,270	7.80	6.61	−13.6[b]	54.4[b]	66.4[b]

[a] real changes in percentage of 1980 values, weighted averages.
[b] weighted averages.

In order to illustrate the findings relating to Irish manufacturing as a whole, we outline the changes that have occurred in a selected set of industries. Table 10.7 lists some examples of sectors that showed pronounced changes in their trading performances. The first seven industries are sectors that expanded their exports relative to competing imports, hence showing high levels of the *B* index. The bottom half of the table lists some industries at the opposite end of the performance scale, Ireland's relative trading position with the EU having markedly deteriorated in these sectors.

This presentation serves to illustrate the broader-based findings reported above. In Table 10.7, the industries with strong trading performance all show high productivity levels relative to the sectors with negative performance. Highly labour-intensive industries thus seem to have lost international competitiveness, while Ireland was specializing into more capital-intensive activities.

In conclusion, the 1980s were a time of considerable *inter*-industry adjustment for Irish manufacturing. During the first half of the decade, characterized by weak domestic demand, the marked improvement in trade performance did not prevent a sharp decline in industrial employment. In contrast, the 1985–90 period was characterized by strong growth of domestic consumption and a modest gain in industrial employment, while the trade surplus kept expanding, even though at a slower rate. Industries with above-average trade performance generally performed better in terms of output and employment. The latter link, however, was relatively weak, since Ireland specialized *out* of labour-intensive sectors *into* activities characterized by high and growing productivity levels.

Table 10.7 Some industries showing pronounced patterns of adjustment, 1980–90

NACE	Description	E^1 1990	O/E^1 1990 (£ 1980)	X/O^1 1990 (%)	ΔE^1 1980–90 (%)	ΔM^1 1980–90 (%)	ΔX^1 1980–90 (%)	B index
Industries with improved trade balance								
413	Milk and dairy products	7,640	161,805	18.4	−24.8	67.4	34.6	0.70
330	Office, data process, machines	7,423	137,080	96.6	59.5	303.2	517.7	0.68
257	Pharmaceuticals	6,220	141,378	22.6	107.5	89.6	316.8	0.46
345	Radio/TV/sound equipment	3,625	137,080	66.0	41.0	252.1	991.5	0.47
417/8/23	Misc. processed foodstuffs	2,540	214,311	43.1	34.0	55.4	489.0	0.74
424	Spirit distilling, compounding	547	254,590	50.6	6.6	18.1	217.4	0.89
Industries with deteriorated trade balance								
453/4	Clothing	10,944	14,758	38.7	−23.2	30.8	23.1	−0.48
419	Bread, biscuits, pastry	5,445	23,635	7.0	−39.8	59.1	39.1	−0.70
471	Wood pulp, paper	3,409	50,446	30.4	−29.8	77.3	71.2	−0.51
351–3	Motor vehicles, parts	3,082	27,327	46.9	−54.1	4.7	−43.5	−1.00
463	Carpentry, joinery	1,959	25,912	7.0	−20.8	40.5	8.4	−0.80
451	Footwear	736	18,626	58.1	−77.4	13.2	−29.6	−1.00

All trade figures relate to intra-EU trade.
[1] E: Employment; O: Output (1980 prices); M: Imports; X: Exports.

10.4   TRADE STRUCTURE AND FOREIGN-OWNED INDUSTRY

The importance of the foreign-owned sector to the Irish economy and the extent of foreign direct investment in Ireland have been well documented (McAleese and Foley, 1991, O'Sullivan 1995). Foreign-owned companies provided over 32 per cent of total industrial employment in 1973, and 44 per cent of the total in 1994. McAleese and Hayes (1995) pointed out that, on average, foreign-owned firms export 86 per cent of their production compared with 33 per cent in the case of indigenous firms.

In a comprehensive cross-country econometric analysis of IIT determinants, Hummels and Levinsohn (1995) noted that 'Ireland, given its small size, has an especially large amount of intra-industry trade. This may be because of Irelands tax policies with respect to multinational corporations'. This link between the foreign-owned sector of the Irish economy, or the presence of MNEs, and the general level of IIT activity in Ireland merits further attention. A logical starting point for such an analysis is to examine the extent to which the behaviour of foreign and domestic firms differ with regard to IIT; that is, to look at IIT and MIIT indices separately for predominantly foreign-owned and predominantly domestic firms. Such an exercise serves to establish what the impact of the foreign owned sector has been on Irish industrial specialization and trade patterns. The separate domestic and foreign MIIT measures might also indicate whether there has been a difference in adjustment patterns between the two sectors.

As a first step we calculated the percentage foreign/domestic ownership in terms of employment for the years 1980, 1985 and 1990 for each of the seventy industries in our NACE data set. Each industry was assigned to one of three categories: (a) over 60 per cent foreign owned, (b) between 30 and 60 per cent foreign owned, and (c) less than 30 per cent foreign owned. This initially revealed some interesting points in relation to ownership. *First*, the percentage of foreign ownership in each of the industries has remained broadly stable during the 1980s. That is, those industries that were domestically (foreign) owned in 1980, were also likely to be domestically (foreign) owned in 1990. *Second*, the types of industries which were predominantly foreign owned were 'high-tech' industries such as electronics, engineering and chemicals. For example, over the period 1983–90, office and data processing machinery was 95 per cent foreign owned, instrument engineering, 95 per cent and pharmaceticals 85 per cent. On the other hand, 'low-tech' industries (some of which are in long-term decline), such as the clothing and footwear (29 per cent) timber (9 per cent) and dairy products (9 per cent), were largely domestically owned. Food sectors such as food processing (38 per cent) and sugar refining (55 per cent) formed the bulk of industries in the intermediate category.

To establish whether domestic and foreign firms displayed significantly different levels of IIT and MIIT, average IIT and MIIT levels were calculated for each of the categories (a) to (c) referred to above. Figure 10.3 shows the average level of IIT by category. It is evident that the level of IIT was higher for foreign than for domestic firms. While IIT in the largely domestic owned firms increased overall from 1980 to 1990, it remained low relative to the other two categories. However, the differences in IIT means across our three industry categories are statistically significant only for 1980 (ANOVA, 1 per cent). Some convergence of IIT levels in the three categories thus appears to have taken place in the 1980s.

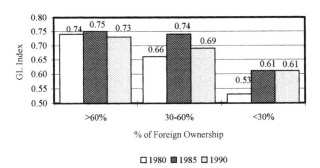

Figure 10.3   Average IIT levels (GL index)

An interesting configuration is revealed by MIIT results. Figure 10.4 shows that for the 1980–90 period, there was little difference in overall levels of MIIT between the three categories. That is, trade induced inter-industry adjustment pressures might have been no stronger in domestic firms than in foreign firms. Looking at the two sub-periods, 1980–85 and 1985–90, we find a marked difference in average MIIT levels between the three categories. Domestic dominated industries displayed significantly lower MIIT than the other two groups in the first sub-period. However, it the 1985–90 period, domestic dominated industries display similar MIIT levels compared to the other sectors. Analysis of variance on MIIT levels between the domestic and foreign dominated industries corroborates the significance of these results. As Table 10.8 shows, while they did differ significantly in 1980–85, there was no significant difference between the two sectors in the 1985–90 period.

Table 10.8   Analysis of variance

A Index 1980–85	SS	DF	MS	F
Between Groups	1.206	2	0.603	6.76*
Within Groups	5.713	64	0.089	
Total	6.919	66		

A Index 1985–90	SS	DF	MS	F
Between Groups	0.016	2	0.008	0.06
Within Groups	8.304	64	0.130	
Total	8.320	66		

* Significant at 1% level

A second exercise involved calculating rank correlations between, on the one hand, the GL index of IIT as well as for the *A* and *B* indices of MIIT, and, on the other hand, the degree of foreign ownership of industries. This was done to test whether the results of our grouped analysis hinged on the delineation of the three categories. Industries were ranked in terms of highest level of IIT/MIIT activity. These same industries were then ranked in terms of the level of domestic ownership (by employment).[12] The rank correlation coefficient allows us to establish where there is a significant relationship between the two sets of rankings, that is if those industries which had high levels of IIT, MIIT, tended to be foreign owned. These results are set out in Table 10.9 and confirm the general patterns indicated by Figures 10.3 and 10.4.

All relationships exhibit a positive rank correlation, with the exception of that for the *B* index for 1980–85. For the GL index, the results indicate that those industries which engaged in high levels of IIT were predominantly foreign owned. This is consistent with Figure 10.3. In relation to MIIT, for the period 1980–85, there is a significant relationship between average IIT levels as indicated by the *A* index and foreign ownership, that is that during this time, high MIIT levels were associated, again, with foreign firms. In the subsequent period however, there is no significant relationship between MIIT and foreign

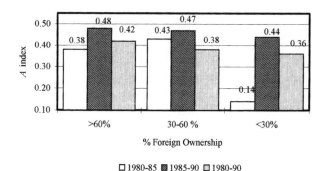

Figure 10.4 Average IIT levels (*A* Index)

ownership, which conforms with our finding based on grouped analysis (Figure 10.4). The *B* correlations suggest that domestic industries performed just as well as foreign-owned firms between 1980–85, but relatively badly in the latter period, 1985–90.

Close inspection of the data shows that the dominant change in trading patterns of domestic-dominated sectors occurred on the *import* side. On average, domestic-dominated industries expanded the real value of their *exports* throughout our sample period, even though at a lower rate than the foreign-dominated industries. Average imports of the domestic-dominated industries, however, fell in real terms between

Table 10.9 Rank correlations between (M)IIT and the degree of foreign ownership

		Industries ranked by percentage of foreign ownership			
IIT Indices	*Year*	*1983*	*1985*	*1990*	*Avg. 1983–90*
GL	1980	0.44**			
	1985		0.32*		
	1990			0.26	
	Avg. 1980–90				0.40*
MIIT-*A*	1980–85		0.35*		0.35*
	1985–90			0.12	0.10
	1980–90				0.13
MIIT-*B*	1980–85		0.00		−0.02
	1985–90			0.36*	0.31*
	1980–90				0.22

$n = 66$: Using a *t*-test, those variables significant at 1% are denoted by **, and those significant at 5% are denoted by *.

1980 and 1985, but surged thereafter. These trade changes led to a rise of IIT, and low MIIT, in domestic industries between 1980 and 1985, as sectoral trade deficits narrowed due to the fall in imports. The strong rise in imports in domestic-dominated industries between 1985 and 1990 resulted in higher MIIT and underlies the negative correlation between an industry's degree of foreign ownership and its trade performance in terms of the *B* index.

In conclusion, we find that the highest IIT levels are apparent in those industries with important multinational presence in Ireland. It is plausible to assume that much of this IIT is re-export trade of similar goods at different processing stages. However, it appears that IIT levels in domestic-dominated industries have converged in the 1980s to IIT levels in the foreign-dominated sectors. At first sight, this might be interpreted as an indication that the trade performance of domestic-owned industry has improved. It appears more likely, though, that this convergence was created by a temporary fall of imports in those industries during the early 1980s, when domestic demand was subdued. Imports in domestic-dominated industries are more likely to be competing with Irish-produced goods than imports in foreign-owned industries, which are largely intermediate inputs and, therefore, complementary to exported products. For this reason, the surge in imports of goods in domestic-dominated industries in the late 1980s, when domestic demand was buoyant, is indicative of a relative weakness of domestic-owned firms to benefit from an upswing in the business cycle. In time, it will be revealing to extend this analysis to the 1990s, in order to ascertain whether the trade performance of domestic firms continued to be relatively weaker than that of foreign subsidiaries under conditions of extraordinary growth in domestic demand and sustained export opportunities.

10.5   SUMMARY AND CONCLUSIONS

This study confirms the considerable involvement of the Irish economy in intra-industry trade (IIT), detected in several previous studies. The relevance of this phenomenon is highlighted by the fact that, even at the five-digit level of the SITC classification, where over 3,000 product groups were distinguished, it was found that, in 1990, 38 per cent of total Irish trade and 44 per cent of trade in manufactured goods was characterized by simultaneous imports and exports of products within the same group.

In addressing the question of how IIT has behaved over time, we found that in line with recently discovered patterns both in Ireland and in other industrialized countries, a stagnation in the growth of IIT was detected for the 1980s. The halt in the rise of IIT particularly affected Irish intra-EU trade. Part of this levelling-off can be attributed to the introduction of more detailed product classifications. Indices of marginal intra-industry trade (MIIT) also indicate that incremental trade flows were predominantly *inter*-industry in character. However, the share of MIIT appears to have been increasing in the 1980s. This warrants a cautious interpretation of IIT developments over time.

In order to investigate whether IIT has had higher adjustment costs that inter-industry trade, a second, less disaggregated data set was employed. The results obtained through the application of various analytical methods together provide a broadly consistent picture of the Irish adjustment experience.

There is a strong link between structural change and sectoral trading patterns. This comes as no surprise, considering the high trade orientation of the Irish economy, geared predominantly towards the EU market. However, it is also found that domestic demand swings are a crucial determinant of industrial growth at the sectoral level. Results obtained by the accounting method suggest that changes in domestic consumption were a somewhat more important determinant of employment growth in Irish manufacturing than changes in the pattern of Irish intra-EU trade.

In investigating the impact of trading patterns in detail, two components of trade flows are distinguished: trade performance, relating to the shifts in Ireland's sectoral trade balances with the EU, and trade structure, which takes into account the proportion of matched import and export changes within each sector (MIIT). It is found that the decline in industrial employment was lower in sectors achieving a strong trade performance during the 1980s, even though these sectors also tended to display the strongest rises in labour productivity. It also appears that sectors characterized by high levels of MIIT performed relatively better in terms of job creation and output growth. The latter somewhat surprising phenomenon is presumably explained by a high involvement of the dynamic foreign-owned sector in the processing and re-export of imported products, and by the fact that MIIT tends to be higher in booming industries, where Irish demand for foreign products increases as well as foreign demand for the Irish-produced varieties. MIIT is thus strongly associated with changes in domestic consumption.

Furthermore, our analysis suggests that Ireland specialized *into* highly trade-oriented and highly productive sectors and *out of* relatively labour-intensive industries during the 1980s. Thus, sectoral employment gains remained far below increases in exports and production, and a net loss in industrial jobs resulted for the 1980–90 period in spite of a sharp improvement of Irish trading performance.

IIT and MIIT levels were then calculated separately for foreign-owned and domestic-owned industries. Given the increasingly important presence of multinational firms in Irish manufacturing, average IIT and MIIT coefficients were calculated separately for three industry categories, defined in terms of the proportion of foreign-owned firms. We found that IIT is generally higher in foreign-dominated industries, but that IIT levels of domestic-dominated sectors increased markedly in the 1980s. The high involvement in IIT by foreign-owned firms is likely to reflect mainly intra-firm re-export trade. Growing IIT in the domestic-dominated industries, however, can be traced mainly to a fall in competing imports in the early 1980s and a resulting narrowing of sectoral trade deficits in that category. The fact that imports in domestic-dominated industries surged in the late 1980s (both in absolute terms and relative to Irish exports) suggests that Irish firms were relatively less successful at exploiting the buoyant demand conditions in that period than exporters in other EU countries.

The entire study of the trade-adjustment link is based on a relatively aggregated data set distinguishing only 70 industrial sectors. This constraint is imposed by the quality of statistical information on Irish industry structure. The inclusion of further time periods might provide a useful test of the robustness of our findings. Further research might fruitfully be conducted on the determinants of productivity changes in Irish manufacturing.

Notes

1. The adjustment to the GL index suggested by Aquino is designed to counteract the impact of overall trade imbalance on the measurement of IIT (see Kol and Mennes (1989)).
2. See Chapter 5.
3. The number of product categories at the five-digit level has increased from 419 in 1961, to 1166 in 1977, to 3023 in 1990.
4. The method has been applied by Wood (1994).

5. This, of course, is an unrealistic scenario, since productivity-growth undoubtedly boosted the amount of output sold by permitting price reductions and quality improvements.
6. Another flaw of the accounting method is the 'index-number problem' arising from the arbitrary weighting of initial and end period productivity. For a comprehensive critique see Martin and Evans (1981).
7. The figures reported in Table 10.4 confirm that the change in IIT indices (ΔGL) is of little use as an indicator of adjustment pressures.
8. If we scale the GHME indices to base-year trade volumes and the C measures to the sum of absolute trade changes within each industry, then the correlations with employment change (1980–90) drop to -0.04 for the GHME measure and to 0.19 for the C measure. The corresponding correlations with output change are 0.02 for GHME and 0.25 for C.
9. The ratios can be calculated from Table 10.6 columns [A] to [D].
10. Note that a country can specialize *out* of an industry without necessarily suffering an absolute decline in employment (as happened, for instance, in Category II). Specializing *out* means that imports are expanding more (or contracting less) rapidly than exports. If domestic demand is growing strongly, this can compensate for 'bad' trade performance and prevent a decrease in the sector's employment.
11. Elsewhere, we have performed a similar grouped analysis for the 1985 to 1990 period (Brülhart and McAleese (1995)). The results for that period were even starker, indicating that industries with high MIIT performed better on all counts (employment, output and trade growth) than industries with strongly increased net exports. That result, of course, conforms with the strong correlations for 1985–90 between MIIT and industrial growth, reported in Table 10.4.
12. Full details of calculations and adjustments to data are given in the Appendix.
13. CSO (1980, 85, 90).
14. As a deflator, we chose the Irish index of manufacturing output prices, since no export or import price index is available for Ireland. The disaggregated results for the 70 industries can be obtained from the authors.

References

Brülhart, M. (1994) 'Marginal Intra-Industry Trade: Measurement and Relevance for the Pattern of Industrial Adjustment', *Weltwirtschaftliches Archiv*, 130, 600–13.
Brülhart, M. and McAleese, D. (1995) 'Intra-Industry Trade and Industrial Adjustment: The Irish Experience', *The Economic and Social Review*, 26, 107–29.
Central Statistics Office (CSO) (1980, 83, 85, 90) *Census of Industrial Production*, Dublin: Stationery Office.
Commission of the European Communities (1993) *European Economy: Annual Report for 1993*. Luxembourg.

Foley, A. (1991) 'Interpreting Output Data on Overseas Industry', in: Foley, A. and McAleese, D. (eds), *Overseas Industry in Ireland*, Dublin: Gill and Macmillan.

Foley, A. and McAleese, D. (eds), *Overseas Industry in Ireland*, Dublin: Gill and Macmillan.

Grubel, H.G. and Lloyd, P.J. (1975) *Intra-Industry Trade*, London: Macmillan.

Hine, R.C., Greenaway, D. and Milner, C. (1994) 'Changes in Trade and Changes in Employment: An Examination of the Evidence from UK Manufacturing Industry 1979–87', SPES research paper, University of Nottingham.

Hummels, D. and Levinsohn, J. (1995) 'Monopolistic Competition and International Trade: Reconsidering the Evidence', *Quarterly Journal of Economics*, 110, 799–836.

Kol, J. and Mennes, L.B.M. (1989) 'Corrections for Trade Imbalance: A Survey', *Weltwirtschaftliches Archiv*, 125, 703–17.

Martin, J.P. and Evans, J.M. (1981) 'Notes on Measuring the Employment Displacement Effects of Trade by the Accounting Procedure', *Oxford Economic Papers*, 33, 154–64.

McAleese, D. (1976) 'Industrial Specialisation and Trade: Northern Ireland and the Republic', *The Economic and Social Review*, 7(2), 143–60.

McAleese, D. (1979) 'Intra-Industry Trade, Level of Development and Market Size', in Giersch, H. (ed.), *On the Economics of Intra-Industry Trade*, Tübingen: J.C.B. Mohr.

McAleese, D. and Hayes, F. (1995) 'European Integration, the Balance of Payments and Inflation', in O'Hagan J.W. (ed.), *The Economy of Ireland*, London, Macmillan.

National Economic and Social Council (NESC) (1989) *Ireland in the European Community: Performance Prospects and Strategy*, Dublin: NESC.

O'Sullivan, M. (1995) 'Manufacturing and Global Competition', in O'Hagan J.W. (ed.), *The Economy of Ireland*, London, Macmillan.

Ruane, F. and McGibney, A. (1991) 'The Performance of Overseas Industry', in Foley, A. and McAleese, D. (eds), *Overseas Industry in Ireland*, Dublin: Gill and Macmillan.

Thomsen, S. and Woolcock, S. (1993) *Direct Investment and European Integration: Competition Among Firms and Governments*, London: The Royal Institute of International Affairs.

Wood, A. (1994) *North-South Trade, Employment and Inequality*, Clarendon Press, Oxford.

APPENDIX 10.1

Data input

Section 10.2

The calculations reported in this section are based on a database covering the 1977–91 period.

Table 10.10   Structure of trade data used

Year	Number of product groups where trade is registered (SITC 5-digit)	Zero-import product groups	Zero-export product groups (in percent of total)	Product groups where GL index > 0.75
1977	1166	1.6	13.8	11.0
1985	1780	1.0	12.5	12.5
1990	3023	1.2	11.3	11.7

IIT was calculated from SITC five-digit OECD trade statistics on Ireland for the eight years 1977, 1978, 1980, 1985, 1986, 1987, 1990 and 1991. Our results are based on 5-digit rather than on 3-digit trade data. Thus, the data sets used were formidable, as trade was reported for up to 3023 product groups. Table 10.10 shows that the number of product groups ('industries') has grown substantially between 1977 and 1990. This development is due, on one hand, to statistical refinement (SITC revisions in 1978 and 1988), and, on the other hand, to the inclusion of formerly non-existent or non-traded products.

Section 10.3

In order to establish a link between the analysis of trade patterns and other economic variables such as industrial output and employment, appropriate matching data are required. Since, in Ireland, no statistics other than trade figures are published according to the SITC classification, and since none can be adequately re-grouped into SITC product categories, different data sources had to be employed.

All calculations reported are performed on three-digit NACE data. The trade figures are taken from the Eurostat microfiche data bank, where Irish intra-EU trade is reported for 126 different three-digit NACE groups. This data set is rearranged so as to match the sectors distinguished in the Irish Census of Industrial Production (CIP) statistics.[13] The CIP product classification is based on the NACE code, but some three-digit NACE groups are left out, because they do not refer to industry, and some are amalgamated because of their small size or to protect confidentiality. We thus achieved a data set distinguishing 70 industrial product groups which comprised figures for both trade and production. In order to retain only *real* changes in trade flows and output, all trade and production figures are converted into 1980 prices.[14]

Section 10.4

In order to establish the breakdown of foreign and domestically owned sectors in Irish industries we referred to data from the Census of Industrial Production (CIP) for the years 1983, 1985 and 1990, which report the proportions of output and employment accounted for by foreign and domestic firms. Since 1983 was the first year for which this breakdown was published, it was necessary to use the information on ownership from the 1983 CIP as a proxy for 1980.

Since the breakdown between foreign and domestic industries was very similar when weighted by output and employment, we chose the employment-weighted data. The calculations reported in this chapter were also conducted using output-weighted data and similar results were obtained (available on request).

The extent of foreign presence in each sector was established by allocating to each industry the percentage of jobs provided by foreign-owned companies. This information is published for a total of 40 two and three-digit NACE sectors. Our initial data set comprised 70 three-digit NACE sectors. The information on ownership is not published for 4 of the industries in our initial data set, so this reduced the number of observations to 66. Because of the discrepancy between the two data sets in terms of the number of industries, each industry in the 66 data set could not be allocated a *separate* index in terms of ownership. We chose to allocate foreign-ownership indices to sub-industries without weighting or adjustment.

This enabled us to divide the industries up into three categories; (a) those that were more than 60 per cent foreign owned, (b) those that were between 30 and 60 per cent foreign owned, and (c) those which were less than 30 per cent foreign owned, with the associated levels of IIT for each group. The average IIT levels for both the *A* index and the GL index were then calculated for each group as illustrated in Figures 10.3 and 10.4.

11. Italy

Gianpaolo Rossini and Michele Burattoni

11.1 INTRODUCTION

Italy appears to be one of the most interesting cases to analyse the effects over time of the establishment of the EU, since many aspects of Italian economy have been shaped by this new political institution. In this chapter, we are interested in a subset of these effects, that is the impact of the EU on the structure of Italian trade specialization.

From an industrial standpoint, the most visible consequence produced by the early Community in Italy was a thorough transformation of manufacturing. Entirely new industries were born and made up of firms having a definite orientation towards the growing European market (Pelkmans, 1984). Two cases deserve to be mentioned. The chemical industry (Burattoni *et al.*, 1994) had been developed during the 1950s with the perception of the Community as the relevant market. The bulk of investment in petrochemicals, in the second half of the 1950s and during the 1960s, was devoted to create productive capacity for the EEC market. Only a European market could justify the building of plants such as those in Southern Italy, exploiting economies of scale at the highest level. The second case concerns the electric appliances industry, created in Italy during the late 1950s. The contemporaneous wave of investment, at the beginning of the 1960s, was undertaken with the explicit intention of selling to the entire EEC market (Pelkmans, 1984; Paba, 1991). These two examples may be taken as evidence that Italian entrepreneurs viewed competition among European countries in terms of inter-industry specialization and inter-industry trade. The same stance was shared by the industrial policy that fostered the development of other smaller sectors, providing financial incentives.

These events may be considered, to a great extent, as the result of the gradual lifting of tariff barriers among the initial six member countries, phased in between 1957 and 1968. The establishment of the EEC has significantly changed the pattern of European trade, leading each country to increase its volume of trade as a percentage of GDP, hence raising the degree of openness of the entire EEC. We shall deal with these phenomena in Italy in Section 2 of this chapter. According to most observers, the structure of European trade should have changed considerably based on comparative advantage liberated from the heavy protective structures imposed between the two World Wars. Adjustment costs were expected to be high, because in each country some industries seemed destined to be unable to compete on the international market. As a consequence, a costly intersectoral shift of resources was anticipated. However, most of these forecasts did not materialize, since they did not take proper account of (a) the degree of similarity of factor endowments of EEC countries, (b) the residual non-tariff barriers in force until 1992, (c) the persistence of several government subsidies all over EEC countries, and (d) the importance of national industrial and regional policies. All these factors can be invoked as causes for the increased share of intra-industry trade (IIT) found in the EU.

Our analysis will cast doubt on the perception that trade of Italy with the EEC has become continuously more intra-industry in nature, since it is true only for the first decade of membership (until 1970). Recently, the outlook has changed substantially for two reasons. One is that the EU has deepened its degree of integration further. Second, new actors have come to the international stage.

This chapter is divided into 5 sections. In Section 2, we describe the aggregate trade specialization of Italy in the last 30 years. A link between changing trade patterns and structural change is established in Section 3 for the 1978–87 period. Section 4 is devoted to an analysis of vertical differentiation in Italian trade, and some conclusions are provided in Section 5.

11.2   A DESCRIPTION OF ITALIAN TRADE PATTERNS, 1961–90

Aggregate trade flows

We first consider aggregate trade flows. In Figure 11.1 we can see the degree of trade integration of Italy with the rest of the world. At the beginning of the 1960s, Italy exported less than one tenth of GDP. In 1990, both imports and exports amounted to roughly one third of GDP.

During the last 30 years Italy had a structural trade deficit that has been reversed only recently after the devaluation of Lira in September

1992. The deficit was compensated by a surplus of the balance of services.

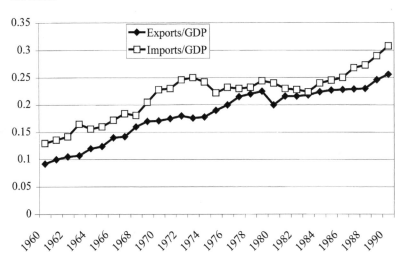

Figure 11.1   Italy's trade exposure, 1960–90

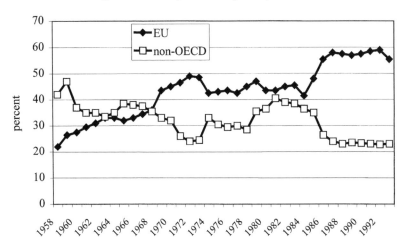

Figure 11.2   EU and non-OECD countries' shares of Italian imports, 1958–93

Figures 11.2 and 11.3 show how the geographical structure of Italian trade has changed between 1958 and 1992. Imports from the EU grew from 20 per cent of total imports to nearly 60 per cent, while the share of imports from non-OECD[1] countries fell from 45 to 20 per cent. On

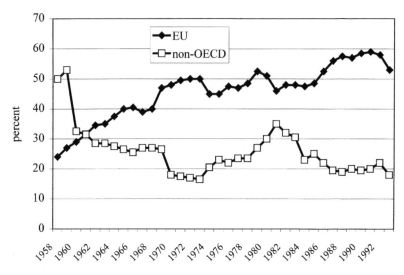

Figure 11.3   EU and non-OECD countries' shares of Italian exports, 1958–93

the export side, we detect a similar re-orientation of trade toward the EU, with the result that, by the early 1990s, more than half of Italian merchandise took place with the EU. This re-orientation of Italian trade flows represents a combination of trade creation and trade diversion, so that it is impossible to assess its welfare implications without a more refined analysis. The main boost from integration appears to have occurred during the 1960s and the beginning of the 1970s, while the two oil shocks (1973 and 1979) led to a resurgence of non-EU trade shares.

Aggregate patterns of intra-industry trade

Italian trade specialization during the last thirty years can be analysed by computing indices of IIT. In Table 11.1 we report the Grubel-Lloyd (GL) indices for Italy, calculated at the 4 and 5-digit levels of dis-aggregation.

We find that IIT increased appreciably only between 1961 and 1967. However, no trend appears afterwards. Our results also confirm that Italian IIT is larger with the EU partners than with outside countries.[2] This gap between IIT with the EU and the rest of the world has remained roughly constant over our sample period.

Table 11.1 GL indices for manufactures (SITC 5–8)

	EU6	*World*	*EU12*	*ROW*
1961	0.40	0.48	0.44	0.35
1967	0.54	0.53	0.56	0.35
1972	0.53	0.53	0.57	0.33
1976	0.54	0.54	0.57	0.35
1977	0.52	0.53	0.56	0.33
1978	0.48	0.50	0.52	0.30
1979	0.46	0.49	0.49	0.31
1985	0.50	0.51	0.52	0.37
1987	0.50	0.54	0.53	0.42
1988	0.47	0.52	0.51	0.41
1990	0.49	0.52	0.51	0.42

The structure of trade changes: marginal intra-industry trade

In order to draw inferences from trade patterns on adjustment pressures, we have complemented our IIT measures by calculations of marginal IIT (MIIT, see Chapter 5). In Table 11.2, we report A indices of MIIT for Italy calculated for 4 areas – all trade partners, the EU6, the EU12 and the rest of the world – for four sub-periods within our sample. Most indices lie below 0.5, hence marginal *inter*-industry trade appears to have prevailed. We find lower average A indices for trade with non-EU countries compared to trade with Italy's EU partners. This gap, however, has narrowed over time, as average MIIT increased with the non-EU countries while it fell with the EU6 and EU12, which points to a convergence of trade patterns between Italy and non-EU countries with Italy's trade inside the EEC (Rossini and Burattoni, 1996).

To discover whether Italy has lost or gained trade competitiveness in any sector we use the B index. We confine the analysis to the period

Table 11.2 A indices of MIIT[3]

	EU6	*EU12*	*ROW*	*World*
61–67	0.42	0.42	0.16	0.32
72–77	0.38	0.41	0.20	0.35
78–87	0.42	0.44	0.31	0.42
88–90	0.37	0.38	0.27	0.37

Table 11.3 Classification of sectors by trade performance, 1978–87

Number of 5-digit sectors	World	ROW	EU12	EU6
B nearly 0	13	15	0	0
$1 >= B > 0.5$	474	638	494	482
$0.5 >= B > 0.25$	164	142	141	142
$0.25 >= B > -0.25$	319	265	307	266
$-0.25 >= B > -0.50$	162	133	159	152
$-0.50 >= B >= -1$	703	642	697	748
Total	1835	1835	1798	1790

1978–87. At that time Italy joined the European Monetary System (EMS) of quasi fixed exchange rates, with important effects on the industrial structure and competitiveness. The Italian inflation rate was higher than the EMS average, and all industrial sectors invested intensively in the restructuring of their production processes to face stiffer price competition from countries with lower labour costs. As a consequence, productivity gains were large, as firms had to adjust to an appreciation of the real exchange rate.

What was the effect on Italian exports? Table 11.3 gives some answers. We classify 5-digit sectors according to the B index. The majority of industries displayed low B values vis-à-vis the EU6 and EU12. In trade with non-members of the EU, however, a narrow majority of industries displayed positive B indices. These results document a reorientation of Italian exports towards non-EU destinations and increased import penetration from the EU during the 1980s.

11.3 STRUCTURAL ADJUSTMENT

Major changes have taken place in Italian industry during the postwar period. One of the principal determinants of adjustment was Italy's integration with the EU. It is important to assess the relative weight of various determinants of change in employment between 1978 and 1987. To this purpose we use the simple accounting methodology applied, for example, by Wood (1994), based on data drawn from the OECD (1994) STAN database, which distinguishes 36 manufacturing sectors.[4]

At the aggregate level, we observe a sharp reduction of employment in Italian manufacturing. Job losses totalled 894,000 (about 15 per cent of the work force). Manufacturing production increased by 3.6 per cent in real terms, productivity by 22 per cent, domestic demand by 8 per cent, real imports by some 20 per cent, while exports decreased by some 3 per cent. The change in employment was due mainly to productivity growth, that was counterbalanced by domestic demand and trade. The components of aggregate demand had a differential impact on employment. Growth in domestic demand would have increased employment by 374,000 (+ 6 per cent) if considered alone. A net increase in imports and a net decrease in exports reduced employment respectively by 169,000 (−3 per cent) and by 29,000 (−0.5 per cent), *ceteris paribus*, resulting in a combined effect of domestic demand and trade of an increase of 176,000 jobs.

Nevertheless, Italy witnessed a decline of the manufacturing sector in terms of employment, because the increase in productivity more than outweighed the positive net effect of domestic and foreign demand.

Another approach underlies the results reported in Table 11.4. We have computed cross-sectional correlation coefficients, relating the change in trade patterns to changes in employment and production. We find a positive correlation between the increase of GL and the increase of employment. This may accord with the view that IIT has a lower cost of adjustment than inter-industry trade. However, we find a negative correlation between the base- and end-year levels of IIT and the net change of employment.

Table 11.4 Changes in manufactures trade and industrial performance 1978–87: (*Correlation coefficients, 36 manufacturing sectors*)

Trade-related variables	Production-related variables			
	Employment change		Gross output change	
	absolute	percentage	absolute	percentage
Trade performance				
Δ Exports	−0.11	−0.02	−0.02	0.21
Δ Imports	0.17	0.16	0.30**	0.22*
B index		−0.16		−0.11
Trade structure				
GL (base year)	−0.13		−0.02	
GL (end year)	−0.08		0.02	
Δ GL	0.13		0.07	
A index		0.05		−0.17

Statistical significance (two-tailed *t* test): 0.1:**, 0.2:*.

Somewhat surprisingly, we find negative correlation coefficients with the *B* index and export growth, and positive ones with import growth. The likely explanation for this counterintuitive result is that, when facing a recovery, Italian imports traditionally grow faster than exports. Until the end of the 1980s the import content of investment in plants and inventories of semi-finished goods and raw materials was higher than that of consumption. In that period, the structural trade deficit was procyclical. This trend was reversed after 1992.[5]

From the above calculations we conclude that Italian trade specialization has on average had an attenuating effect on industrial growth. It will be interesting to extend this analysis to the 1990s, as trade performance has changed substantially since the Lira's 30 per cent devaluation in 1992. Furthermore, there is early evidence that the productivity gains of the 1980s have increased the competitiveness of Italian exports in the 1990s.

11.4   VERTICAL DIFFERENTIATION IN ITALIAN IIT

Most models of IIT are based on the assumption that goods are horizontally differentiated and sold at the same price regardless of their specification (Krugman, 1980). The existence of IIT between countries having different standards of living and casual observation suggest that quality differentiation is relevant for IIT (Flam and Helpman, 1987).

Our approach to differentiation and trade is largely descriptive. We assess the relative importance of horizontal and vertical differentiation in overlapping trade, by calculating the ratio of export price over import price for each 5-digit industry on a bilateral basis. Then we classify all industries into 3 intervals.

If V_x/V_m (unit value of export over unit value of imports) lies below 0.85, Italy exports goods of lower quality than those imported. We call this *disadvantaged vertical* trade. Between 0.85 and 1.15, we have horizontal differentiation or even homogeneous goods, since price differences are negligible. We call this horizontal trade. Above 1.15, exports have higher prices than imports in the same 5-digit sector. We call this *advantaged vertical* trade. Then, we compute the volume of IIT for each 5-digit level and allocate them to one of the three categories. In Table 11.5 we report these values aggregated over trade in all manufactures. The highest levels of IIT appear in horizontally differentiated industries. In 1961 IIT was mostly in goods where Italy

Table 11.5 IIT in vertically and horizontally differentiated manufacturing
sectors, 1961–90

	Below 0.85	0.85 to 1.15	Above 1.15
1961	0.34	0.31	0.26
1967	0.41	0.46	0.30
1972	0.45	0.46	0.27
1976	0.39	0.47	0.31
1977	0.41	0.45	0.28
1978	0.41	0.39	0.26
1979	0.40	0.36	0.27
1985	0.41	0.34	0.33
1987	0.42	0.38	0.34
1988	0.39	0.39	0.28
1990	0.39	0.42	0.31

exported lower quality goods, while in 1990 the highest level of IIT is
the horizontally differentiated range. Italy faces strong price competition owing to the high level of IIT in the horizontally differentiated
sector.

Looking at total trade, that is inter- as well as intra-industry trade,
Table 11.6 shows that the share of vertically advantaged sectors increased from 39 to 63 per cent in our sample period. The share of
vertically disadvantaged sectors decreased from 46 to 32 per cent and a
pronounced reduction also appears for horizontally differentiated
sectors.

Table 11.6 Vertical/horizontal differentiation in total manufacturing trade,
1961–90

	Above 1.15 (%)	Below 0.85 (%)	0.85 to 1.15 (%)
1961	39.06	46.05	14.89
1967	40.08	45.45	14.47
1972	47.14	41.83	11.04
1976	52.95	37.77	9.28
1977	54.77	36.52	8.71
1978	57.29	35.92	6.78
1979	58.85	34.29	6.86
1985	57.99	34.64	7.37
1987	60.63	33.73	5.64
1988	61.61	32.81	5.58
1990	63.63	31.67	4.70

This is one of the most important features of the changing Italian trade pattern during the last 30 years. Starting from a position of exporting predominantly low-price low-quality goods, Italy's specialization patterns evolved towards the export of high-price and high-quality goods.

11.5   CONCLUSIONS

The structure of Italian trade has undergone fundamental changes during the last 30 years. Trade orientation, relative to GDP, increased threefold. This evolution was shaped to a significant extent by the European integration process.

IIT is an important feature of Italy's trade, particularly in intra-EU flows. We find that Italian IIT expanded in the 1960s, that is during the first phase of EEC integration. Subsequently, average IIT remained roughly unchanged for about 15 to 20 years. We detect some indications of a reduction in IIT at the end of the 1980s, possibly as a result of further progress in integration within and outside the EU. This result may point to a sort of 'IIT life cycle'. IIT grows when integration starts and there is a convergence of per capita income among countries (Rossini and Burattoni, 1996). Once the integration process slows down, IIT levels out. If integration then progresses beyond a certain critical threshold, IIT might fall again, since comparative advantage emerges liberated from most residual trade barriers (Rossini, 1996).

The analysis of MIIT shows that Italy has partly lost competitiveness and restricted its export specialization to fewer sectors. Given the close relationship between trade changes and structural adjustment, we have linked the analysis of trade patterns to data on employment and output change. A net decline in manufacturing employment can be traced mainly to productivity gains. Trade also appears to play a role, since Italy saw its export market share reduced during the 1980s, mainly due to an appreciation of the real exchange rate.

Italy's revealed comparative advantage in the 1960s was in low-quality low-price goods. We find that this situation had been reversed by 1990, and an advantage in higher quality goods had been attained. Even if the decline in IIT with the EU were not to materialize, price competition is more important with non-EU countries, and the level of IIT is lower, imposing higher adjustment costs. The apparently smooth adjustment to progressing integration in the EU will have to be set against potentially substantial adjustment costs implied by trade with emerging economies.

Notes

* We wish to thank Furio Camillo, Roberto Cellini, Roberto Golinelli, Luca Lambertini, Stefano Zecchi for useful support and advice. Prometeia Calcolo has kindly provided free computer facilities. The comments of an anonymous referee have highly improved the content of this work. The usual disclaimer applies.

1. In Figures 11.2 and 11.3, the share of trade with non-EU OECD countries can be calculated as the residual of the sum of the two reported percentages.
2. See Rossini (1983).
3. MIIT indices have been calculated on current values deflated using the GDP deflator (base year: 1980).
4. Detailed numerical results can be obtained from the authors on request.
5. See *Relazione annuale della Banca d'Italia*, various issues.

References and Further Reading

Brülhart M. (1994) 'Marginal IIT: Measurement and Relevance for the Pattern of Industrial Adjustment', *Weltwirtschaftliches Archiv*, 130, 600–13.
Burattoni M, Lambertini, L. and Rossini, G. (1994) 'The Chemical Sector in Europe: Productive Structure and Trade Specialisation', mimeo, University of Bologna.
Flam H. and Helpman, E. (1987) 'Vertical Product Differentiation and North-South Trade', *American Economic Review*, 77, 810–22.
Hamaguchi N. and Sazanami, V. (1978) 'Intra-Industry Trade in EEC: 1962–1972', *Keio Economic Studies*, 15, 53–68.
Helpman E. (1981) 'International Trade in the Presence of Product Differentiation, Economies of Scale and Monopolistic Competition: A Chamberlin-Heckscher-Ohlin Approach'. *Journal of International Economics*, 11, 305–40.
Krugman P. (1980) 'Scale Economies, Product Differentiation and the Pattern of Trade', *American Economic Review*, 70, 950–59.
OECD (1994) *The OECD Stan Data Bases for Industrial Analysis*. Paris: OECD.
Paba S. (1991) 'Brand Reputation, Efficiency and the Concentration Process. A Case Study', *Cambridge Journal of Economics*, 15, 21–43.
Pelkmans J. (1984) *European Economic Integration in Theory and Practice*, Amsterdam: Martinus Nijdoff.
Rossini G. (1983) 'Intraindustry Trade in Two Areas: Some Aspects of Trade Within and Outside a Custom Union', *Keio Economic Studies*, 20, 1–26.

Rossini G. (1996) 'Integration and the Life-Cycle of Intraindustry Trade', *Mimeo*, University of Bologna.

Rossini G. and Burattoni, M. (1996) 'Trade and Convergence Between Rich and Developing Countries: Some Empirical Evidence on Macro-determinants of Specialisation', *Weltwirtschaftliches Archiv*, 132, 75–96.

United Nations (1975) 'Standard International Trade Classification: Revision 2', *Statistical Papers Series M No. 34/Rev. 2*, New York: Department of Economic and Social Affairs, Statistical Office.

United Nations (1986) 'SITC: Revision 3', *Statistical Papers Series*, New York: Department of Economic and Social Affairs, Statistical Office.

Wood, A. (1994) *North-South Trade, Employment and Inequality*. Oxford: Clarendon Press.

12. The Netherlands

Jacob Kol and Bart Kuijpers

12.1 INTRODUCTION

Having stated the fallacy of the mercantilist system, Adam Smith (1776) observed that of all the countries of Europe, Holland most closely approached the situation of free trade, although it was still very remote from it; and furthermore that 'Holland, it is acknowledged, not only derives its whole wealth, but a great part of its necessary subsistence, from foreign trade'. In an overview of the Dutch economy in the twentieth century, De Vries (1977) observed that, during the industrialization in the late nineteenth century, the tendency toward free trade has remained the undercurrent in the Netherlands' trade policies. After World War II, the Netherlands concluded temporary bilateral trade and payments agreements, but the government recognized that a liberal multilateral trading system was in the interest of the country, given its small domestic market and geographical position. This long-term stance on foreign trade policy has induced the government of the Netherlands to seek economic cooperation in Europe, while at the same time trying to retain openness towards the rest of the world.

Consequently, this chapter reports on developments in the international trade of The Netherlands with its European partners as well as with the world at large; the focus is on developments in intra-industry Trade (IIT) in the period 1961–90. Developments in merchandise trade and in the openness of the Dutch economy since 1960 are described in Section 2. The database is presented in Section 3. Empirical evidence on IIT in the period 1961–90 is given in Section 4. Within measured IIT, a distinction can be made between horizontal and vertical IIT, the latter allowing the distinction between high-quality imports and high-quality exports. Section 5 gives the relevant empirical results. Traditionally, the measurement of IIT has been related to economic integration and industrial specialization; this issue is studied in Section 6, where we link changes in output, employment and labour productivity in 36 industries to developments in trade performance.

12.2 FOREIGN TRADE OF THE NETHERLANDS

On 5 September 1944, the governments in exile of Belgium, Luxembourg, and The Netherlands agreed in London on the formation of a customs union between their countries: the Benelux. A common import tariff was introduced on January 1, 1948. The Benelux partners abolished quantitative restrictions on trade among them in 1949. In 1958 a new treaty transformed the customs union into an economic union, which became effective in 1960.

By then, other forms of economic cooperation among European countries had been established as well. Financial aid under the Marshall Plan had been granted on the condition of economic cooperation among the recipients. This led to the foundation in 1948 of the Organization for European Economic Cooperation (OEEC, later OECD). After the signing of the Treaty of Rome in 1957, the European Economic Community (EEC) came into force on 1 January 1958. The Common Commercial Policy (CCP) of the Member States vis-à-vis non-members was subsequently developed in accordance with Article 110 of the EEC Treaty. Given these relations of economic cooperation, the scope for an independent national trade policy of The Netherlands was limited in the period 1960–90, which is the period considered here.

In the 30-year period 1961–90 exports from The Netherlands increased from 4.3 to 125.8 billion US dollars at 1972 prices, slightly above the 28-fold increase in world exports in the same period. The openness of an economy is usually measured by the ratio of total trade (exports plus imports) to national income. Table 12.1 shows that this ratio for The Netherlands increased from 87 per cent in 1961 to 104 per cent in 1990. This is well above the EC-12 average which was 56 per cent in 1990, but below the figures for Belgium (147 per cent), Ireland (130 per cent) and Luxembourg (145 per cent). The figures of openness for Japan and the USA in 1990 were 21 and 22 per cent respectively.

Appendix 12.1 shows the product composition of exports at the SITC 1-digit level. Food and live animals (Section 0) continue to have a characteristically high, though declining, share of around 20 per cent in Dutch exports. Mineral fuels (including natural gas) (Section 3) also have an important share in exports, the value of which however fluctuates with price changes. Manufactures (Sections 5 to 8) comprise between 50 and 60 per cent of total exports of The Netherlands in the period 1961–90. Within this broad sector, chemicals (Section 5) almost doubled its share from 9 to 16 per cent. The share of raw-material

Table 12.1   Total trade as a share of GDP, The Netherlands, EC-12, Japan and USA, 1961–90

| | Total exports + imports in percent of GDP | | | | | |
	1961	1967	1972	1977	1985	1990
The Netherlands	86.8	78.3	83.4	89.8	116.8	103.8
EC-12	37.3	37.7	42.6	52.9	60.4	55.6
Japan	20.2	19.0	18.9	24.6	25.6	20.9
USA	9.4	10.2	11.9	17.2	17.8	21.5

Source: OECD (1994)

based manufactures (Section 6) declined steadily, whereas those of machinery and transport equipment (Section 7) and miscellaneous manufactures (Section 8) increased.

The product composition of imports is similar to that of exports. The Netherlands ran pronounced and persistent trade surpluses for food and live animals (Section 0) and for chemicals (Section 5), and trade deficits for the other manufacturing industries (Sections 6 to 8).

Germany is by far the most important trade partner of The Netherlands, accounting for a quarter on average of both exports and imports in the years 1961–90. There is a marked increase in the share of Germany in Dutch trade up to 1972, with the share declining and levelling out at a somewhat lower level since then. A similar pattern is found for trade with the EC-6, as if the intensification of trade relations upon the founding of the EEC in 1958 with the early partners had been completed by 1972, the intensification then being taken over by other member countries. The figures for the EC-12 support this view: the shares of the EC-12 in exports and imports of the Netherlands increased in the period 1960–72 but to a lesser extent than for the EC-6; after a decrease in 1977 the shares for the EC-12 however continued to rise, especially after 1985 (see Kol and Kuijpers, 1994).

12.3   THE DATABASE

Data for measuring intra-industry trade

Trade data were obtained from the OECD according to SITC Revision 1 for the years 1961, 1967, 1972 and 1977, Revision 2 for 1985 and Revision 3 for 1990. Tables of correspondence between Revisions 1, 2 and 3 were applied to compare the trade data for the various sample years.

Basic headings of the trade data were used to measure the amount of IIT. The number of basic headings increased from 625 SITC 4-digit sub-groups in 1961 to 3118 SITC 5-digit items in 1990. The increasing refinement of the SITC leads to an increasing percentage of basic headings for which no exports or imports are registered, this percentage being 3.5 in 1961 and 6.8 in 1990 in the foreign trade of The Netherlands. The basic headings with a Grubel-Lloyd (GL) index of 0.75 or more increased from nearly 23 per cent in 1961 to 28 per cent in 1990, notwithstanding the 5-fold increase in the number of basic headings.[1]

Data for measuring structural adjustment

Measuring structural adjustment requires data on output, employment and trade, which are comparable with respect to the classification of economic sectors and consistent over the years. To that end for the two benchmark years, 1972 and 1990, the 59-sector classification of the input-output tables for the Netherlands has been used. Data on *output* and *employment* for 1972 and 1990 were obtained from the Central Bureau of Statistics (CBS, 1986 and 1993).

As described above, data on *trade* were available according to the SITC. In order to match them with the data on output and employment, a concordance table was used to allocate SITC basic headings to 3-digit industries of the Dutch Standard Industrial Classification (SIC) (see Kol and Kuijpers, 1994). Data on trade and output for 1990 have been converted to 1972 prices using the consumer price index reported in CBS (1991).

12.4   EMPIRICAL ANALYSIS OF INTRA-INDUSTRY TRADE

Table 12.2 presents the development since 1960 of IIT with the other five founding members of the EC-6. The results confirm that the scope for IIT is in manufactures rather than in primary commodities.

Within manufactures, IIT levels differ considerably among the four manufacturing sections of the SITC (5-8). There is a marked decrease in IIT for chemicals (SITC Section 5) since 1967. IIT in raw material based manufactures (Section 6) and in miscellaneous manufactures (Section 8) has remained fairly stable around 60 and 65 per cent

Table 12.2   IIT indices for trade with EC-6 by SITC section,
The Netherlands 1961–90

SITC Section		1961	1967	1972	1977	1985	1990
		Grubel-Lloyd index[a]					
0	Food, live animals	0.21	0.29	0.32	0.37	0.37	0.35
1	Beverages, tobacco	0.45	0.59	0.62	0.59	0.46	0.38
2	Crude materials	0.41	0.41	0.37	0.37	0.39	0.37
3	Mineral fuels	0.56	0.58	0.20	0.17	0.16	0.20
4	Animal/vegetable oils, fats	0.30	0.44	0.44	0.62	0.47	0.42
5	Chemicals	0.57	0.71	0.60	0.62	0.52	0.45
6	Raw material based manufactures	0.54	0.61	0.61	0.64	0.61	0.58
7	Machinery, transport equipment	0.43	0.46	0.51	0.51	0.57	0.62
8	Miscellaneous manufactures	0.68	0.61	0.60	0.58	0.67	0.70
9	Commodities n.e.s.	0.62	0.71	0.52	0.59	0.79	0.28
5–8	Manufactures	0.52	0.56	0.57	0.58	0.58	0.58
0–9	All commodities	0.47	0.52	0.49	0.49	0.45	0.51

Note: [a] Grubel-Lloyd index calculated from SITC 4-digit level (1961 and 1967) and from SITC 5-digit level (1972, 1977, 1985 and 1990).
Source: OECD Trade Data

respectively. IIT in machinery and transport equipment (Section 7) increased considerably from 43 per cent of total trade in these products in 1961 to 62 per cent in 1990. This Section 7 represents of course the type of products most prone to product differentiation and consumers' preference for variety, the production of which, moreover, is likely to have considerable scope for the exploitation of scale economies.[2] Consequently, an increase of IIT is in line with expectations regarding the effects of economic integration among developed countries.

Since the founding of the EEC in 1958, the original six members have been joined by nine additional members. Most of them had been members of an EEC–EFTA free-trade agreement in industrial goods since 1973. This may have given scope for intra-industry specialization in manufactured products among these countries and the EC-6 to a similar extent as among the EC-6 countries themselves. Dutch trade with the original EC-6 partners accounted for some 80 per cent of trade with the EC-12 partners. Consequently, IIT patterns record-ed for trade with the EC-12 do not differ substantially from those recorded in trade with the partners of the EC-6. (see Kol and Kuijpers, 1994).

IIT in manufactures shows an increase from 1961 to 1977, and a levelling out since then. This may well correspond to the finding in Torstensson (1994) that initial phases of regional integration are generally associated with rising IIT, while later stages can reverse this increase.

Table 12.3   Horizontal and vertical IIT, The Netherlands trade with the EC-12, 1972 and 1990

SITC		Horizontal IIT	Vertical IIT		
			VIIT	of which:	
		HIIT		HQIM	HQEX
		Share in IIT (in percentages)			
	1972				
0	Food, live animals	51	49	11	39
1	Beverages, tobacco	52	48	37	11
2	Crude materials	45	56	17	39
3	Mineral fuels	72	28	25	4
4	Animal/vegetable oils, fats	50	50	23	27
5	Chemicals	36	64	41	23
6	Raw material based manufactures	59	41	17	23
7	Machinery, transport equipment	55	45	9	36
8	Miscellaneous manufactures	38	63	33	30
9	Commodities n.e.s.	0	100	100	0
0–9	ALL COMMODITIES	51	50	21	28
	1990				
0	Food, live animals	45	55	13	42
1	Beverages, tobacco	37	63	7	56
2	Crude materials	32	68	8	60
3	Mineral fuels	72	28	22	6
4	Animal/vegetable oils, fats	77	23	9	14
5	Chemicals	50	51	25	26
6	Raw material based manufactures	55	45	26	19
7	Machinery, transport equipment	39	61	22	40
8	Miscellaneous manufactures	53	47	25	22
9	Commodities n.e.s.	93	70	0	7
0–9	ALL COMMODITIES	47	53	22	31

Notes: r: unit value of exports/unit value of imports; HIIT: $0.85 \leq r \leq 1.15$; VIIT: $r < 0.85$ or $r > 1.15$; HQIM: $r < 0.85$; HQEX: $r > 1.15$; Shares in IIT do not always add up to 100 due to rounding.
Source: own calculations from OECD Trade Database.

12.5 HORIZONTAL AND VERTICAL INTRA-INDUSTRY TRADE

In 1972 as well as in 1990 horizontal IIT (HIIT) and vertical IIT (VIIT), defined by the standard unit-value interval of $+/-0.15$, each accounted for roughly half of total IIT in *all commodities* with the EC-12 partners (Table 12.3). Significant improvements over time in the relative quality of exports to the EU partners is found for *beverages and tobacco* (Section 1) and for *chemicals* (Section 5). The same tendencies are found for trade with the EC-6 partners and with all countries (Kol and Kuijpers, 1994).

During the period 1972–90 covered in this chapter, Dutch policy on non-border measures, such as state aids to industry, changed considerably. The policies of supporting sectors in decline, together with protecting employment especially in depressed areas, which had been pursued actively, were discontinued. Policies changed from supporting specific industries to general measures, and within the context of this section, if support was directed to specific industries, these were not in decline, but innovative and high value added industries (Kol and Mennes, 1992). This policy shift is a probable cause of the detected quality shift in Dutch trade flows.

12.6 INDUSTRIAL STRUCTURE AND SECTORAL TRADE PERFORMANCE

During our sample period, the industrial structure of the Dutch economy changed substantially. Appendix 2 shows that, on average, growth in *output* between 1972 and 1990 was relatively low in agriculture, mining and manufacturing, textiles, clothing and footwear industries, and high in gas production, the chemical industries and in the automobile industry. In terms of *employment*, only some of the industries with above-average output growth also experienced an increase in employment. Through gains in labour productivity, employment declined in 30 out of the 36 industries.

The real value of *exports* with the world and with the EC-12 and EC-6 partners tripled between 1972 and 1990, far outweighing the real increase in output values of 117 per cent. The average, however, conceals substantial differences across individual industries. Especially in some of the food-processing industries export increases were substantially above average: in grain processing, the sugar industry, in beverages and tobacco processing, but also in wood and furniture production, and in machinery. Well below-average increases in exports are found for the gas, petroleum and chemical industries.

Table 12.4 Industrial structure and sectoral trade performance, 1972–90

Class	Number of sectors	Average B	ΔQ (%)	ΔL (%)	ΔX (%)	d(Q/L) (% per year)
Trade with the World						
Class I	3	−1.00	18	−55	−6	5.5
Class II	16	−0.13	126	−13	232	5.4
Class III	12	0.24	114	−17	212	5.4
Class IV	5	0.64	145	−28	191	7.0
Total	36	n.a.	117	−18	202	5.5
Trade with the EC-6						
Class I	2	−1.00	−45	−72	−47	3.8
Class II	19	−0.15	110	−17	194	5.3
Class III	10	0.19	122	−15	227	5.5
Class IV	5	0.75	149	−25	179	6.7
Total	36	n.a.	117	−18	191	5.5
Trade with the EC-12						
Class I	2	−1.00	−45	−72	−36	3.8
Class II	19	−0.09	116	−16	261	5.4
Class III	11	0.33	117	−17	201	5.5
Class IV	4	0.73	150	−27	206	7.1
Total	36	n.a.	117	−18	216	5.5

Notes: Only sectors involved in international trade are included. 1990 values are converted into 1972 prices using the CPI.

Classification of sectors according to the Brülhart (1994) B index:

Class	Definition	MIIT	Specialization
I	$-1 \leq B < -0.5$	low	out
II	$-0.5 \leq B < 0$	high	out
III	$0 \leq B < 0.5$	high	into
IV	$0.5 \leq B \leq 1.0$	low	into

ΔQ: Change in production between 1972 and 1990 (in %)
ΔL: Change in employment between 1972 and 1990 (in %)
ΔX: Change in exports between 1972 and 1990 (in %)
d(Q/L): Average annual growth of labour productivity, 1972–90 (in %)
Source: own calculations from CBS (1986, 1987, 1991, 1993) and OECD trade data.

The Brülhart (1994) *B* index is used as a measure of sectoral trade performance and MIIT. Table 12.4 classifies the 36 economic sectors of the Dutch economy into four categories according to the size and the sign of this index. Negative values of *B* indicate that the economy specialized out of that particular industry in terms of trade flows. The opposite holds for positive values of *B*. The grouped analysis is performed for trade with the EC-6, the EC-12 and with all countries.

A majority of sectors display *B* indices between −0.5 and 0.5, hence relatively high MIIT (see Table 12.4). This applies to trade relations with the world, the EC-12 and the EC-6. Hence, adjustment to Dutch trade expansion appears to have been predominantly intra-industry. Nevertheless, trade performance appears to have been a significant determinant of structural adjustment, as output and labour productivity increased more strongly in sectors with high *B* indices.

The observations above correspond to the findings of a recent study on the structure of economic sectors in the Netherlands by the Central Planning Bureau (CPB, 1996). It is found that per working hour the employee in the manufacturing industry has a higher productivity in The Netherlands than in Germany. The CPB (1996) mentions three reasons:

1. Difference in sector composition. The sectors with a relative high productivity are represented to a larger extent in the manufacturing sector in The Netherlands than in Germany.
2. The Dutch manufacturing industry has a relative high capital intensity.
3. The skills and participation in training activities of the work force in the Netherlands are relatively high.

The analysis in CPB (1996) points also to the above mentioned special successful development of the food and chemical industries. With respect to the chemical industry in particular the CPB (1996) points to a clear change in strategy in the 1980s; this implied a break with the past when the chemical industry in The Netherlands was very raw-material and energy intensive. The introduction of new process technologies, that are efficient in the use of raw material and energy, improved the value added and profit position of the chemical industry considerably.

Within the context of the present chapter it is worth observing that the process of economic integration in Western Europe has certainly created opportunities for an improved economic structure of the economy of the Member States, but that the intentional design of

Table 12.5 Correlation between trade and employment changes, 1972–90

	ΔX^1	ΔM^1	GL72	GL90	ΔGL	A	B
	\multicolumn{7}{l}{*Correlation coefficients between changes in employment (ΔL) and various trade variables*}
ΔL	0.50*	0.69*	−0.42*	−0.11	0.43*	0.37*	0.24

[1] percentage changes
* statistically significant at 95% level of confidence

ΔL : percentage change in employment (1972–90)
ΔX : percentage change in total exports (1972–90)
ΔM : percentage change in total imports (1972–90)
GL72 : Grubel-Lloyd index (1972)
GL90 : Grubel-Lloyd index (1990)
ΔGL : GL90–GL72
A, B : as defined in Brülhart (1994) and in Chapter 3

policies and strategies both in the public and private sector are the major factors shaping structural change.

12.7 CONCLUSIONS

The Netherlands are among the small open economies in the EU and have historically pursued a relatively free trade policy, actively seeking economic cooperation in Europe while supporting a liberal multi-lateral trade system for the world at large.

In the period considered, 1961–90, IIT with the EC-partners increased up to 1972, levelling out since then; this corresponds to theoretical findings on economic integration and its effects on the share of IIT in total trade.

In the period 1972–90 the quality of exports to the EC-partners improved considerably in some sectors. This may reflect a switch in policy in the Netherlands in the same period from giving support to declining sectors to innovative and high value added industries.

Correspondingly, in the same period the economy of the Netherlands has been specializing out of sectors with a low labour productivity and into sectors where labour productivity is relatively high and rising further.

This leads to the conclusion that economic integration in Western Europe has certainly created opportunities for an advanced division of labour, but that the exploitation of these opportunities is due to the intentional design of policies and strategies both in the public and private sector.

Establishing a firmer relationship between economic integration and IIT could benefit from using more elaborate econometric analysis of both industry and country factors, as well as from studying the role of multinational corporations and intra-firm trade, as suggested in Greenaway and Torstensson (1997).

Notes

1. For details, see Kol and Kuijpers (1994).
2. The increase in recorded IIT within Section 7 becomes even more pronounced against the background of the addition of many new headings in the SITC Revision 3 since 1985, testifying to the generally advanced and innovative character of the products involved.

References

Brülhart, Marius (1994) 'Marginal Intra-Industry Trade: Measurement and Relevance for the Pattern of Industrial Adjustment', *Weltwirtschaftliches Archiv*, 130, 600–13.

CBS (1986) *Revised Input-Output Tables for the Years 1969–1976: Production Structure of the Dutch Economy Based on the Revised Reporting Year 1977, Voorburg: Netherlands Central Bureau of Statistics.*

CBS (1987) *National Accounts: Time Series 1969–1984*, Voorburg: Netherlands Central Bureau of Statistics.

CBS (1991, 1993) *National Accounts*, Voorburg: Netherlands Central Bureau of Statistics.

CPB (1996) *Central Economic Plan 1996* (Central Economisch Plan 1996), The Hague: Central Planning Bureau.

Greenaway, D. and Torstensson, J. (1997) 'Back to the Future: Taking Stock on Intra-Industry Trade', *Weltwirtschaftliches Archiv*, 133, 249–65.

Kol, J. and Mennes, L.B.M. (1992), 'Trade policies in the Netherlands', in Salvatore, D. (ed.), *National Trade Policies*, Amsterdam/New York: North-Holland.

Kol, J. and Kuijpers, B. (1994) 'IIT and Structural Adjustment in The Netherlands: 1961–1990', mimeo, Erasmus University, Rotterdam, 1994.

OECD (1994) *National Accounts 1960–1992*, Paris, OECD.

Smith, A. (1776) *An Inquiry into the Nature and Causes of the Wealth of Nations*, Indianapolis USA: Liberty Classics, (1981).

Torstensson, J. (1994) *Economic Integration, Market Size and the Location of Industries*, Lund University, Sweden, (Research Paper).

Vries, Joh. de (1977) *De Nederlandse economie tijdens de 20ste eeuw* (The Netherlands economy in the 20th century), Haarlem: Fibula/van Dishoeck.

APPENDIX 1   TOTAL TRADE BY SITC SECTIONS, 1961–90

Table 12.6   The Netherlands total trade and distribution over SITC sections, 1961–90

		1961	1967	1972	1977	1985	1990
						(in billion US dollars)	
Total Exports		4.3	7.3	17.0	43.6	66.4	125.8
Distribution over SITC sections						(in percentages)	
0	Food, live animals	24.0	22.4	20.4	19.3	16.6	17.9
1	Beverages, tobacco	1.2	1.3	1.3	1.3	1.7	2.3
2	Crude materials	7.2	8.0	6.1	5.3	5.1	5.8
3	Mineral fuels	11.9	7.9	12.1	18.2	23.4	10.2
4	Animal/vegetable oils, fats	1.0	0.8	1.0	1.0	1.3	0.7
5	Chemicals	8.8	12.3	13.7	14.5	15.4	16.4
6	Raw material based manufactures	18.6	19.2	17.7	14.8	12.5	13.7
7	Machinery, transport equipment	18.6	20.4	19.7	18.8	16.8	23.7
8	Miscellaneous manufactures	5.2	6.5	7.4	6.4	6.6	9.2
9	Commodities n.e.s.	3.5	1.2	0.6	0.4	0.5	0.2
5–8	Manufactures	51.2	58.4	58.5	54.5	51.3	62.9
0–9	All commodities	100.0	100.0	100.0	100.0	100.0	100.0
						(in billion US dollars)	
Total Imports		5.1	8.3	17.0	45.5	64.2	123.3
Distribution over SITC sections						(in percentages)	
0	Food, live animals	11.5	12.3	11.7	12.5	11.1	9.9
1	Beverages, tobacco	1.6	1.4	1.4	1.2	1.3	1.3
2	Crude materials	11.9	10.0	7.9	6.9	6.0	5.4
3	Mineral fuels	12.9	10.4	13.2	18.4	22.3	10.5
4	Animal/vegetable oils, fats	1.1	1.0	1.0	1.0	1.2	0.5
5	Chemicals	6.0	7.9	8.0	8.0	9.5	10.1
6	Raw material based manufactures	22.4	21.7	20.1	16.6	14.6	17.6
7	Machinery, transport equipment	23.6	24.0	24.3	23.1	22.9	30.9
8	Miscellaneous manufactures	6.4	9.8	11.5	11.5	10.3	13.7
9	Commodities n.e.s.	2.7	1.5	0.9	0.8	0.7	0.2
5–8	Manufactures	58.3	63.4	63.9	59.1	57.4	72.2
0–9	All commodities	100.0	100.0	100.0	100.0	100.0	100.0

Note: Percentage shares do not always add up to 100 due to rounding
Source: OECD Trade Data.

APPENDIX 2   INDUSTRIAL STRUCTURE OF THE NETHERLANDS

Table 12.7   Industrial structure of the Netherlands: Output, employment, labour productivity and exports; percentage changes from 1972–1990

Sector	ΔQ (%)	ΔL (%)	d(Q/L) (% per year)	ΔXtot (%)	ΔXEC12 (%)	ΔXEC6 (%)
1 Agriculture, horticulture and forestry	97	−17	4.9	179	174	142
2 Fishing	111	−14	5.1	203	151	134
3 Petroleum and gas production	367	133	3.9	270	271	273
4 Other mining and quarrying	89	−73	11.4	71	68	63
5 Meat-processing industry	84	−27	5.2	122	141	91
6 Manufacture of dairy products	71	−21	4.4	135	125	122
7 Processing of fish, fruit and vegetables	135	−9	5.4	306	304	217
8 Grain-processing industry	50	−18	3.4	224	232	165
9 Sugar industry	67	−40	5.8	362	667	702
10 Flour-processing industry	84	−19	4.6	234	175	143
11 Manufacture of cocoa and chocolate	119	−42	7.6	152	155	132
12 Manufacture of other food products	83	−8	3.9	227	230	173
13 Beverage industry	105	−31	6.3	446	367	280
14 Tobacco-processing industry	130	−33	7.1	466	539	631
15 Wool industry	−69	−86	4.4	64	42	36
16 Cotton industry	−45	−77	5.1	−36	−42	−54
17 Knitting and hosiery industry	−46	−60	1.7	−17	−27	−35
18 Textile industry (other enterprises)	51	−38	5.1	161	163	118
19 Clothing industry	−36	−63	3.1	189	185	160
20 Leather, footwear and other leather goods	21	−47	4.7	200	247	196
21 Wood and furniture industry	85	−28	5.4	355	352	318
22 Paper and cardboard industry	143	−25	6.7	298	274	200

Table 12.7   (contd.)

Sector	ΔQ (%)	ΔL (%)	d(Q/L) (% per year)	ΔXtot (%)	$\Delta XEC12$ (%)	$\Delta XEC6$ (%)
23 Paperware industry	151	−11	5.9	244	222	148
24 Printing and publishing industries	180	7	5.5	207	229	246
25 Petroleum industry	129	−18	5.9	128	133	179
26 Chemical basic products industry	225	−6	7.2	251	275	249
27 Chemical final products industry	205	3	6.2	239	257	196
28 Rubber and plastic-processing industry	259	35	5.6	438	405	350
29 Manufacture of building materials	102	−29	6.0	256	262	234
30 Basic metal industry	64	−22	4.2	124	141	132
31 Manufacture of metal products	144	−16	6.1	260	249	243
32 Machinery	157	−9	5.9	443	487	428
33 Electrotechnical industry	99	−7	4.3	151	242	215
34 Automobile industry	273	61	4.8	529	518	451
35 Manufacture of transport equipment	45	−47	5.8	18	68	85
36 Manufacture of goods n.e.s.	158	32	3.8	255	313	247
Total (international sectors)	117	−18	5.5	202	216	191

Notes: Only sectors which are involved in international trade are included. 1990 values are deflated into 1972 prices using the CPI.
ΔQ: Change in production between 1972 and 1990 (in %)
ΔL: Change in employment between 1972 and 1990 (in %)
d(Q/L): Average annual growth of labour productivity between 1972 and 1990 (in %)
ΔXtot/$EC12$/$EC6$: Change in exports to the world/EC-12/EC-6 between 1972 and 1990 (in %)
Sources: own calculations from CBS (1986, 1987, 1991, 1993) and OECD trade data.

13. Portugal

Manuel Porto and Fernanda Costa

13.1 INTRODUCTION

The main purpose of this chapter is to analyse intra-industry trade and adjustment in the Portuguese economy.[1] Portugal has traditionally been quite open to international trade – having been referred to already by Ricardo in his famous example of the theory of comparative advantage. It is still a moot point among economic historians, however, whether free trade was a priority of Portuguese policy in the postwar years. Salazar's political ideology would have favoured a more inward-looking approach, but the realization of its external economic dependency as a small nation led Portugal to follow the main integration movements. Portugal was a founder member of the OEEC and EFTA, joined the GATT in 1962, signed wide-ranging free-trade agreements with the EEC in 1972 and 1976 and joined the Community in 1986.[2]

The dependence of Portugal on international trade is reflected in the degree of openness of the economy, which is surpassed in the EU only by Ireland, the Benelux and the Nordic countries. The importance of external trade is particularly marked in certain key economic sectors such as textiles and clothing, cars and forestry products.

This chapter provides a comprehensive overview of Portuguese trade developments since 1960, with a particular emphasis on the extent, composition and effects of intra-industry trade.

The chapter is structured as follows. In Section 13.2 we show the increasing role of international trade for the Portuguese economy and some of its features. In Section 13.3 the evolution of intra-industry trade (IIT) is presented, including its sectoral and geographical evolution. We distinguish trade in homogeneous and differentiated goods in Section 13.4. In Section 13.5 we correlate the evolution of IIT with other features of the Portuguese economy, and in Section 13.6 we report patterns of marginal intra-industry trade. Some conclusions are drawn in Section 13.7.

13.2 PORTUGAL'S INTERNATIONAL TRADE

Since 1961, Portuguese trade orientation has generally been increasing (Figure 13.1). In 1990, imports amounted to 41.6 percent and exports to 27.3 per cent of the country's GDP (in the EU, only the values for Ireland and the Benelux countries were higher).

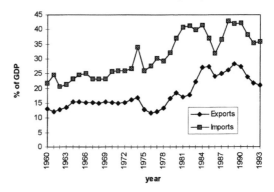

Figure 13.1   Portuguese merchandise trade 1960–93; all countries
Source: Commission of the European Communities (1993) *European Economy*, No. 54

The geographical composition of Portuguese trade has changed dramatically over the last three decades. Since 1984, trade with EU countries has grown strongly, while trade with third countries has

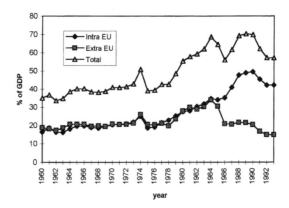

Figure 13.2   Total portuguese merchandise trade 1960–93: Intra and extra-EU
Source: Commission of the European Communities (1993) *European Economy*, No. 54

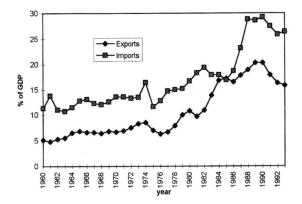

Figure 13.3 Portuguese merchandise exports and imports 1960–93: Intra EU
trade

Source: Commission of the European Communities (1993) *European
Economy*, No. 54

Figure 13.4 Portuguese merchandise exports and imports 1960–93: Extra EU
trade

Source: Commission of the European Communities (1993) *European
Economy*, No. 54

fallen in proportion to GDP. Commodity exports to EU countries
increased from 10.8 per cent of GDP in 1960 to 20.3 per cent in 1990,
and imports from 16.7 to 29.2 per cent; while the value of exports to
third countries decreased from 7.6 to 7.2 per cent of GDP, and the
value of imports decreased from 20.3 to 13.1 per cent (see Figures 13.2,
13.3 and 13.4). It was therefore intra-EU trade which fuelled the

increasing trade orientation of the Portuguese economy in the past decade.

Important changes have also occurred in the sectoral structure of Portuguese trade, with a clear increase in the role of manufacturing relative to the role of primary products. Manufacturing products (sectors 5 to 8 of the SITC) increased from 60 to 73 per cent of total imports and from 53 to 80 per cent of exports between 1961 and 1990.

It is interesting to note, however, the different evolution of trade with EU and with non-EU countries. With EU countries, the percentage of manufacturing *imports* was already very high in 1961, 88 per cent of the total, and have remained stable at that level ever since. In contrast, manufactured goods represented only 40 per cent of total *exports* in 1961, but this share has increased substantially to 82 per cent in 1990. The big imbalance registered in 1961, with manufactured goods representing much more in imports than in exports, therefore disappeared by 1990.

With non-EU countries, however, the share of manufactured goods has always been much higher in exports than in imports. The proportion of manufactures in extra-EU trade increased over the thirty years of our study from 25 to 44 per cent for imports and from 62 to 76 per cent for exports. Hence, the rate of this increase was lower than the increase registered for trade with EU countries.

13.3   THE EVOLUTION OF INTRA-INDUSTRY TRADE

In order to allow for sectoral comparisons over time, we report GL indices calculated at the SITC five-digit level.

Figure 13.5 shows a general increase in IIT, with the exception of a decrease in the 1970s. It is also apparent that IIT in manufacturing has always been higher than IIT in the whole of the economy.

A more disaggregated picture (reported at the one digit level) can be seen in Figure 13.6, focusing on the evolution between 1985 and 1990.

We can note that the upward trend in Portuguese IIT was evident in each SITC 1-digit sector, including the manufacturing industries (SITC 5–8), where average IIT is generally higher than in the primary sectors. Given the trends in the composition of aggregate trade flows, it can be hypothesized that the growth in IIT in manufacturing is primarily a result of increased Portuguese exports in industries where trade was traditionally dominated by imports. The reverse is likely to

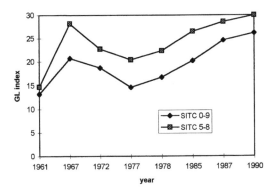

Figure 13.5   GL indices for total trade
OECD data: calculated from 4-digit (1961, 1967) and 5-digit (1972 , 1977, 1978, 1985, 1997, 1990)

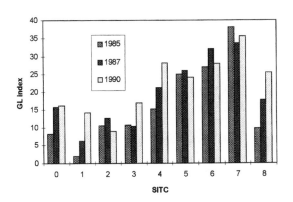

Figure 13.6   GL indices for total trade by sector
OECD data, calculated from 5-digit, SITC Rev. 2. Sector 0 includes food, live animals, 1 drink, tobacco, 3 raw materials, 3 mineral fuels, 4 animal/ vegetable oils, 5 chemicals, 6 manufactures, classified by materials, 7 machinery, transport equipment, 8 miscellaneous manufactures.

be driving IIT growth in primary sectors: increasing import penetration of traditional export commodities.

In Figure 13.7 we can see the different evolution of IIT with EU and with third countries. A steady increase of IIT with the EU contrasts with broadly stable levels of extra-EU IIT. Until 1977, IIT with other EU countries was lower than with third countries. Since then, certainly due to structural convergence of the economies, the role of the EU in

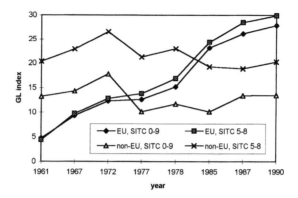

Figure 13.7 GL indices for trade with EU and non-EU countries
OECD data; calculated from 4-digit (1961, 1967) and from 5-digit (1972, 1977,
1978, 1985, 1987, 1990)

Portugal's IIT became more important. The GL indices in 1990 for all
products were 27.9 for Union trade and 13.5 for extra-Union trade.[3]

13.4   VERTICAL AND HORIZONTAL PRODUCT
DIFFERENTIATION

Another feature worth investigating is whether Portuguese IIT has
been mainly with similar-quality goods (horizontal IIT) or with goods
of unequal quality (vertical IIT).

With this purpose, calculations were made to find whether the unit
values of exports have been greater or lower than those of imports.
Furthermore, we explored whether, in a given industry, exports are
predominantly of products of higher or of lower 'quality' as reflected
in unit values.

To calculate the unit values for each SITC 5-digit industry, we
compared exports and imports in value and in quantity terms (tonnes).
For export values and for import values we distinguished matched
exports and matched imports, and net exports and net imports (the
quantities having been determined as a proportion of the values). With
this distribution the unit values of exports and of imports were calculated according to the type of trade and for each industry, ag-
gregating values and quantities at the 3 digit level of the SITC.[4]

The upper panel of Table 13.1 shows that for Portuguese *trade with
the EU* the average unit value of exports is inferior to the unit value of

Table 13.1 Intra EU trade ratio of export/import unit values

	Total			SITC 0–4			SITC 5–8		
	1979	1987	1990	1979	1987	1990	1979	1987	1990
Intra-EU trade									
matched 5 digit	0.89	0.88	0.89	1.09	1.01	0.99	0.74	0.79	0.76
net exports/imports	0.62	0.83	0.75	0.92	1.18	1.09	0.72	0.75	0.73
total trade	0.66	0.87	0.79	0.92	1.15	1.05	0.76	0.78	0.77
Extra-EU trade									
matched 5 digit	0.86	0.86	0.97	0.91	0.90	1.00	0.82	0.80	0.85
net exports/imports	3.55	3.81	3.65	2.06	1.88	2.11	0.55	0.86	0.79
total trade	3.47	3.61	3.46	2.08	1.91	1.99	0.58	0.85	0.80

imports. The overall average masks an important difference between manufacturing goods (SITC 5–8), where the average unit values of exports is lower than that of imports, and primary products (SITC 0–4), where exports tend to have higher unit values than imports. We therefore conclude that Portugal has specialized in relatively low-quality industrial goods and in relatively high-quality primary products.

The lower panel of Table 13.1, however, shows that for *trade with non-EU countries* export unit values generally exceed import unit values, the reverse situation compared to trade with EU members. However, manufactured goods in extra-EU trade, as in in-EU trade, have higher unit values for imports than for exports. Hence, the average quality differential between extra-EU imports and exports is determined mainly by the larger share of primary products in those trade flows.

In Table 13.2, 5-digit manufacturing industries are grouped according to the ratio of export and import unit values. Following the standard criterion, 5-digit industries with unit value ratios between 0.85 and 1.15 were considered to exhibit horizontally differentiated trade; while trade in the remaining industries is deemed vertically differentiated.

It can be seen that a relatively small proportion of trade that is captured as IIT by the conventional measures was characterized by horizontal differentiation. Yet, the number of such sectors has been growing during the period under analysis from 9 to 27 per cent of the total. Furthermore, this presentation confirms the prevalence of exported manufactures with lower quality compared to the quality of imports, when considering intra-EU trade flows. Within matched

Table 13.2   Intra EU trade – matched trade, SITC 5–8

Ratio of export/ import unit values	Number of product groups			% of import/export		
	1979	1987	1990	1979	1987	1990
Intra-EU IIT						
≥ 1.15	127	174	326	44	33	24
0.85–1.14	55	150	282	9	16	27
< 0.85	399	597	986	47	51	49
Total (matched)	581	921	1594	100	100	100
Total	1216	1280	2293			
Extra-EU IIT						
≥ 1.15	215	263	513	22	32	36
0.85–1.14	62	105	200	24	21	21
< 0.85	503	437	727	54	47	43
Total (matched)	780	805	1440	100	100	100
Total	1216	1212	2116			

trade flows, specialization in low-quality product varieties appears to have intensified during the 1980s, since the percentage of products with unit values below 0.85 increased from 47 to 49 per cent, while the percentage of sectors with values over 1.15 decreased form 44 to 24.

We notice also in Table 13.2 that the relative quality of exports in IIT with non-EU destinations has been improving, the percentage of sectors with unit values over 1.15 growing from 22 to 36 between 1979 and 1990.

It can be concluded that Portuguese trade increasingly comprises exports of relatively lower quality to EU members – a fact to which special attention should be paid, bearing in mind that competitiveness in Europe is likely to be difficult to sustain in low-quality products, in which Eastern European and less developed countries have a comparative advantage relative to Portugal.

13.5   PORTUGUESE INTRA-INDUSTRY TRADE AND EUROPEAN INTEGRATION

The general evolution of IIT in Portugal (Figure 13.5) shows a remarkable similarity with that of trade liberalization in Portugal, represented in Figure 13.8.[5]

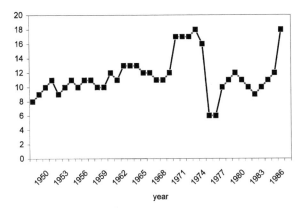

Figure 13.8 Index of trade liberalization, 1948–86

It can be seen that from 1961 to 1972 the increase of IIT accompanied an increase in liberalization. Subsequently, the IIT decrease of the 1970s coincided with a policy reversal towards protection. From 1977 onwards, an increase in the level of IIT again corresponded to increased liberalization.

Liberalization in Portugal has mainly been the result of steps taken within multilateral agreements. It thus appears that the increase in IIT was related to policy-led integration of the country with its trading partners.[6]

13.6 MARGINAL INTRA-INDUSTRY TRADE AND ADJUSTMENT

To analyse trade-related adjustment in the Portuguese economy, compatible data are required on trade and industry variables. Such compatibility could be achieved for 1986 and 1989, but not for earlier years, as the classification of the national statistics was changed in 1986. Information on 81 sectors could be obtained at the three digit NACE level. To examine the evolution in real terms, the values of 1989 were deflated according to the index of manufacturing output prices.

To see whether adjustment problems were related to changes in the structure of trade flows, we employed different variables to measure those changes (see Chapter 3). Correlations between these trade variables and changes in employment and production are reported in Table 13.3.

Table 13.3   Changes in manufactures trade and industrial performance, 1986–89

		Employment change		Production change	
		absolute	%(a)	*absolute* (b)	%(c)
ΔM		0.03		0.31(**)	
ΔX		0.56 (*)		0.56 (*)	
GL index	1986	−0.13	0.20	−0.08	0.17
	1989	−0.05	0.25	−0.07	0.17
ΔGL		0.14	0.06	0.02	0.00
A index		0.26(***)	0.27(**)	0.08	0.26(***)
GHME		0.35(*)	0.12	0.40(*)	0.16

a) % of (employment 1986 + employment 1989)/2
b) 10^6 Escudos at 1986 prices
c) % of (production 1986 + production 1989)/2
(*) significant at 0.005 confidence level
(**) significant at 0.01 confidence level
(***) significant at 0.025 confidence level

All the correlations with static IIT measures are statistically insignificant. However, Table 13.3 suggests that MIIT does relate significantly to both employment and output growth. This is confirmed by the positive correlation between output and employment growth and the GHME and *A* indices.

Table 13.4 categorizes industries into four groups using two criteria: MIIT (the *A* index being higher than 0.5 in the first case and lower than 0.5 in the second case); and the relative growth of imports and exports (the *B* index being < 0 or > 0).

Table 13.4   Industrial specialization 1986–89, by MIIT categories

Category	No. of indust.	Empl. 1986 (%)	Prod 1986 (%)	Δ Emp. (%)	Δ Prod (%)	Δ Trade (%)
I *B* < −0,5						
(*A* index < 0,5)	41	46.6	47.3	0.7	6.4	36.9
II −0,5 ≤ *B* < 0						
(*A* index ≥ 0,5)	16	10.1	11.7	12.6	17.9	73.1
III 0 ≤ *B* < 0,5						
(*A* index > 0,5)	9	24.4	18.8	8.7	6.8	29.2
IV *B* > 0,5						
(*A* index < 0,5)	15	18.9	22.2	6.8	11.7	30.3
TOTAL	81	100.0	100.0	5.1	9.1	38.9

This analysis confirms that employment growth was above average in sectors with high MIIT (that is groups II and III). Group II also had the largest increase in production. The most successful industries in terms of job creation and output growth were therefore characterized by simultaneous increases in imports as well as exports.

13.7 CONCLUSIONS

During the last thirty years important changes occurred in the patterns of Portugal's international trade, with significant implications for industrial specialization and adjustment. The Portuguese economy increased its trade orientation continuously, with a certain bias towards EU countries. The redirection of Portuguese trade flows towards the EU was particularly evident after accession to the EU in 1986. An important source of trade reorientation came from Portugal's participation in the Common Agricultural Policy, which led to a marked increase of imports of primary products from the EU, which had not been covered by the trade agreements of 1972 and 1976.

The structure of Portuguese exports, however, changed in favour of manufactures. Portugal witnessed an overall increase in the share of manufactured exports, from 53 per cent of the total in 1961 to 80 per cent in 1990. A balance was, therefore, achieved relative to the share of manufacturing in imports.

The quality of exports and of imports in Portugal's trade, measured by unit values, has varied across sectors and partner countries. Exports to EU countries tend to be of lower quality than imports. This is confined to trade in manufactured products, as in primary products the quality of exports is higher than the quality of imports. Given the role of manufacturing in Portuguese trade, there are reasons to be worried with this situation, particularly given our finding that this situation has become more pronounced in the 1980s. Having specialized in goods of lower quality, Portugal will find it difficult to compete with goods coming from potential new EU members. In trade with non-EU countries Portugal appears to have a quality advantage, exports being of higher quality than imports. However this is due to the very significant differential in the quality of primary products; exports of manufactured goods being generally of lower quality than imports in extra EU trade as well.

Finally, correlation and grouped analysis was used to examine whether IIT has been related to changes in employment and output.

Some evidence was found to suggest that adjustment problems are easier when MIIT is high.

Notes

1. Up to now, only a few studies have been devoted to IIT in Portugal (see Chouzal, 1992; Africano Silva, 1995 and 1996; Dias, 1996; and Faustino, 1996). IIT results for Portugal were also reported in Aquino (1978), Havrylyshyn and Civan, (1983), Buigues *et al.* (1990), and Greenaway and Hine (1991).
2. On the changing attitudes of the Portuguese authorities towards trade see Porto (1984) and Macedo *et al.* (1988).
3. Measurements with the use of the Aquino index led to similar results.
4. Trade of each product was assigned to one of four categories: (a) matched imports, (b) net imports, (c) matched exports, and (d) net exports. The values of (a) and (c) are identical in value terms and add up to the absolute value of IIT. Import quantities were allocated to categories (a) and (b) in proportion to the value shares, and the same imputation was carried out for export quantity data.
5. From Macedo *et al.* (1988); see also Papageorgiou *et al.* (1991). This index was constructed attaching a number on a same scale from 0 to 20 to different types of policy-led integration steps.
6. This relationship was confirmed by Africano Silva (1995 and 1996) and Dias (1996).

References

Africano Silva, A. (1995) *The Impact of European Community Membership on Portuguese Trade in Manufactured Goods*, PhD thesis, University of Reading.

Africano Silva, A. (1996) *The Nature of Trade Changes Associated with Portuguese Membership of EC*, in Curso de Estudos Europeus da Faculdade de Direito da Universidade de Coimbra, (ed.: Porto, M.) *Integration and Specialization*, Coimbra, 191–205.

Aquino, A. (1978) 'Intra-Industry Trade and Inter-Industry Specialization on Concurrent Sources of International Trade in Manufacturing'. *Weltwirtschaftliches Archiv*, 114, 275–96.

Buigues, P., Ilzkovitz, F. and Lebrun, J.F. (1990) 'The Impact of the Internal Market by Industrial Sector: The Challenge for the Member States', *European Economy, Social Europe*, special edition.

Chouzal, C. (1992) *Comércio Intra-Industrial. O Caso das Relações Comerciais entre Portugal e a Comunidade Europeia*, Masters thesis, Economic School, University of Coimbra.

Dias, J. (1996) 'Comércio Intra-Ramo, Integração Europeia e Competitividade: Uma Análise do Caso Português', in Porto, M. (ed.), *Integration and Specialization*, Coimbra, 123–41.

Faustino, H. (1996) 'Análise do Comércio Intra-Sectorial e das Vantagens Comparativas entre Portugal e Espanha para o periodo 1983–1992', *Notas Economicas. Revista da Faculdade de Economia da Universidade de Coimbra* 17, 66–88.

Greenaway, D. and Hine, R.C. (1991) 'Intra-Industry Specialisation, Trade Expansion and Adjustment in the European Economic Space', *Journal of Common Market Studies*, 24, 603–22.

Grubel, H.C. and Lloyd, P.J. (1975) *Intra-Industry Trade*, London: Macmillan.

Havrylyshyn, O. and Civan, E. (1983) 'Intra-Industry Trade and the Stage of Development: Regression Analysis of Industrial and Developing Countries', in Tharakan, P.K.M. (ed.), *Intra-Industry Trade: Empirical and Methodological Aspects*, Amsterdam: North Holland.

Macedo, J.B., Corado, C. and Porto, M. (1988) 'The Timing and Sequencing of Trade Liberalization Policies: Portugal 1948–1986', Working Paper No. 114, Faculdade de Economia da Universidade Nova de Lisboa.

Papageorgiou, D., Choksi, A. and Michaely, M. (1991) *Liberalising Foreign Trade in Developing Countries*, Oxford: Blackwell.

Porto, M. (1984) 'Twenty Years of Change', in Williams, A. (ed.), *Southern Europe Transformed: Political and Economic Changes in Greece, Portugal and Spain*, London: Harper and Row.

Index

A index   (see Brülhart)
Abd-el-Rahman, K.   70, 74, 75,
   142, 158
Adjustment
   inter-industry   8, 36 *et seq.*, 55,
      101, 113–14, 133, 158, 191,
      193, 200
   intra-industry   36 *et seq.*, 101 *et
      seq.*, 113
Adjustment costs   39, 41 *et seq.*,
   56, 57, 101, 113, 121, 125,
   152–3, 156, 207, 222, 250
   short run   36
   trade induced   36 *et seq.*, 64,
      98, 189, 194
Adler, M.   39
Africano Silva, A.   250
Alexakis, P.   169
Aquino index (see Grubel)
Australia   40
Aw, B.   74

B index   (see Brülhart)
Balassa, B.   37, 71, 72
Balasubramanyam, V.   38
Baldwin, R.   64, 65
Barriers to trade   (see trade
   impediments)
Belgium   6, 121 *et seq.*, 226
Benelux   226, 239, 240
Bergstrand, J.   31
Bhagwati, J.   15
Bonnaz, H.   143
Brander, J.   15, 55
Brecher, R.   64
Brenton, P.   73
Brülhart, M.   6, 28, 46, 48, 49, 65,
   66, 111, 114, 128, 131, 158, 183,
   191, 196, 209, 233, 234, 235
   A index   49 *et seq.*, 60 *et seq.*,
      111, 131, 158–60, 163,
      166, 174, 183, 193, 197,
      198–200, 204–5, 217, 219,
      234, 248

B index   49 *et seq.*, 60 *et seq.*,
   128, 158–63, 166, 183,
   196–7, 204–5, 217–8, 226,
   232–4, 248
C measure   49 *et seq.*, 60 *et seq.*,
   197, 209
Buigues, P.   130, 250
Burattoni, M.   6, 213, 222

C measure   (see Brülhart)
Cadot, O.   38
Calfat, G.   6, 64
Canada   44
Categorical aggregation   20, 54
Caves, R.   34
Central Planning Bureau,
   Netherlands   233
CEPII   38
Choudhri, E.   64
Chouzal, C.   250
Civan, E.   72, 250
Cohesion Fund   3
Commission of the European
   Communities   129
Comparative advantage   3, 98,
   122, 214, 222
COMTAP database   19
Concentration   3, 29, 87–8,
   98, 109
Cooper, D.   73
Costa, F.   6
Courtot, N.   143
Customs Union   2, 92, 226

Davis, D.   15
Dean, J.   28, 101
Denmark   103 *et seq.*
Determinants of IIT   13 *et seq.*,
   30, 70, 93, 202
Developing countries   26
De Vries, J.   225
Dias, J.   250
Dixit, A.   13, 15, 64, 71
Dixon, P.   38, 49, 65

Djankov, S. 38
Dollar, D. 16
Drábek, Z. 38
Drysdale, P. 38

Economic geography 30
Economic integration 41, 102, 109, 125, 233, 234
ECSC 39
EFTA 239
Elliott, R. 6, 44–6, 49, 64, 124, 142, 158, 174, 178, 183, 248
EMU 189
Endogenous growth (models of) 30
EU 2, 37, 98, 102, 124, 135, 149, 229, 239, 249
  Common Agricultural Policy 110, 157, 249
  Common Commercial Policy 226
  & enlargement 36
European integration 1, 98, 114, 135–6, 149, 151, 154, 181, 185, 213, 222, 246
European Monetary System (EMS) 218
Evans, J. 209
External economies 98
Extreme bounds analysis 22–4, 34–5

Factor-market adjustment 36 *et seq.*, 58, 114
Faini, R. 75
Falvey, R. 15, 72, 123
Faustino, H. 250
Feenstra, R. 64, 74
Finger, J. 15
Fischer, R.D. 38
Flam, H. 220
Foley, A. 202
France 6, 104 *et seq.*, 135 *et seq.*
Future of IIT 27

Garnaut, R. 38
GATT 1, 36, 135, 188, 239
Germany 6, 73, 103 *et seq.*, 151 *et seq.*, 227, 233
GHME measure (see Greenaway)

Giannitsis, A. 169
GL index (see Grubel)
Globerman, S. 28, 38, 101
Gonzalez, J. 38
Grant, R. 37, 38, 63
Gray, H. 21
Greece 6, 103 *et seq.*, 168 *et seq.*
Greenaway, D. 6, 13, 23, 25, 26, 28, 35, 38, 44–6, 49, 64, 75, 87, 98, 101, 124, 158, 163, 173, 174, 178, 183, 194, 248, 250, 255
Greenaway-Hine-Milner-Elliott (GHME) measure 45–6, 174, 178, 183, 209, 248
Grubel, H. 13, 72, 117 (see also Grubel-Lloyd index)
Grubel-Lloyd (GL) index 7, 18, 22, 43–4, 46–7, 52–3, 58, 60, 64, 101–2, 111–12, 114, 122, 124, 128, 140, 147–8, 153–6, 158, 165–6, 171, 173–5, 178, 190, 197, 204, 216–7, 219, 228, 242, 244
  Aquino adjustment 190, 191, 208, 250

Hamilton, C. 38, 43–5, 65, 101
  Hamilton-Kniest index 44–5, 64, 65
Hansson, P. 19, 24, 31, 34, 35, 39, 64
Harfi, M. 6, 143
Harrigan, J. 35
Havyrylyshyn, O. 72, 250
Hayes, F. 202
Heckscher-Ohlin model
  Neo H-O 15, 26
  Traditional 15
  Chamberlin 71, 73, 83
Heimler, A. 75
Helpman, E. 9, 14–16, 26, 31, 71–3, 85, 115, 220
Hine, R.C. 6, 25, 26, 28, 38, 44–6, 49, 98, 101, 124, 142, 158, 173, 174, 178, 183, 194, 248, 250
HK index (see Hamilton)
Hoekman, B. 38

Horizontal IIT (HIIT)   4, 8, 25,
    27, 30, 38–9, 55, 70 *et seq*., 85,
    87, 89 *et seq*., 124, 136, 142,
    149, 156, 158, 166, 220, 230
    et seq., 244
  measuring   24, 25, 73
Human capital   26, 123
Hummels, D.   26, 31, 202

Ilkovitz, F.   130
Imperfect competition   30
Imperfect information   4
Increasing returns   3, 98
Inter-industry trade   4, 5, 37, 38,
    43, 44, 73, 140, 149, 152, 169,
    185, 189, 199, 207, 213
  Marginal inter-industry trade
    49, 217
Inter-industry labour
    movements   52
Inter-industry specialisation   110,
    129, 132, 161, 213
Intra-EU trade   101, 129–30,
    143, 152, 191, 194, 207,
    235, 241, 245
Intra-industry labour
    movements   51–2, 57
Intra-industry trade (IIT)
  & employment   7, 88–9, 143–9,
    125 *et seq*., 163–5, 181–5,
    194 *et seq*., 207, 218 *et seq*.,
    247–9
  Intra-EU IIT   8, 28–9, 106
    et seq., 122, 132
  Intra-firm IIT   90, 149
Ireland   6, 103 *et seq*., 188 *et seq*.,
    226, 239–40
Italy   6, 103 *et seq*., 213 *et seq*.

Jacobsson, S.   128, 147, 133
Jacobsson index   128–30, 133,
    147–8
Japan   226
Jayasuriya, S.   40
Jordan, T.   26, 63

Katseli, L.   168, 169, 180
Katsos, G.   169
Kennedy Round   64

Kerstens, B.   26, 133
Khalifah, N.   38
Kierzkowski, H.   15, 72, 123
Klepper, S.   24, 31
Kniest, P.   38, 43–5, 65, 101
Kol, J.   6, 31, 208, 227, 228,
    230, 231
Kostecki, M.   38
Krugman, P.   9, 13–16,
    29, 31, 37, 38, 55, 71,
    72, 98, 115, 220
Kuijpers, B.   6, 227, 228, 230, 231

Lambertini, L.   213
Lancaster, K.   71
Leamer, E.   21, 22, 24, 31
Leamer, E.   22
Lemoine, F.   38
Leonard, H.   22
Levine, R.   22
Levinsohn, J.   26, 31, 202
Lewis, T.   64
Lincoln, E.   38
Linder   84, 93
Little, J.   38, 44
Lloyd, P.   13, 72, 115 (see also
    Grubel-Lloyd index)
Loertscher, R.   72, 73
Lundberg, L.   24, 31, 34, 35,
    38, 39, 64
Luxembourg   133, 226

Machine-tool industry   39
Macedo, J.   250
Maddala, G.   24
Mardas, D.   169
Marginal IIT (MIIT)   4–5, 7–8,
    40, 43 *et seq*., 101, 112 *et seq*.,
    128, 131, 146, 158–60, 165,
    173–5, 191, 197–9, 203–4,
    217, 233, 247, 250
  & measurement of   58–63, 183–4
    (see also Brülhart)
Marshall Plan   226
Martin, J.   209
Marvel, H.   63
Mathieu, C.   143
Mavrogiannis, A.   6, 178, 185
Mazerolle, F.   140

McAleese, D. 6, 190, 191, 202, 209
McGibney, A. 193
Mennes, L. 31, 208
Menon, J. 38, 49, 65
Messerlin, P. 143
Milner, C. 6, 13, 23, 25, 26, 35, 44–46, 49, 64, 75, 87, 124, 142, 158, 163, 174, 178, 183, 194, 248
Monopolistic competition 4, 16 *et seq.*, 26, 37, 55, 90
Montet, C. 6
Mucchielli, J. 140
Mucchielli, J. 102
Multinational firms 85, 90, 202–8, 235
Murshed, M. 65
Mussa, M. 56

NAFTA 36
Neary, P. 56
Neo-factor-proportions model 92
NESC 189
Netherlands 6, 104 *et seq.*, 225 *et seq.*
Neven, D. 38
New economic geography 3
New trade theory 3, 14, 36, 98
Nivaz, D. 143
Noland, M. 38
Non-tariff barriers 2–3, 41, 129–33, 186, 214
Noonan, D. 65
Nordic countries 19, 239
Norman, V. 13, 15, 64

O'Donnell, M. 6
OECD 38, 218
Oligopolistic market structure 15, 55, 89–90
Oligopoly models, large-number 90, 93
Oligopoly models, small-number 4, 39, 55
Oliveras, J. 65
O'Sullivan, M. 202
Oulmane, N. 143
Oulton, N. 73, 74, 92

Paba, S. 213
Papadimitriou, P. 6, 178, 185
Papageorgiou, D. 250
Parr, R. 38
Pearson coefficients 5
Pelkmans, J. 213
Porto, M. 6, 250
Portugal 6, 104 *et seq.*, 239 *et seq.*
Primo Braga, C. 38
Product differentiation 13–4, 16, 71, 121, 140
  horizontal 25, 37, 55, 70–1, 75, 85, 123–4, 244
  intermediate 39
  vertical 25–6, 70–5, 85, 88, 93, 244

R&D-intensive industries 113
Rajan, R. 38
Ratnayake, R. 40
Ray, E. 63
Rayner, A. 174
Reciprocal dumping 15, 39
Regional policy 214
Reker, C. 39, 124
Renelt, D. 22
Ricardo 239
Richardson, J. 39
Roberts, M. 74
Rodrik, D. 38
Rossini, G. 6, 213, 222, 223
Ruane, F. 193

Salazar 239
Sapir, A. 38
Sarris, A. 6, 168, 178, 185
Saudi Arabia 94
Scale economies 13–4, 16, 18–20, 27–30, 85, 87, 123, 129, 149
Schuhmacher, D. 153
Serra, P. 38
Shaked, A. 73
Shelburne, R. 38, 65
Single Market 3, 5, 8, 36, 98, 101, 109, 113, 128–30, 132–3, 135, 167–8, 188, 201–2
Smeets, D. 6, 124
Smith, Adam 36, 225
Smith, Alasdair 38

Smooth-Adjustment Hypothesis
36 *et seq.*, 146 (see also
Adjustment)
definition of 42 *et seq.*
Social dumping 135
Spain 103 *et seq.*
Spanakis, N. 169
Steel industry 39, 64
Sterdyniak, H. 143
Stiglitz, J. 71, 73
Strategic trade policy 14
Structural adjustment 5, 124–5,
143–4, 147–9, 152, 163 *et seq.*
Structural Funds 3
Sutton, J. 72
Sweden 39–40, 75

Terra, I. 65
Tharakan, P. 6, 26, 64, 73, 133
Thomsen, S. 189
Torstensson, J. 13, 16, 19, 22–8,
31, 34, 65, 74, 230, 255
Trade barriers (see trade
impediments)
Trade impediments 1, 19, 20, 55,
78, 85, 98, 129, 168, 213, 222
iceberg type 16
preference barriers 29
Trade liberalisation 1, 2, 36–9,
55, 121, 130–2, 135, 143, 148,
166, 186, 246–7

Trade theory 1, 13 *et seq.*, 55, 169
Transfer pricing 90
Transitional costs 1, 38 *et seq.*
Transport costs 78, 85
Treaty of Rome 226

United Kingdom 6, 71, 73 *et seq.*,
103 *et seq.*
United States 29, 44, 63, 64,
135–7, 140, 226
Unit values 73–4, 158

Velez, A. 38
Venables, A. 9, 55, 115, 133
Vertical IIT (VIIT) 4, 5, 8,
25–27, 30, 70 *et seq.*,
88 *et seq.*, 123–4, 136, 142,
156, 158, 176–8, 185, 193,
220–2, 225, 230 *et seq.*, 244
high quality 80
measuring 73 *et seq.*
Vimont, C. 143

Winters, L.A. 73, 133
White, H. 20
Wolff, E. 16
Wolter, F. 72, 73
Wood, A. 208, 218
Woolcock, S. 189

Xanthakis, M. 169